GP

BAINTE DEN STOC

WITHDRAWN FROM DLR LIBRARIES STOCK

The Microdot Gang

The Microdot Gang

The Rise and Fall of the LSD Network That Turned On the World

James Wyllie

The History Press

First published 2022

The History Press
97 St George's Place, Cheltenham,
Gloucestershire, GL50 3QB
www.thehistorypress.co.uk

© James Wyllie, 2022

The right of James Wyllie to be identified as the Author
of this work has been asserted in accordance with the
Copyright, Designs and Patents Act 1988.

All rights reserved. No part of this book may be reprinted
or reproduced or utilised in any form or by any electronic,
mechanical or other means, now known or hereafter invented,
including photocopying and recording, or in any information
storage or retrieval system, without the permission in writing
from the Publishers.

British Library Cataloguing in Publication Data.
A catalogue record for this book is available from the British Library.

ISBN 978 0 7509 9600 6

Typesetting and origination by The History Press
Printed and bound in Great Britain by TJ Books Limited, Padstow, Cornwall.

Trees for Life

Contents

Part Four   Come-Down

Dramatis Personae

(In Order of Appearance)

GERALD THOMAS: A scientist, LSD enthusiast and small-time hashish smuggler, THOMAS was both friend and foe of the Microdot Gang.

DAVID SOLOMON: The New Yorker SOLOMON was part of the Beat generation; a jazz critic and editor who compiled the first authoritative and accessible anthology about LSD before settling in the UK and forming the Microdot Gang.

BILLY HITCHCOCK: A member of the mighty Mellon family, HITCHCOCK was a Wall Street trader who helped acid entrepreneurs launder their money.

PAUL ARNABOLDI: A boat-sailing, college-educated hippy and part-time smuggler based in Majorca, ARNABOLDI was involved in several of the Microdot Gang's business ventures.

AUGUSTUS OWSLEY STANLEY THE THIRD: OWSLEY was a wayward polymath and the original acid alchemist; his LSD launched San Francisco's Summer of Love.

NICK SAND: A self-taught chemist who followed in OWSLEY'S footsteps. Based in California, SAND created the legendary Orange Sunshine.

JOHN GRIGGS: GRIGGS was the leader of an LA motorbike gang before taking LSD and forming The Brotherhood of Eternal Love, a hippy mafia that collaborated with the Microdot Gang.

RONALD STARK: Anarchist, con-man, alleged secret agent, the Brooklyn-born STARK was a major international LSD producer and distributor who worked with The Brotherhood of Eternal Love and the Microdot Gang.

TORD SVENSON: A trained chemist and psychedelic pioneer, SVENSON made huge quantities of acid for STARK in various European labs.

STEVE ABRAMS: A parapsychologist and legalise cannabis campaigner, ABRAMS moved in the same circles as members of the Microdot Gang.

RICHARD KEMP: A hugely talented chemist and political radical, KEMP was an LSD idealist who was determined to make the Microdot Gang's acid the purest ever.

CHRISTINE BOTT: A qualified doctor who worked as a GP and in hospitals, BOTT had been with KEMP since they met at university and shared his revolutionary beliefs.

HENRY BARCLAY TODD: A drop-out with a taste for fine living, TODD organised and ran the Microdot Gang's distribution network.

GEORGE ANDREWS: ANDREWS was an American acid poet who ended up in London, edited an anthology about Indian hashish culture and collaborated with SOLOMON on several books.

ALSTON 'SMILES' HUGHES: One of the Microdot Gang's main dealers, SMILES ran his operation from a small village in Wales.

DICK LEE: Head of the Thames Valley Drug Squad, LEE spearheaded the massive police investigation into the Microdot Gang's activities.

MARTYN PRITCHARD: PRITCHARD was an undercover hippy cop who posed as a dealer and penetrated the Microdot Gang's distribution network.

ANDREW MUNRO: A gifted if eccentric chemist, MUNRO knew the Microdot Gang's key personnel and would turn his hand to LSD after observing KEMP at work.

BRIAN CUTHBERTSON: A Reading University drop-out, CUTHBERTSON oversaw the tableting of the Microdot Gang's LSD.

RUSSELL STEPHEN SPENCELEY: A bon viveur, SPENCELEY acted as a go-between in the Microdot Gang's supply chain connecting London to Wales.

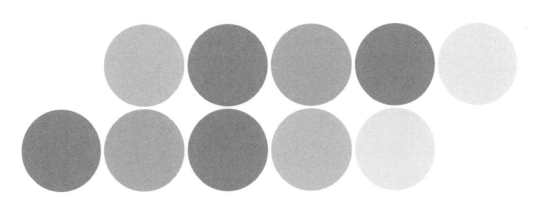

Part One

DAYDREAM BELIEVERS

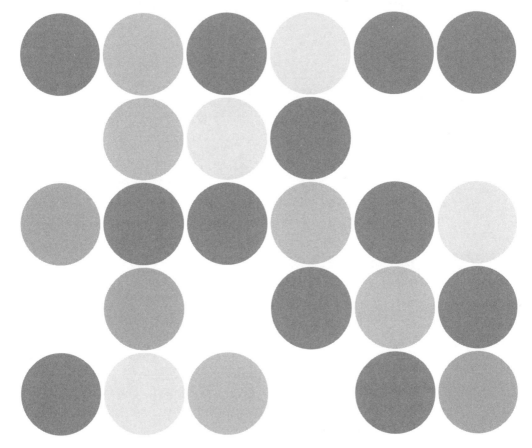

Prologue

Grass

Gerald Thomas had every reason to be nervous as he strolled through the terminal at Montreal airport on 3 June 1973. He was carrying 15 pounds of hashish in his luggage. He was a self-employed dope entrepreneur, a travelling salesman with a reputation for taking risks, or being sloppy, depending on your point of view. No major drug dealer or international player of any consequence would be caught dead in an airport transporting anything more suspicious than a change of clothes, toothbrush and shaving kit.

For the big-time smuggler, air travel was a necessary evil and airports a potential hazard. You were vulnerable entering and leaving countries, assuming you were always of interest to the DEA (Drug Enforcement Administration), the FBI, Interpol and every other law-enforcement agency engaged in the global war on drugs, and they were waiting for you every time you got off a plane. You never knew when your passport was going to be flagged or when you'd be invited into a little room for a thorough examination. If you had to move product by air you did it by cargo, not in your hand luggage; if you could do it by boat, even better.

But Gerald Thomas was not a major trafficker. And he wasn't nervous. Sure, there was a certain amount of inevitable anxiety, but more satisfying was the feeling of sticking it to the Man, each time striking a blow against the system as he passed by undetected with his beloved marijuana. Risking a long prison sentence so he could get paid and the people get high. He was the rebel bandit, hero of the oppressed, defying tyranny wherever he went. He was Zorro. On one occasion he shipped a consignment of weed across the Atlantic concealed in a dead elephant.

When he first arrived at Montreal airport, Thomas stashed the dope in a locker and took a short flight to Boston to check out its customs and security arrangements in preparation for returning there with the marijuana. Satisfied with what he saw he hopped back to Montreal and retrieved the stuff, confident that he'd complete the transfer successfully. That morning his luck ran out. As it happens they weren't waiting for him; it was just some canny customs official with a hunch. Though Thomas' appearance was smart and conventional – not John Lennon glasses, faded flares and a flower in his hair – something wasn't right. Why the quick trip to Boston and back? If that was his destination, why transit through Montreal? The answer was in his suitcase.

● ● ●

Thomas was not a hardened criminal. He'd not grown up on any mean streets or graduated from juvenile detention centres or committed any crime other than the import and export of controlled substances, which he did more out of faith than necessity. For over a decade he'd been fully committed to an alternative lifestyle that involved the consumption of large quantities of cannabis and LSD. Given his hostility to work – the soul destroyer – to wage labour and the 9–5 hell, to paying taxes to support the hated system or being part of that system in any shape or form, it was a logical step to become a dealer. You got an income while remaining unemployed. You guaranteed your own supply. Your colleagues were usually friends or fellow believers, every customer a potential recruit to the cause. It was an open market and demand was consistently growing. It was the perfect 'job'. Even though penalties were harsh and the law brutal in its application, this added to the attraction; not only did it bring drama, it meant you remained an outlaw and a revolutionary. For Thomas, and many like him, part of this image was wish-fulfilment, glamorising the inconvenient reality that they really were out to get you. But part of it was also a lingering conviction that they were on the right side of history.

Unfortunately for Thomas – when faced with the full might of the forces of law and order – he was nothing more than an amateur enthusiast who'd hit on the happy circumstance of making money out of his hobby. He'd been caught with a substantial amount of hashish. There were no mitigating circumstances. He was facing anything between seven and twenty-five years locked up with real criminals in a real prison, with murderers, rapists, child molesters and organised gangs. He was a college-educated hippy with three science degrees approaching middle age. What did he know about hard time?

One possible way out was to go underground. Become a fugitive. There were established routes and contacts. False IDs and passports could be provided. However, Thomas didn't think that way. Released on bail, he stayed put and asked his friends in the UK to send him some money and clothes; he was unprepared for a Canadian winter. Nothing happened. Then he tried to get them to clear valuable drug-making equipment out of his London-based warehouse. Instead of preserving it, like he asked, they destroyed it. Infuriated, Thomas demanded compensation, but was bluntly refused. Disappointed and feeling betrayed, Thomas contemplated another option. Turn informer. He had a wealth of knowledge, in particular the inside track on the Microdot Gang, a massive LSD network based in the UK that produced millions of tabs a year – each acid trip potentially powerful enough to change a person overnight and make them question the very nature of reality. Thomas knew the key figures well and the intimate details of their operation. Surely this would be of interest to the authorities?

April 1974, with the tape machine rolling and two Scotland Yard officers present, Thomas began at the beginning. Late summer 1969: David Solomon, Ronald Stark and Richard Kemp met for the first time at Solomon's cottage nestled in bucolic Grantchester Meadows to discuss how their LSD was going to change the world …

1

Jazz Head

Aged 43, David Solomon was the oldest member of the Microdot Gang and represented the vanguard of LSD culture, pioneers whose youth was played out against the backdrop of world war, nuclear bombs, anti-communist witch-hunts and rapacious consumerism. People like Solomon were part of a slow-burning protest against the mainstream, an informal underground. When their experiments went spectacularly over-ground during the 1960s, they faced a clear choice. Embrace the new generation or step back. Some did, appalled by the flower children's apparent naivety and reckless hedonism. Others claimed the mantle of leadership – Solomon included. Ironically, a movement associated primarily with youth followed gurus and prophets who were often middle-aged or older.

David Solomon was born in California in 1925. During the war he was called up but spared combat duties after his two brothers were killed on a bombing run over Germany. Instead he did clerical work for the OSS – the forerunner of the CIA – before being discharged in 1946. Solomon headed for New York, enrolled at NYU to study English literature, and dived into the city's pulsing jazz scene where he discovered a new form of music: be-bop. A dazzlingly fast, rhythmically complex, harmonically adventurous and blues orientated style that sent convulsions through the jazz world and eventually the wider one, be-bop's main practitioners adopted a provocative anti-establishment stance with a distinctive style and their own hipster language.

Solomon was an instant convert and quickly befriended one of be-bop's leading lights, the trumpeter Dizzy Gillespie. At the same time, Solomon was introduced to cannabis, which had been circulating in the jazz community since the 1920s and spawned a sub-genre of tunes known as 'reefer music'; Dizzy Gillespie observed that 'jazz musicians, the old ones and the young ones, almost all smoked pot'. On graduation, Solomon settled with his wife Pat in Greenwich Village – ground zero of the post-war counter-culture – and began working as a critic for the jazz magazine *Metronome*, which championed be-bop. Working for *Metronome* gained Solomon kudos, but not much income. By the early 1950s, he had two daughters to support. Thankfully, his credentials were good enough to land him a job as an editor at *Esquire* magazine.

Founded in 1933, *Esquire* mixed high-brow fiction and topical discussion with life-style features, sports profiles, motor cars and drawings of naked ladies. *Esquire* also had a strong tradition of jazz coverage – running a Jazz Forum and a yearly Jazz Awards – and welcomed be-bop. Solomon slotted in nicely, working on articles like 'Dizzy's Jazz' (June 1957), and 'The Golden Age of Jazz' (January 1959). As the decade progressed, *Esquire* picked up on messages from the underground transmitted by creatures known as the Beats who attempted to capture the intensity, freedom and spontaneity of be-bop; shared a fondness for drugs and Paris; and lived hand to mouth from city to city, rubbing shoulders with the marginalised and dispossessed. Head tribesmen were the poet Allan Ginsberg and fellow writers William Burroughs and Jack Kerouac. Though both Ginsberg and Burroughs transcended the Beat label, Kerouac was shackled to it due to his staggeringly successful set text *On the Road* (1955). Solomon's home turf of Greenwich Village was one of the nexus points of the Beat scene, showcased in the November 1954 issue of *Esquire* in 'The Lives and Loves of Greenwich Village'. Other Beat hotspots were given similar treatment; in the May 1958 edition it was 'San Francisco: The Magnet City'.

As well as being deeply embedded in the same cultural milieu as the Beats, Solomon was prepared to take similar risks to achieve a heightened state of awareness. During his tenure at *Esquire*, Solomon embarked on his psychedelic initiation when he ingested 400 milligrams of mescaline, a by-product of two strains of cactus – the San Pedro, a mountain plant from Peru, and peyote, a desert variety found in Mexico – that had been central to sacred rites and rituals for thousands of years before Spanish conquerors arrived in the sixteenth century along with Christianity. Determined to crush any indigenous religions, the emissaries of the Church demonised mescaline. According to them, the 'devilish root' opened a gateway for Satan to enter and possess his victims. During the nineteenth century, peyote was adopted by Native American tribes after they were shunted onto reservations, in the hope that it would give them access to the spirit world. Their use of mescaline was studied by anthropologists, which led to it gaining the attention of scientists, psychologists, philosophers and artists and writers, whose experiments with mescaline in the first half of the twentieth century laid the groundwork and created the terms of reference for the first generation of LSD consumers. For Solomon, his encounter with mescaline was like nothing he'd ever experienced before: 'I had never seen, touched, tasted, heard, smelled and felt so profound a personal unity and involvement with the material world.'

● ● ●

Solomon's first psychedelic adventure occurred because of his involvement with the English writer and intellectual Aldous Huxley, best known for his sci-fi masterpiece *Brave New World* (1932). During 1953, Solomon contacted Huxley about a newspaper article he'd written about drugs: Solomon suggested he might like to do a longer version for *Esquire*. Huxley agreed in principle, but publication was delayed and then abandoned when the material appeared as *The Doors of Perception* (1954), perhaps the most significant single work on hallucinogens.

Marked by the horrors of the First World War, alienated by industrial society and materialism, fearful of the rise of Communism and Fascism, Aldous Huxley rejected modern society and dedicated himself to finding ways to overcome the human malaise and reconnect to spiritual values. Having settled in California, Huxley was contacted by a psychiatrist working in a state mental hospital in Canada who was researching the effect of mescaline on schizophrenics. He began a correspondence with Huxley. Spring 1953, Huxley offered himself as a test subject; 'thus it came about that one bright May' he 'swallowed four-tenths of a gram of mescaline dissolved in half a glass of water and sat down to wait for the results'. After about half an hour some flowers caught Huxley's eye and he saw not merely a set of well-arranged blooms but the essence of life itself: his trip had begun. Time and space became dislocated and displaced. Everything around him, including the folds in his trousers, revealed themselves in microscopic depth and detail.

LSD followed on 23 December 1955 and, a year later, Huxley coined the term 'psychedelic'. Meanwhile, his writings on the subject, though mauled by the critics, quickly gained traction and hit a nerve with legions of potential followers, Solomon included: 'my own excursions … were largely the result of a deep curiosity engendered by reading such books as *The Doors of Perception*'. Suitably inspired, Solomon moved onto psilocybin – a synthetic derivative of magic mushrooms that first emerged from a Swiss lab in 1958 – and LSD two years later. By then, Huxley was increasingly preoccupied with how best to harness LSD's potential for the good of mankind. His solution was essentially elitist; LSD would benefit the more enlightened members of society, but the masses would be overwhelmed and disorientated by it. Solomon shared Huxley's concerns, but came to less conservative conclusions. Solomon wanted to spread the word and help LSD gain wider acceptance. So he decided to compile an anthology of writing about acid.

LSD: The Consciousness-Expanding Drug (1964) was a varied collection that mixed scholarly articles on the subject that Solomon selected from a range of scientific journals with more mainstream offerings, including material he'd commissioned and edited for his new employers at *Playboy* – which Solomon joined in the early 1960s after leaving *Esquire*. Hugh Hefner had launched *Playboy* in 1953 with capital from his mom as a raunchier version of *Esquire*, with real nude ladies rather than drawn ones. Within a few years, it was outselling its rival and shifting millions of copies. Though Hefner essentially reproduced *Esquire*'s basic formula – and its extensive jazz coverage – *Playboy* was more explicitly attached to the counter-culture. As a result, Solomon was able to push his agenda and he recycled three articles from the magazine in his LSD book, each one a personal account of a psychedelic experience.

To guarantee the anthology's success, however, Solomon needed to acquire some new material by 'celebrity' authors. Solomon contacted

Alan Watts – a well-known expert on Buddhism who had married LSD to Zen philosophy. In his piece for Solomon, Watts asked whether 'the risks involved in using these chemicals was worthwhile': his answer was 'yes' on the basis that LSD could help us throw off our 'insular identity' and become 'thoroughly at home in our own world … swimming in the ocean of relativity as joyously as dolphins'.

More significant was a contribution by William Burroughs, one of the few '60s icons to be equally revered by the '70s punks and '80s ravers: Solomon called him a 'reformed junky turned literary genius'. A pathologically secretive man who felt like an alien on an undercover mission to Earth, Burroughs had been thrust into the limelight because of his experimental novel *The Naked Lunch* (1959), which had inspired rave reviews and moral outrage. Burroughs welcomed Solomon's request as he'd gone out on a limb to showcase the author's work in *Metronome*. Solomon was now overall editor at the jazz magazine and was trying to steer it in a more avant-garde direction; one of his staff recalled that 'under Solomon's leadership we were publishing a magazine that featured something truly revolutionary … the young black jazz performers who were transforming music in America'. Keen to add literary fuel to the fire, Solomon got Burroughs' permission to run extracts from the author's latest novel, *The Soft Machine* – where characters, plotlines and locations were chopped up and spliced together in fractured sentences and repetitive patterns – alongside an essay about ninth-century hashish-eating Arabic assassins: not exactly what the average *Metronome* reader was expecting to find next to reviews of the latest Miles Davis album.

Burroughs was grateful for the commission – and the $50 that came with it – and wrote to Solomon thanking him for 'the excellent job you did with the two pieces I sent you'. When he next passed through New York, Burroughs dropped by the *Metronome* offices to see Solomon, but was informed that he no longer worked there. After over fifteen years as a contributor and barely a year into his editorship, Solomon had been 'let go'. His determination to push the boundaries (he encouraged his reporters to take acid and then write about it) had backfired. At least Solomon had the LSD book to fall back on, and Burroughs duly submitted *Points of Distinction between Sedative and Consciousness-Expanding Drugs* for inclusion in the anthology. As a long-term heroin addict and authority on drugs of all kinds, Burroughs approached the subject with scientific rigour; his forensic analysis of the differences between stimulants – LSD, cannabis, amphetamines and cocaine – and depressants – alcohol and heroin – ended with the claim that 'hallucinogens provide a key to the creative process'.

Another coup for Solomon was securing an appearance by Aldous Huxley. *Hallucinogens: A Philosopher's Visionary Prediction* was the last thing Huxley wrote before his death and was trailed in the November 1963 issue of *Playboy*. Huxley warned that the world was suffering a life-or-death crisis caused by 'explosive population increase' and 'head long technological advance and militant nationalism'. Action was needed to transform humanity through education, meditation and 'the use of harmless psychedelics'.

To complete the line-up, Solomon roped in Dr Timothy Leary, the poster boy of acid who exhorted the youth to 'turn on, tune in and drop out'. Vain and narcissistic, Leary had the ability to relay sophisticated and complex ideas in readable and memorable prose, which he combined with an instinctive understanding of how to manipulate the media to propel himself into the limelight. When Solomon first entered Leary's orbit in 1961, the self-appointed 'high-priest' of LSD hadn't even tried acid yet, despite studying the effects of mescaline and psilocybin as part of a research programme that he'd started at Harvard after his introduction to magic mushrooms, during which he claimed to have learnt 'more in the six or seven hours of that experience than in all my years as a psychologist'. When Leary finally took LSD – not long after he'd met Solomon – he called it 'the most shattering experience of my life'.

Solomon and Leary shared a mutual acquaintance in the jazz world, the trumpeter and big band leader Maynard Ferguson, a precocious talent who had just finished a lucrative gig writing and performing the soundtrack for a primetime TV drama about racing drivers. Ferguson and his wife Flo – 'a radiant redhead in her mid-forties' – ran an open house that attracted a steady stream of bohemians like Solomon, all drawn by the easy-going atmosphere, stimulating company and availability of drugs. A young writer remembered participating in a psilocybin session there in April 1961 after Ferguson urged him to sample the fruits of the 'sacred mushroom'. Arriving at Ferguson's house, he was ushered into a dimly-lit room with a huge fireplace, 'dark woodwork, heavy beams' and 'leaded windows'. Also present were Leary, a prison psychiatrist and about eight others. Leary handed him a pink pill 'the size of a baby aspirin' from 'an amber plastic bottle' and off he went into the realms of supercharged consciousness and sensory overload.

Recognising that Solomon was a potential ally with access to all sorts of interesting people, Leary gave him eight psilocybin pills to distribute as he saw fit. Solomon needed no encouragement as he was already dishing out acid to his contacts in the jazz community. One of those Solomon introduced to LSD was the young free jazz clarinettist Perry Robinson, who regarded Solomon as a 'progressive leftie' and 'family friend'. Solomon convinced Robinson that he needed to take acid ('you're ready for it, and I'm going to turn you on'), and invited him over to his Bronx apartment for an LSD session. Robinson remembered how fascinated he was by 'an oil painting of Dave's wife' and how he immersed himself in its colours before reaching a transcendental state of awareness as he glimpsed 'the pure undulating energy of the universe' and understood 'the true one-ness of life'.

Throughout, Solomon was at his side giving encouragement. Reminding Robinson that 'you can do anything you want to', Solomon urged him to experiment with his facial expressions and watch himself transform. Robinson went to the bathroom, stared in the mirror and decided he 'wanted to be a werewolf'. Then Solomon took his pupil out for a walk in the park – 'I had an impulse to fuck a tree' – and then across the bridge to a Manhattan bank where Solomon kept his drugs in a safety-deposit box. According to Robinson, Solomon was able to score pharmaceutical-grade LSD from local hospitals because 'he knew all the doctors and nurses'.

● ● ●

Solomon dedicated *LSD: The Consciousness-Expanding Drug* to Huxley – 'guru extraordinaire'. In his preface, Solomon observed that psychedelic drugs were seen as a threat because they 'enable one to see through the myriad pretensions and deceits which make up the mythology of the social lie'. However, LSD wisely used could 'offer hope and encouragement to a democratically orientated social structure'. The book was released in 1964 by G.P. Putnam's Sons, a long-established publisher whose list of authors included nineteenth-century giants like Edgar Allan Poe and

Herman Melville as well as current literary stars like Vladimir Nabokov, whose *Lolita* (1958) had caused a sensation. Solomon's debut garnered generally favourable and respectful reviews. *The New York Times* recommended it to 'all who wish to learn about the way in which the mind of man may be influenced' and praised Solomon's 'erudite treatment' of a 'difficult and possibly personal topic'; *The Berkeley Daily Gazette* gave its seal of approval: 'an interesting and informative book' that provided 'fresh insight into new and fascinating frontiers'.

The book's appearance coincided with an outbreak of media interest in LSD. Overall, the tone of the coverage was cautiously positive, but tempered by anxiety over the potential effects on society if LSD got into the wrong hands. *The Saturday Evening Post* ran an article with the headline 'The Dangerous Magic of LSD', while *Cosmopolitan* breathlessly declared that LSD was 'the sophisticated' and 'fun thing' to take if you ran with 'the fast set and the beat set'. Thanks to all this attention, Solomon's anthology sold well and a sequel was on the cards. Solomon chose cannabis as his next subject, signed a contract with a different publisher – The Bobbs-Merrill Company, which had been turning out bestsellers for over a century – and began assembling *The Marijuana Papers: An Examination of Marijuana in Society, History and Literature*.

As cannabis had been around for thousands of years, the anthology had a wider range than the LSD one. There was the history of the plant, its cultural and social uses, and a selection of dope literature featuring Rabelais, Baudelaire and the Beats. Solomon also assembled a number of papers and lectures examining the therapeutic and medical applications of the herb, and once again reached out to Burroughs, who let him reprint the essay that had previously appeared in the LSD book. The two of them had stayed in touch since the *Metronome* incident and, in a letter dated 20 April 1964, Burroughs told Solomon that his cannabis book sounded 'great' and would act as a corrective to the American government's 'pernicious falsification of facts' and suppression of any 'scientific evaluation of marijuana' that contradicted its propaganda.

Solomon also commissioned a piece by Leary on the politics and ethics of marijuana. By then, Harvard had expelled Leary after the good doctor had 'tested' some trainee priests from Andover Theological Seminary – half with LSD, half with amphetamines – and sat back to watch the results. Cut loose from Harvard, Leary and his co-conspirators immediately started the International Federation for Internal Freedom and launched a serious-minded journal called *The Psychedelic Review*. At the same time, Leary began looking for 'a setting free from secular distractions'. After several aborted attempts to establish a base, a suitable resting place was found thanks to the intervention of Peggy Hitchcock – 'a free-spirited jazz buff' – who'd met Leary at the Ferguson home. A jet-setting party animal with a mischievous streak, Peggy took pity on Leary and his failed attempts to find a safe haven. She asked her twin brothers if Leary could use the 'lovely big property' they'd recently acquired.

Of the two siblings, Billy Hitchcock was particularly taken by Leary. According to a close family friend, Hitchcock was easily influenced – 'he never liked to confront anybody about anything' – and quickly fell under Leary's spell: 'he got Billy totally enthralled and became a sort of father figure to him'. Hitchcock's own father – who died when Hitchcock was a child – was an impossible act to follow. Aside from being a successful banker who helped set up Lehman Brothers in 1937, Hitchcock's father had distinguished himself in the First World War by escaping from a POW camp and walking several hundred miles to safety, lit up the inter-war years as a star polo player – considered to be one of the best ever – and was killed test-flying a prototype fighter plane during the Second World War. If that wasn't enough of a legacy to contend with, his mother's side of the family was even more intimidating. Billy Hitchcock was the great-grandson of Thomas Mellon, who established the Mellon Bank in 1869, and grandson of William Mellon Snr, who set up Gulf Oil in 1901. The Mellon family also had controlling interests in US Steel, Heinz, Credit Suisse Bank and General Motors and were patrons of Yale and the University of Pittsburgh, while the Carnegie Mellon University was named after the family. Aside from Hitchcock's lucrative job at Lehman Brothers, his trust fund provided him with a further $15,000 a week.

The property Hitchcock offered to Leary was called Millbrook, a sixty-four-room Gothic mansion – though the word mansion hardly does it justice – surrounded by 25,000 acres of land featuring orchards, forests, rivers and waterfalls, 80 miles north of Manhattan in Duchess County. Hitchcock used Millbrook as his weekend pad, staying in a complex of buildings – a bungalow and a four-bedroom cottage – a mile from the main house. Hitchcock handed the keys to Leary and a small tribe of devotees moved in. The rent was $500 a month. LSD was acquired from chemical traders in London and brought in via Montreal. Leary installed himself as resident 'spiritual teacher', hoping to combine 'the humility and wisdom of a Hindu guru … the sensitivity of a poet and the imagination of a science fiction writer'. The emphasis was on LSD sessions that incorporated elements of Eastern religions. Hinduism was popular, particularly after Leary had made the pilgrimage to India. The *I Ching* did its work. *The Tibetan Book of the Dead* loomed large. Visitors paid $60 for a weekend's reprogramming. They wore togas, ate their meals – consisting of dyed food – in silence, took part in role-playing games and produced primitive art. One resident compared Millbrook to an 'orbiting astral space station, where beings on different levels of consciousness converged to exchange communications'.

Solomon frequently visited the house to soak up the atmosphere and mingle with his jazz buddies: Maynard Ferguson was an almost permanent fixture, as was the explosive bassist and virtuoso composer Charles Mingus. Solomon had known Mingus for years and lobbied hard to get extracts from the musician's devastatingly honest autobiography reproduced in *Playboy*. Aside from these familiar faces, there were many new ones as word of Leary's acid hotel spread – including a certain Gerald Thomas who, some years later, would be in a Canadian jail ratting out his colleagues. Thomas was in his early 30s, a chemical engineer with degrees in physics, maths and chemistry. While still on the fringes of academia he had developed a serious interest in LSD. Solomon and Thomas became friends and stayed in touch outside the magic kingdom.

When he wasn't at Millbrook, Solomon was trying to capitalise on the success of his books. There were various creative projects: an unpublished humorous piece called *Psychedelic Satire* and a feature film project about LSD – *Flight to Reality* – that Solomon developed a screenplay for but never got off the ground. These failures, added to a dearth of magazine work, must have been frustrating for Solomon, who was approaching 40. However, 1966 promised to be a good year for him, kicking off with the publication of his cannabis book on 1 January with a photograph on the cover of a neatly rolled joint resting under a brass microscope. Reviews were universally good. *The Washington Post* called it 'interesting and controversial'. Following on its heels was the paperback edition of the LSD book, which appeared with an eye-grabbing marine blue cover that displayed a distorted image of a human face blurred and twisted out of focus and a quote from *The LA Times* describing it as 'the most balanced and informative book on the subject'. The blurb on the back boldly asserted that Solomon's 'lucid, provocative and totally absorbing account' would reveal the truth behind 'the intriguing and revolutionary world of consciousness expanding drugs'.

The paperback hit the stores in the midst of a growing media furore over LSD, with newspapers and magazines competing to see who could print the most shocking scare stories. Both *The Washington Post* and *The New York Times* were worried about a potential LSD epidemic when students returned to college. The front cover of *Life Magazine* (March 1966) warned of 'The Exploding Threat of the Mind Control Drug that Got Out of Control'. *Reader's Digest* featured tales of students being hit by cars and middle-aged women committing suicide on LSD. One report described how a man drilled a hole in his skull while under the influence. More ominously, the slumbering American Leviathan finally woke up to the LSD 'problem', flexed its muscles and extended its tentacles. On 7 June 1965, New York State reacted to reports of LSD use in high schools by outlawing the 'possession, sale, exchange or giving away' of 'hallucinogenic drugs or preparations', with the exception of 'licenced physicians' buying from 'registered manufacturers'. Shortly afterwards, Washington introduced an amendment to section 201 of the Federal Food, Drug and Cosmetic Act, which came into effect on 1 February 1966 and added LSD to the list of controlled substances only available to authorised healthcare professionals, while criminalising 'the widespread illicit trade'. By that summer, three other state legislatures – California, Nevada and New Jersey – had passed similar measures.

Meanwhile, the authorities went after leading figures of the counterculture. The easiest way to bring down heat was by exploiting America's draconian anti-cannabis laws, which were considerably more severe than the ones introduced to police LSD. First offence for simple possession of marijuana was two to five years; second offence, five to ten years; third, twenty years with no possibility of parole. Leary was busted December 1965 on the Texas/Mexico border carrying $10 worth of weed. He was charged with smuggling and transporting narcotics, a felony. At Leary's trial a few months later he was sentenced to thirty years and given a $40,000 fine. He immediately launched an appeal, increased the self-promotion and did the prestigious *Playboy* interview.

Solomon's reaction was much less cavalier. He saw the writing on the wall. The cannabis book, coupled with the one on LSD, made him a prime target. As he had no intention of changing his behaviour – he was known to stroll through customs with marijuana in his pipe and drive round with a big joint on the go – he was vulnerable to arrest and incarceration at any time. Rather than take the risk, Solomon and his family high-tailed it to Europe and ended up in Deya, a small Majorcan fishing village just north of the capital Palma.

● ● ●

Close to the beach, on the slopes of a beautiful valley rich with olive groves, consisting of 200 solid stone houses and a church built on the shrine of an Iberian moon goddess, Deya was a magical place. Before the Spanish Civil War it attracted writers, painters, musicians, academics and Buddhists. After the Second World War, they returned, and during the 1950s they were joined by holidaymakers who flocked to the island, sucked in by Majorca's 200 miles of unspoilt beaches. Hotels and villas sprang up on Palma's Golden Mile. By 1965, 5,000 charter flights were landing a month. But Deya was spared the tourist invasion. Instead, it got hippies. By 1966, when Solomon arrived, 'the village had become … increasingly a centre of the hippie culture … pot and acid were readily available in the cafes, lacing people's drinks was common'.

Solomon was quick to seek out Deya's most famous resident: the English poet, author and classical scholar, Robert Graves, who was the same generation as Aldous Huxley. He endured the trench hell of the First World War, recorded this nightmare in his autobiography *Goodbye to All That* (1929) and quit the UK for good. Graves was searching for a refuge from modernity, which he regarded as a purely destructive force: 'the indiscriminate use of scientific invention without regard for consequences and devoted solely to commercial gain is poisoning earth, sea and atmosphere to a degree which threatens soon to destroy populations'.

Deya offered him the perfect 'background to my work as a writer'. Immersed in ancient Greek and Roman culture, he produced his most famous works of prose, *I Claudius* and *Claudius the God* (1934), and continued to produce love poetry at a prodigious rate. Keenly interested in all things mystical, Graves experimented with psychedelic substances while investigating their role in early European religions. On 31 January 1960 in a darkened hotel room in New York, Graves ate mushrooms while listening to a recording of a Mexican priest: 'this was not merely a red-letter day but a day marked with all the colours of the celestial rainbow'. After repeat performances, Graves concluded that this sacrament was ideal fuel for 'poets and artists'.

Graves accepted invitations to Solomon's frequent parties and was introduced to two of his American associates who'd recently landed in Deya: the ubiquitous Gerald Thomas and Paul Arnaboldi, who'd befriended Solomon at Millbrook. Born in New Jersey in 1938, Arnaboldi graduated college and worked for a construction company in the Middle East, before a car accident curtailed his career. A handsome, buccaneering type, Arnaboldi bummed around, did the occasional male modelling job – he got the nickname 'Captain Bounty' after appearing in an ad for the chocolate bar – and lived off compensation from the crash. Together with Thomas, Solomon and Arnaboldi began planning for the future; that future was THC. Extracting the psychoactive element from the cannabis plant was something of a Holy Grail for heads in the late '60s. If pure THC could be produced successfully, the sky was the limit.

However, not everybody in Deya welcomed the hippies. The locals didn't like the loud music, the mess they left their rented houses in and the fact their children 'were openly handed marijuana to share with their friends'. The villagers blamed Graves for the invasion as 'the hippies seemed to be friends' of his. The local police warned Graves' son William that Solomon and co. thought they were untouchable when they were with his father, but 'one day we will have orders from Madrid and we'll have to pull him in'. Desperate, William asked one of his father's old friends – a thriller writer – to seek out and destroy any marijuana in Graves' house. After Graves gave up his stash, the friend ceremoniously burnt it on a compost heap 'then summoned Solomon and lectured him on the dangers of getting caught'.

Solomon did take the hint and relocated to Palma. However, by spring 1967, Solomon was in jail: according to Graves, he'd made the mistake of smoking dope with a local teenager whose father happened to be a cop. Released on bail, but with a huge fine hanging over him, Solomon prepared to quit Majorca, but not before confirming with Gerald Thomas and Paul Arnaboldi that the THC plan was worth pursuing. They agreed that Arnaboldi would buy a boat, stay on the island and await further instructions; Thomas would remain in Deya a bit longer before joining Solomon in England; and Solomon would leave immediately to begin searching for THC.

———

2

Agent Provocateur

Across the Atlantic, one of Solomon's old haunts was shutting down. Billy Hitchcock – owner of Millbrook, site of Leary's acid holiday camp – had grown tired of his increasingly degenerate and aimless guests and the unrelenting pressure from the police: the mansion was regularly raided, visitors were routinely stopped and searched, and there were arbitrary arrests. In 1967, Hitchcock boarded up the main house and headed west. Once settled in Sausalito, Hitchcock tapped into the local acid scene, whose key figures had all visited Millbrook at one point or another and included Augustus Owsley Stanley the Third. Owsley was a hippy folk hero, the first person to synthesise high-quality acid outside of a laboratory, and his timing was perfect, making his breakthrough before the various anti-LSD laws came into effect. When they did, Owsley supplied what was needed in greater quantities than ever before.

From an elite Southern family – his grandfather was a senator and his father practised law in Washington – Owsley was a child prodigy who refused to listen to anybody and constantly clashed with authority, flunking out of a series of schools, the army and college before winding up at Berkeley and quitting his studies after two semesters. Keen to explore the meaning and nature of existence, Owsley soon tracked down some LSD, which had a profound effect on him. Ever curious, Owsley wondered how difficult it would be to cook some up. Using the bath tub in his cramped apartment and begging and borrowing the various ingredients he required from science students he knew, Owsley went to work, cranking out batch after batch, his product getting better all the time.

Despite being an erratic salesman (with an aristocrat's disdain for money, Owsley gave away nearly half his LSD for free) his reputation grew and, in October 1965, he was invited to a party at a secluded ranch owned by Ken Kesey – author of *One Flew Over the Cuckoo's Nest* (1962). Kesey got involved with LSD while attending a prestigious writing course at Stanford University. This all-American boy settled in an artists' community near campus and signed up to be part of a series of trials, which were being funded by the CIA, on the effects of psychoactive drugs. Based at the local veterans hospital, volunteers were paid $75 a session.

For Kesey, LSD was the undisputed highlight. When the programme ended, Kesey took a job at the hospital as a psychiatric aide, often hallucinating his way through shifts. Out of these experiences came *One Flew Over the Cuckoo's Nest*. Owsley was less than impressed by Kesey; however, he bonded with some of the other guests at Kesey's party who were members of the Oakland Hells Angels – the most feared and loathed biker gang in America. They'd met Kesey through Hunter S. Thompson, who was writing a book on their shocking exploits. Two Angels in particular – Terry the Tramp and Chocolate George Hendricks – were fascinated by LSD and when they learnt about Owsley's achievements they offered to help him offload his product.

Glad to be rid of that responsibility, Owsley ramped up his output and started branding his acid with names like Blue Cheer, White Lightning and Pink Floyd, most of which landed on the streets of Haight-Ashbury, setting off a chain reaction that transformed this down-at-heel neighbourhood into the epicentre of hippydom and fertilised the Summer of Love. LSD ceased to be a fringe phenomenon – more talked about than taken – and entered the mainstream of American life. At the same time, Owsley was hired as a sound engineer by the Grateful Dead – the band that invented acid rock – after approaching them at a gig. Owsley travelled with the band, endlessly fussed over their amps and monitors, and dished out his acid wherever they went – including back-stage at the legendary Monterey Pop Festival. It was during the band's East Coast tour, spring 1967, that Owsley visited Millbrook and got pulled over by the cops. Though there was nothing illegal in his vehicle, the contents were seized, including the key to a safety-deposit box lodged in a Manhattan bank that was stuffed with between $100,000 and $200,000 of his LSD profits. Terrified that the law would discover his stash, Owsley begged Hitchcock to make his money disappear. Hitchcock removed the bundles of cash and went to the Bahamas – where he made regular trips on 'business' – and put it in an account at the Fiduciary Trust, an investment company run by an old friend of his.

Over the next six months, Owsley and his new apprentice – a Millbrook alumnus and borderline genius who'd built a computer when he was a teenager – managed a series of labs together in obscure locations, abandoning one for another if they sensed the cops were getting too close, and farming out their product to the Hells Angels. But time was running out. Owsley was a marked man; his antics had made him a celebrity. The more his fame grew, the more desperate the FBI and state police were to bring him down. After months of on–off surveillance and several near misses, they sprang into action on 21 December 1967: the lab was raided and Owsley taken into custody. Released on bail and facing a long prison sentence, Owsley cut his losses, reunited with the Grateful Dead, and went back on the road.

Owsley's assistant slipped the net and contacted Hitchcock about bankrolling a new venture. Hitchcock weighed in with $12,000 and access to the Fiduciary Trust. Next, Hitchcock recruited Nick Sand, a young Brooklyn-born chemist who was capable of replicating Owsley's magic formula. Sand had spent time at Millbrook and was an old-hand at DIY psychedelics; in his teens, he began brewing up intoxicants and selling them on to street dealers. While at college studying sociology and anthropology, he ran a manufacturing and wholesaling operation, shifting large quantities of his own mescaline and DMT – an incredibly intense and short-lived hallucinogenic – under the cover of a fake perfume company. When the local cops started sniffing round, Sand packed up his stuff and drove to San Francisco. Once Sand had been welcomed on board, Hitchcock took him to the Bahamas so he could make use of the same money laundering service as the others. Next, the team needed to arrange sales and distribution. For this, they contacted an organisation based in Orange County: the Brotherhood of Eternal Love.

● ● ●

Two years earlier, the Street Sweepers were a biker gang operating out of Anaheim and Long Beach, south of Los Angeles. Led by John Griggs, they raided supermarkets, sold cannabis and got into fights. At the time, Griggs was struggling to kick his heroin habit. Having heard stories about LSD's healing properties, he decided to give it a try. One night, the gang broke into a Hollywood producer's house and stole his LSD from right under his terrified nose. The gang mounted their machines, headed for the Arizona desert, stopped near Joshua Tree and dropped the acid. By the next morning they had renounced their biker existence. Instead they would dedicate themselves to psychedelic exploration.

For Griggs, the desire to attain a higher state of being – mediated by LSD – was genuine and sincere. He was also sufficiently charismatic to pull other members of the gang along with him and dynamic enough to lead his motley crew further than they'd ever imagined possible. But before Griggs embarked on his quest, he travelled east to sit at Leary's feet, showing up at Millbrook in the summer of 1966. The two of them bonded instantly. Leary was fascinated by this working-class former high-school wrestling champion turned petty criminal – who'd suddenly seen the light – and gladly gave Griggs his blessing.

Having returned to California, the ex-biker and his clan decided to make their new beliefs official by forming their own religion. Setting up a legal acid church became a possibility after a 1962 test case involving Navajo Indians who'd been arrested because they used peyote during their sacred rituals. However, their appeal against the charges was successful; the judge ruled that peyote was essential to their religion and could be classed as a sacrament. Would this dispensation apply to LSD and cannabis? It was worth a try. The first to succeed were Dr John Aiken and wife who were seeking an 'appreciation of Transcendental Reality' aided by mescaline and peyote. In 1963, their Church of the Awakening based in New Mexico opened its door to fellow worshippers, and David Solomon was one of the first to attend their bizarre services.

Griggs and co. took advantage of these rulings and in October 1966 the Brotherhood of Eternal Love became an incorporated religion with legal status and tax breaks. In their founding statement, the Brotherhood vowed to uphold the 'sacred right of each individual to commune with God in spirit and in truth as it is empirically revealed to him'. Their first 'church' was a large stone building in Modjeska Canyon that stood in the shadow of the towering Santiago Peak: the walls were covered with images of Christ, Buddha and a whole range of Hindu gods, and incense burned day and night. Outside, there was an orange grove and land where they cultivated vegetables. Every Wednesday, they gathered the 'disciples' together – there were around a hundred regulars and as many as 500 floating members, mostly working class, many of whom had criminal records.

To fund their movement, the Brotherhood wanted to expand their drug-dealing activities. Before this ambition could become a reality, however, the Brotherhood needed to find somewhere else to live. In late December 1966, their 'church' was destroyed by fire when some candles set the Christmas tree alight. The Brotherhood shrugged off this setback and moved south to Laguna Beach, home to an artist's community and a thriving surfer scene – which would provide customers and new recruits. Griggs and his wife moved into a two-bedroom cottage in the canyons that ran inland from the sea and opened the Mystic Arts and Crafts Shop. In the front of their boutique they sold hippy merchandise; in the back they ran their marijuana business. At first, they smuggled grass in from Mexico by truck and boat. But then they discovered hashish (cannabis resin), which was practically unheard of in the US until bedraggled seekers of enlightenment carved out a route from Europe to Afghanistan – home of the finest hashish in the world – and small amounts of it started appearing in southern California.

Aside from loving the smoke, Griggs and co. were excited by the commercial possibilities. Two Brothers were sent to find the source. Travelling via the UK, they drove their beat-up van to Kabul where they hooked up with a local producer, made a bulk purchase and laid the groundwork for regular consignments – which were flown back to the US hidden in the panels of camper vans or in stereo equipment. Within months, they were shipping tons of it into the country to satisfy the huge demand they'd generated, creating a nationwide monopoly in the process. The Brotherhood had quickly morphed from local suppliers to global players – two of them were caught in the sleepy British fishing town of Tilbury moving Afghani hash.

As for LSD – the Brotherhood's holy sacrament – they continued to score their supplies from Owsley's Hells Angels connections up north and were actively looking to increase the size of their inventory. What they lacked was know-how, so when Hitchcock – who'd met Griggs at Millbrook – introduced Nick Sand to the Brotherhood, everything went smoothly. An agreement was made to flood the US with their LSD, and Hitchcock opened accounts for Sand and the Brotherhood at the Swiss branches of the Paravicini Bank and the Vontobel Bank, registered in the names of phony corporations, shell companies that consisted of nothing more than a postal address in Lichtenstein.

In an especially constructed and extremely well-hidden lab in Windsor, California, Sand refined and improved Owsley's recipe: the result was Orange Sunshine, the most famous brand of LSD. Buoyed by their success – Sand had made enough acid for millions of doses – the consortium discussed opening another lab in Hawaii. However, Hitchcock was in no mood to celebrate. He was in the midst of a messy divorce. His financial affairs were being forensically examined by the Internal Revenue Service (IRS). During the course of its agent's investigations into the links between organised crime and the Bahamas, the IRS uncovered Hitchcock's ties to a conglomerate called the Mary Carter Paint Factories (MCP), a shady company that had begun life as a humble paint manufacturer before being absorbed by the mafia; they used it to take control of a chunk of valuable real estate in the Bahamas that boasted several casinos.

In 1967, MCP began constructing a major hotel complex under the name Resorts International. A year earlier, the Fiduciary Trust – Hitchcock's preferred acid cash laundry – had invested $612,000 in this new venture, while Hitchcock kicked in $5 million from his own funds. With the whole Resorts International project under scrutiny, Hitchcock did his best to conceal his involvement and shifted his colleagues' assets out of the Fiduciary Trust and into the same Swiss bank that was looking after the Brotherhood. Nevertheless, Hitchcock knew it was only a matter of time before the IRS started delving into those accounts as well.

Given the trouble he was in, Ronald Stark was not the type of person Hitchcock wanted to be associated with. Stark had arrived in San Francisco having established himself as Europe's foremost LSD dealer and was looking for a partner to help him break into the US market. Stark was born Ronald Shitsky in April 1938 and grew up on New York's Depression-scarred streets. In 1953, when he was 15, his father died and his mother changed the family name from Shitsky to Stark. Whatever the nature of his relationship with his father, Stark was at a volatile and vulnerable age and his father's death knocked the teenager's world out of joint. Stark hung out with a bad crowd, flirted with trouble and, though he graduated high school, he failed to complete his studies in bio-chemistry at any of the three colleges he attended over a four-and-a-half-year period.

Nevertheless, Stark managed to secure an apparently innocuous civil service desk job, only to sabotage his chances of a stable career by submitting a fraudulent application for another government position. Stark was arrested and charged with a federal crime. He served some of his sentence at Lewisburg Penitentiary, a high security jail that held senior mob figures and their associates: one section of the prison was simply known as 'the Mafia wing'. Stark was placed with non-violent white-collar criminals: expert con-men, smugglers, embezzlers and tax-dodgers who could teach him all the tricks of their trades. On release, he immediately headed for Europe; though the details are hazy, it appears that he was initially based in Paris – where he got into difficulties over the theft of a rare book – then moved to Italy – probably Rome or Milan – and returned to France in early 1968.

Quite when or how Stark entered the LSD trade is hard to know for sure. Assuming he began as an entry-level dealer – gaining knowledge of the market and his customer base before making the quantum leap into manufacturing – Stark's supply of LSD probably came from Czechoslovakia. In 1954, the Communist regime in Prague began sponsoring an ambitious and long-running investigation into the therapeutic properties of LSD, based primarily at the Psychiatric Research Clinic and the Research Institute for Human Nutrition, where psychologists conducted thousands of sessions with hundreds of patients over the next twenty years. At first, the Czechs sourced their LSD from the Swiss firm Sandoz, but in 1961, after local chemists had managed to create good-quality acid, they went into production. From 1966, the state-owned company SPOFA began exporting millions of doses. When the laws regulating LSD in the UK, US and much of Europe were tightened, the Communist government – which was always looking for sources of foreign currency – allowed SPOFA to carry on manufacturing for the black market and customers like Stark.

Stark's success as an acid entrepreneur suggests that he would have prospered whatever field of criminal activity he entered: Stark chose to sell LSD because he believed it was a weapon that could 'facilitate the overthrow of both the capitalist West and the communist East by inducing altered states of consciousness in millions of people'. Stark was an anarchist, an engine of chaos out to destabilise the status quo and stir up an insurrection that would reduce the old order to ashes, clearing the way for a glorious new dawn. His character shared much with certain anarchists of the late nineteenth and early twentieth centuries; rogue individuals primed to attack the system – and all systems were as bad as each other: assassinating an Emperor here, a foreign dignitary there; planting bombs, robbing banks, stirring up trouble; living as fugitives in constant fear of arrest or exile.

Stark walked in their footsteps: he even resembled them with his stocky build, receding brown hair, intense, piercing blue eyes, Mexican bandit moustache and chunky sideburns. Like his nihilistic forebears, Stark was a man of action not words: theory was a dead end. However, there was one book that Stark could not live without: a sci-fi novel by Robert Heinlein, a libertarian who occupied the space where the extreme Right and extreme Left sometimes meet. Since his first story appeared in the legendary pulp magazine *Astounding*, Heinlein had churned out material of varying quality – from juvenilia to classics like *Starship Troopers* (1959) and *Stranger in a Strange Land* (1961) – which frequently tackled controversial themes and ideas. Stark was fascinated by Heinlein's *The Moon is a Harsh Mistress* (1966); he referred to it as his 'revolutionary guidebook'.

Stark was not alone in finding inspiration in sci-fi. It was the defining genre of the hippy movement. It spoke directly to the acid culture. Offering an oblique critique of society, sci-fi dealt with philosophy and theology; imagined alien beings and strange worlds in even stranger galaxies; featured telepathy, telekinesis, teleportation, technological aberrations; and altered states of consciousness. The biggest sci-fi novel of the decade was Frank Herbert's *Dune* (1965), which revolved around a spice with psychedelic properties. Herbert took mescaline in 1953 and found it exhilarating – 'you have grasped the tail of the ultimate tiger' – and terrifying – 'you are a shaman, alone and forced to master your own madness'. The success of sci-fi was reinforced by comic books. At Marvel, Stan Lee and Jack Kirby created *Spiderman*, *The Incredible Hulk*, the *Fantastic Four* and the *X-Men* among others. There were big movies like *2001: A Space Odyssey* and *Planet of the Apes*, and the *USS Enterprise* toured the universe on TV screens. Alleged UFO sightings and encounters with extra-terrestrials multiplied to such an extent that it was necessary to form the Amalgamated Flying Saucer Clubs of America.

● ● ●

Heinlein's *The Moon is a Harsh Mistress* is set in the twenty-first century and charts the course of a revolt against the Lunar Authority based on Earth that administers the colony and bleeds it dry. The leader of the insurrection is an aging professor, an anarchist whose vision of personal liberty – 'I am free no matter what rules surround me. If I find them tolerable, I tolerate them, if I find them obnoxious, I break them' – appealed directly to Stark. The professor's clandestine rebel network was connected by a system of interlocking cells arranged in an open pyramid to ensure that 'communications never break down because they run sideways as well as up and down'. Each of these cells had three members each equipped with false IDs, addresses and phone numbers. Only one of them would have contact with the adjoining cell, limiting the risk of betrayal or penetration by enemy agents. Stark adopted this approach, keeping numbers to a minimum and operating on a strictly need-to-know basis.

More significantly, Stark saw the professor's vision play out during the student uprisings that rippled across Europe, first in Italy where students occupied Turin University for a month at the end of 1967. Their actions unleashed a wave of demonstrations, protests and further occupations at colleges across the country; tens of thousands took part and thousands were arrested during violent confrontations with heavy-handed police. Further confirmation that Heinlein's professor knew what he was talking about came in Paris during the May 1968 uprisings, during which Stark added LSD to the revolutionary cocktail and took part in the protests around the Sorbonne University.

In 1958, France had 175,000 students; by 1968, there were 530,000 living in cramped sexually segregated dorms, attending overcrowded lectures, enduring a conservative, dated curriculum. Simmering discontent was channelled by a handful of left-wing activists who preferred Trotsky to Stalin; took inspiration from Mao's China, Castro's Cuba, the Vietcong and various anti-colonial independence movements; and absorbed recent works by French philosophers who had performed an autopsy on consumer capitalism and revealed its barren soulless core. At Nantarre University, Daniel Cohn-Bendit, who would become the face of the revolt, fronted a protest. The authorities overreacted. There were more protests. More overreaction. The police charged in. On 6 May, Cohn-Bendit reported to the disciplinary board at the Sorbonne while students gathered outside. The CRS – France's riot squad – confronted them. There was fighting. The Latin Quarter was in flames. Paving stones were torn up to make barricades. The CRS ramped up the violence. The more beatings they dealt out, the more people took to the streets. On Tuesday 7 May, 25,000 demonstrators, who wanted the police to release all the students they'd arrested, converged on the city centre waving 'the red flag of communism and the black flag of anarchism' and marched 'up the Champs Elysée to the Arc de Triomphe, singing *The Internationale*'.

Events were unfolding just as Heinlein's professor predicted. In *The Moon is a Harsh Mistress*, he argued that the most effective way to raise public support was to provoke the state to use disproportionate force against 'peaceful' demonstrations. In Paris, a poll of its citizens found that only 6 per cent thought police tactics were justified, while 71 per cent thought the students had been badly treated. Stark also saw the professor's approach to propaganda adopted by the Parisian rebels. In *The Moon is a Harsh Mistress*, the professor orchestrated a guerrilla publicity campaign that covered every available public space with posters and graffiti as his foot-soldiers hit the streets and distributed handbills, pamphlets and one-page tracts. Similar tactics were employed by the students in Paris; art schools were creating 350 different poster designs every day and Stark would have seen walls covered with proverbs and slogans – 'I am in the service of no-one', 'the people will serve themselves', 'the barricade blocks the street but opens the way', 'I am a Marxist of the Groucho faction' – and various groups issued dozens of statements and manifestos and handed them out wherever people congregated. Thesis 12 of *The Amnesty of The Blind Eye* – a leaflet that gained wide circulation – reminded its readers that 'revolution is neither a luxury nor an art. It is a necessity when every other means has failed'. Another method for mobilising the masses employed by both Heinlein's professor and the students was agitprop: in Paris, the Revolutionary Committee for Cultural Agitation (CRAC) tried to 'open a breach in the cultural system of the bourgeoisie' by occupying theatres, art galleries and cinemas, and filling them with 'the excluded, the poor and the oppressed'.

For a moment it seemed that the workers might join the students after a general strike on 13 May, but once they were granted pay hikes and better conditions their support fizzled. It also appeared that President De Gaulle might topple from his lofty perch, but he rallied to win handsomely in the June elections. This outcome echoed the downbeat ending of *Moon*: The Lunar Authority was overthrown only to be replaced by another oppressive system. But Stark was not as pessimistic as Heinlein. Revolution was still in the air and Stark was briefly in Milan when student demonstrations and massive trade union action rocked the Italian state. Back in Paris, he had business to attend to; Stark was going into LSD production for himself and rented several spaces in the Thirteenth Arrondissement to use as labs. This was a major step-up for Stark. In order to accumulate the organic materials, chemicals and specialised lab equipment needed to operate on an industrial scale, he created a legitimate front. Armed with an invented CV that claimed he'd studied at Harvard, the Rockefeller Institute, Bellevue Hospital and Cornell University (and having already set up one fake company – Calbiochem – that was registered in California), Stark bought into a series of firms – some active concerns, others just shells – in countries where due diligence and oversight were slack. Stark had a 40 per cent stake in Inter-Biochemical Ltd, based in Ghana, and holdings in various Nigerian companies.

Having laid the groundwork, Stark tracked down a chemist who had the ability to synthesis laboratory-grade LSD. Tord Svenson – who'd swapped the US for Paris to escape the consequences of a drug bust – was a charming Swedish giant with an easy-going nature and a passion for all things psychedelic. Tord rode motorbikes, lifted weights, kept up with the latest trends in psychology, sociology and politics, and was constantly testing his own boundaries. After graduating from the University of Massachusetts in 1959, Tord got a job with a chemical firm near Boston. In 1965, he joined the higher echelons of East Coast LSD society after being warmly embraced by the citizens of Millbrook. Hitchcock enjoyed his company, while a long-term member of the Millbrook scene and founder of the Neo-American Church (which preached that 'everyone has the right to expand his consciousness' using psychedelic drugs) fondly remembered that Tord, despite looking like 'he'd stepped out of a movie about the Vikings', was 'sweet and childlike'.

In his spare time, Tord experimented in his basement with a variety of substances, including a powerful psychedelic that comes from the glands of the Australian Cane Toad. To produce it, Tord ran a weak electric current through a toad, causing it to secrete a toxic hallucinogenic compound that had to be heavily diluted before being safe to drink. On his first visit to Millbrook, Tord brought a vial of it with him. After an hour's preparatory meditation, he consumed the potion while sitting by a lake. Four hours later, Tord came back to reality. Impressed, the leader of the Neo-American Church gave him an official title: 'Keeper of the Divine Toad'. Tord's 9–5 job prevented him from becoming a regular at Millbrook, but in early 1967 he was made redundant after the company he worked for was taken over by New England Nuclear. Tord's previous boss had ignored pressure from the FBI to have him fired, but the new owners weren't so charitable. Unemployed and at a loose end, Tord was invited to stay in the medieval style gatehouse that guarded the main entrance to the Millbrook estate. Once there, the casual debauchery and obscene wealth of his host troubled Tord's conscience and his 'Scandinavian, populist principles were constantly violated in front of his eyes'.

That autumn, however, Tord was arrested after his Boston home was raided by local police and federal agents who believed Tord was running a 'psychedelic drug laboratory'. In the basement, they found small quantities of peyote and cannabis. Out on bail, Tord and his Millbrook buddies wondered if they could get the charges dropped on the basis that he was an honorary member of the Neo-American Church and these substances were an essential part of his religion. A lawyer was contacted who agreed to take the case, but wanted $25,000 up front. Though this fee would have barely scratched the surface of Hitchcock's fortune, he refused to help because the payment wasn't tax deductible. Left high and dry, Tord pleaded guilty. He was fined $200 and put on probation for three years. This onerous restriction on his freedom was too much to bear; Tord skipped town and headed for Paris. His reputation preceded him, and Stark was quick to take advantage. A deal was done and Tord went to work in Stark's labs, where he conjured up several kilos of pure LSD, enough for millions of tabs of acid.

● ● ●

During his time in Europe, Stark frequently popped over to New York. With his profits well hidden in the same Swiss banks Billy Hitchcock used to launder his money, Stark was now a wealthy man and behaved accordingly. He drove fast cars, wore expensive clothes, ate at up-scale restaurants, owned a deluxe pad in a swanky building in Greenwich Village with a Picasso hanging on the wall, and indulged in casual sex. According to those who witnessed him in action, Stark slept mostly with women, but occasionally men as well, and participated in threesomes, foursomes and genuine orgies. To fend off questions about how he became rich overnight, Stark followed the bigger the lie principle. Either he was a not-too-distant relative of the Austrian branch of an uber-rich family who lived off his trust fund, or he was the son of a brilliant biochemist who'd inherited a fortune in patents from his father.

Using samples of Tord's LSD to attract interest, Stark was looking for somebody to sell his European-made acid in the US. Several people pointed him in Hitchcock's direction. Stark reached out to him through an intermediary and Hitchcock agreed to a meeting, reassured by Stark's connection to his old friend Tord. Stark arrived in Sausalito, only to be disappointed by Hitchcock's reaction to his plan. Beset by legal problems and the IRS, Hitchcock heard Stark out, politely declined his offer and told him to get in touch with the Brotherhood of Eternal Love. By then, the Brotherhood had moved to Arizona, next to the San Jacinto Mountains, close to Palm Springs: one visitor remembered that 'their haven lay in a spectacularly beautiful niche … There was a small lake, a rambling ranch house, corrals, a huge barn, tack houses, and cabins'. This move to such an idyllic location was partly practical; the Laguna Beach scene was spinning out of control with mobs of stoned youths fighting running battles with the police and each other, threatening to drag the Brotherhood down with them.

However, by shifting to this new environment, Griggs was also chasing a dream that had been awakened in him by Aldous Huxley's final novel *Island* (1962), a detailed portrait of an ideal community based on a remote

Pacific island that has a decentralised democratic system, an economy based on alternative technologies and sustainability, extended family networks, tantric sex and a hallucinogenic toadstool that produced a state of 'luminous bliss', which could 'take you to heaven' or 'to hell' or – if you were receptive enough – 'beyond either of them'. Though Huxley's utopia is eventually corrupted and despoiled, Griggs was fascinated by the promise it held and hoped to reconstruct the Brotherhood along similar lines; and the Arizona ranch would act as the starting point. A core of Brothers with their partners and children formed a tight circle around Griggs and together they began their journey towards true self-knowledge: one visitor fondly remembered nights in the desert soaring on acid while recreating Native American ceremonies around a campfire and scanning the sky for UFOs.

Before long, they were joined by good old Timothy Leary and family. With Millbrook under siege, Leary had shifted his attention to the West Coast, determined to stay at the head of the rapidly evolving LSD movement. Griggs had befriended Leary's wayward eldest son and reconnected with his idol when Leary delivered some lectures at California State University Long Beach. But having Leary as a house guest meant that the Brotherhood came under increased scrutiny from the FBI – in addition to mounting harassment from local cops. Trouble followed Leary wherever he went and, over Christmas 1968, he was busted driving through Laguna Canyon with two roach ends in his ashtray. Leary was now facing twenty years behind bars, ten for the joint butts and another ten from the 1965 conviction that had finally caught up with him. The heat was on. Police helicopters buzzed overhead. The roads in and out of the ranch were under surveillance. Then tragedy struck in July 1969: a friend of Leary's teenage daughter drowned on Brotherhood property. Traces of LSD were found in her system. A raid followed. Five Brothers were arrested on pot charges. Then Griggs took a dose of psilocybin, unaware that it had been cut with strychnine. He fell into a coma and died ten hours later at Idyllwild Hospital.

Nevertheless, when Ronald Stark – acting on the advice he'd been given by Hitchcock – appeared at the Brotherhood ranch, they welcomed him with open arms. Having won their confidence and entertained them with tall tales of his drug-dealing exploits – like smuggling dope from Japan concealed in electrical goods – Stark laid out his grand plan: he would manufacture LSD in Europe for them to sell in the US. Impressed by Stark's business acumen, international profile and claim to speak ten languages, the Brotherhood instantly agreed to join forces with him. Stark enjoyed their hospitality for a few days then returned to Paris to set the wheels in motion.

3

Brit Pop

When David Solomon picked Grantchester Meadows as his new home after arriving in the UK from Majorca during the spring of 1968, he was well aware of its rich literary heritage, stretching back to Chaucer and into Anglo-Saxon folklore. As an East Coast intellectual, the sheer Englishness of the place can't have failed to appeal, captured forever by Rupert Brooke in his poem 'The Old Vicarage, Grantchester', which famously asked if the church clock stood at 'ten to three' and whether there was 'honey still for tea'? But Grantchester's allure wasn't merely located in the past; its proximity to Cambridge was a massive bonus. For nearly a decade, the city had been a counter-cultural hub. According to one undergraduate, the 'student scene was one of the hippest in the country'. Modern jazz and the Beat movement arrived in the late 1950s. Cannabis appeared in 1960. Membership of CND (the Campaign for Nuclear Disarmament) was disproportionately high. Apart from London, the grand old university town was one of the few places that witnessed an influx of acid: a former student recalled how 'Cambridge was a wonderful place to take LSD, as there were loads of fascinating places you could go'.

As a venerable authority on LSD and cannabis – his books were required reading – who'd rubbed shoulders with iconic jazz musicians and figures like Leary and Huxley, Solomon was guaranteed a captive audience and quickly gained guru status: students flocked to his cottage for parties, which never seemed to end. His main problem was money. His only source of income was royalties from his books, which were boosted after *The Marijuana Papers* came out in paperback in the US with the backing of a heavyweight publisher; Signet was an imprint of the colossal New American Library, which shifted millions of books a year – everything from Shakespeare to James Bond. The new edition bore praise from a selection of reviews. *Bookweek* called it 'the basic reference work on marijuana' and trumpeted its scholarly credentials: 'this volume provides illuminating answers with a wealth of evidence'.

More important for building his profile, however, was getting the book out in the UK and in 1969 it was published by Panther, one of the market leaders in popular paperback fiction. Panther was launched in 1953 under the wing of Hamilton Ltd – a pulp sci-fi outfit who pumped out magazines with titles like *Fantastic Stories* and *Strange Adventures* – as a showcase for novel-length material. By the late 1950s, Panther was issuing the work of US sci-fi writers as well as local ones, and by the mid-1960s it dominated the market, releasing new work by the current crop of authors alongside reprints of classics from the so-called Golden Era of Asimov and Heinlein. Solomon's book was part of a new series of titles – *Panther Modern Society* – and sat alongside a history of the relationship between pornography and literature, and two works that tackled environmental issues like over population and wasteful food production.

In a new foreword written at his desk in Grantchester, Solomon described how marijuana has been consumed throughout human history, not only for recreation but as part of folk rituals and sacred ceremonies in Africa, Asia and Latin America; dispelled some of the myths surrounding it; noted its spread from the margins of Western society to centre stage; and demanded that 'the use of marijuana should be legalised'. To support his theses, Solomon commissioned a new piece for the UK edition. *Cannabis Law Reform in Britain* was by Steve Abrams, an American academic who studied under Jung and was head of the Parapsychology Department at the University of Chicago, before joining St Catherine's College, Oxford, where he studied extrasensory perception (ESP). In his essay for Solomon's book, Abrams argued that 'the social cost of prohibiting cannabis is becoming difficult to justify', not only on moral grounds but also practical ones, as 'only a considerable intensification of police powers and activity could hope to halt the spread'. He concluded that 'cannabis smoking will have profound long-term effects on society' leading to a 'far more sophisticated and humane mass culture'.

In 1967, Abrams had set up the Society of Mental Awareness (SOMA) to campaign for legalisation of cannabis after a police raid on the Redlands home of Keith Richards. The cops found drugs and a naked Marianne Faithfull. Mick Jagger was sentenced to three months for possession, Keith Richards a year. SOMA ran an ad in *The Times* criticising the judgement, which was signed by sixty-five eminent scientists, artists, writers, thinkers and musicians. That summer SOMA marched through Fleet Street and held a rally in Hyde Park attended by 10,000 supporters. The noise generated by SOMA prompted a reaction from the government. *The Wootton Report* – January 1969 – was based on an exhaustive study of the available data: though it conceded that 'in terms of physical harmfulness' cannabis was 'much less dangerous' than opiates, amphetamines, barbiturates and alcohol, its 'mental effects were much less clear', which meant that it was 'necessary to maintain restrictions on the availability and use of the drug'.

Solomon's publisher, Panther, was determined to cash in on these debates about the rights and wrongs of cannabis. The enthusiastic pitch on the back of the book described it as 'the first paperback of such scope to appear in Britain', and it came with a recommendation from R.D. Laing, the most famous psychiatrist in the UK, a bestselling author who made frequent appearances on radio and TV and had integrated LSD into his therapeutic practice. Laing may have met Solomon on a tour of the US – during which he visited Leary at Millbrook – or through their shared involvement with SOMA (Laing was one of the signatories of *The Times* ad). Laing informed prospective readers that *The Marijuana Papers* was 'indispensable' because it contained 'all the significant references on the subject up to 1969' and praised 'David Solomon' for collecting 'much more than we expect to find in one volume'.

Unfortunately, even if *The Marijuana Papers* sold well, it would take a while before Solomon saw the benefits. It was time to resuscitate the plan to extract THC from its host, especially as Abrams was pursuing the same goal and was currently locked in a Cambridge lab trying to pull the rabbit out of the hat with the help of his co-conspirator Francis

Crick, the Nobel Prize winning biochemist who unravelled the mysteries of DNA. Based in Cambridge since 1950, Crick was a social animal. By 1962, he was hosting fancy-dress parties where the unmistakable smell of marijuana hung in the air. Within a few years, Crick was sporting shaggy sideburns, jackets with wide lapels and multi-coloured shirts. Solomon was eager to tap his brain. He invited Crick to the cottage and sweet-talked him. Would he share his findings? Crick's response was guarded. Solomon tried the same with Abrams but got nowhere.

Then another option presented itself. Gerald Thomas – who'd settled in London with £20,000 ready to invest in the THC venture – introduced Solomon to a young postgraduate biochemist called Richard Kemp. Thomas had met Kemp at a scientific conference. Kemp told him about a forthcoming event in Cambridge. Thomas suggested that they meet up and visit his friend David Solomon. At 25, Kemp was an earnest young man who had so far avoided all contact with cannabis and LSD. Lack of availability may have been a factor. It was perfectly possible that Kemp simply couldn't find any acid after parliament had introduced a range of penalties for unauthorised use and added it to a list of substances that could only be obtained 'on prescription from a registered premises or under the supervision of a qualified pharmacist'. These measures were followed in August 1966 by a modification to the 1964 Drugs (Prevention of Misuse) Act. Though it continued to grant 'psychiatrists' and 'bona-fide research workers' the right to play around with LSD, it also gave the police greater powers to 'take action'. These changes severely limited imports from European manufacturers, and there was no British equivalent of Owsley to fill the gap. The vast majority of the population remained untouched. During the whole of 1968, there were just seventy-two convictions for unlawful possession of LSD.

Kemp may have resisted for political reasons: he was a radical and many on the Left were wary of the hippy drugs, fearing they encouraged introversion, self-absorption and a hedonistic attitude that would blunt revolutionary potential and undermine commitment to the struggle. However, Solomon wasn't your average stoner. And his expertise on the subject was hard to deny. Disarmed, Kemp smoked his first joint in the grounds of Solomon's Grantchester cottage. Kemp was pleasantly surprised. Whatever his concerns, they quickly evaporated the moment he inhaled.

● ● ●

Richard Kemp was born on 17 June 1943 in Bedford. He was a bright kid from a working-class background with an early gift for science. Aged 11, he embarked on that great adventure in post-war social mobility when he won a scholarship to Bedford Grammar. His talent and background made him something of an outsider there, but he performed well and earned a place at St Andrews University to study inorganic chemistry in 1961. Entering higher education, Kemp took an irreversible step away from his roots and up the social scale. Despite a big increase in student numbers in the UK during the 1960s, by the end of the decade only 25 per cent were from a working-class background. When Kemp went to St Andrews, the proportion was far lower. Though university and college attendance had risen from 122,000 in 1954 to 216,000 in 1962, this amounted to just 7 per cent of those leaving school that year: Kemp had joined the elite. This transition – leaving one class behind without being fully accepted into a new one – was difficult and Kemp may have nursed resentments and unresolved feelings of both inferiority and superiority: he was often a difficult man to be around, testy and prickly, prone to sudden flashes of temper. Kemp shared something with the Angry Young Men, who entered the nation's consciousness during his teens. They came from the provinces. They were either lower middle or working class. Their anti-heroes were alienated and dissatisfied, full of contempt for mainstream society.

Nevertheless, Kemp's rebellious streak did not emerge until his second year at university. Up to that point, his extra-curricular activities had gone no further than drinking beer, playing squash and joining the bridge club. But in 1962, Kemp bought a motorbike. At that time – when British manufacturers were turning out machines that were more than a match for US imports like the legendary Harley Davidson – any young man astride a motorbike was seen as a potential menace to society. Marlon Brando's brooding, surly performance in *The Wild Ones* –which came out when Kemp was 10 – set the template for the biker sub-culture that had sprung up by the end of the 1950s. Emulating their stateside brethren, the 'rockers' greased their hair, wore denim and studded leather jackets and continually clashed with the scooter-riding, smart suit and narrow tie-wearing 'mods', a battle for supremacy that peaked in 1964 with mass brawls at seaside towns that shocked and horrified the nation.

It's hard to know if Kemp took sides or to what extent he identified with the 'rockers'. He may simply have relished the freedom of the open road and the independence his bike gave him. Nevertheless, it was a clear sign that Kemp wanted to cultivate a bad-boy image and, within months, he'd managed to get himself expelled from St Andrews after entering the women's dormitory at night, which was strictly forbidden. Such was his scientific ability that he was quickly snapped up by Liverpool University. In autumn 1963, Kemp resumed his studies. Liverpool was buzzing with the energy unleashed by the Beatles' sudden fame. It had its own pop genre, Mersey Beat; its own brand of literature performed by the Mersey Poets; and a thriving art scene.

But just as the 60s started to swing Kemp's college life was violently interrupted. In May 1964, he had a serious motorbike accident. It took him a year to recover. After this second hiatus in his university career he knuckled down, completed his BSc in the summer of 1966 and embarked on an MA that he finished a year later, before pursuing further studies in organic chemistry. By then, Kemp had a girlfriend. Christine Bott was a tall blonde with striking looks. Born on 26 November 1943 in leafy Surrey, her father was a boat builder. Bott attended Suffolk Grammar School, where she excelled at science, and went up to Liverpool University in 1965 to study medicine. At the time, women were heavily outnumbered on most campuses and many female students were at single-sex institutions. When Bott went to university, women accounted for around 30 per cent of undergraduates; of these, 12 per cent were studying medicine. The overall disparity between the number of male and female students was even wider when it came to her chosen subject. Throughout the 1960s only about 23 per cent of those training to be doctors were women.

Bott was from a generation whose involvement with left-wing politics would shape the development of feminism, providing valuable experience in organising protests, demonstrations and direct action. She was already a committed radical when she met Kemp – who had so far shown little interest in politics aside from a short-lived association with right-wing groups during his biker days – and she soon brought him round to her way of thinking. By the mid-1960s, the inheritors of the fractured Marxist tradition were gaining a foothold in universities, attracting a dedicated hardcore on the fringes of student life, but largely ignored by the majority. This didn't mean that British students didn't face the same restrictions and hardships that so enraged their European counterparts. Course content was overwhelmingly old-fashioned and lacking imagination, tied to an archaic exam system. There was intense pressure on accommodation, forcing a large proportion into the world of private landlords and barely habitable dwellings, where the rent and daily outgoings ate up most of their funds leaving them permanently broke.

However, the leadership of the student union (the NUS) was generally more concerned with their career prospects than upsetting the status quo and did the bare minimum required to fulfil their narrow range of responsibilities. Then, seemingly out of nowhere, students at the London School of Economics occupied one of the college buildings and refused to move. Suddenly, there was a groundswell of copy-cat protests: strikes and sit-ins occurred at sixteen different institutions. In Cambridge, there was a campaign directed at the hated exam system; the organisers of the demonstrations thought the whole examination process was 'a direct expression of class warfare' that softened students up for 'mastication in the jaws of the ruling class'. Running through finals week, there were pamphlets, posters, graffiti and the 'March of the Academic Cripples', a burlesque parade 'complete with bandaged heads, burning gowns, street theatre, and a fire-hose employed by an unfriendly porter'.

Elsewhere, moves were afoot to supplant the NUS leadership. At the February 1967 conference, the radicals split from the main body and directly challenged its authority by reconvening as the Revolutionary Socialist Student Federation. Though it struggled to bring all the revolting students under its control, on 1 July the group gathered 3,000 of them outside parliament to demand greater control over their education. Demonstrations against the Vietnam War attracted a large following, but after several rallies turned violent the anti-war movement quickly ran out of steam. Otherwise the student radicals spent most of their time endlessly squabbling over the finer points of ideology and splitting into ever tinier groups: a meeting of the Cambridge Revolutionary Socialist Student Federation to discuss their future plans ended with one irate member expressing his frustration that 'we've been talking for three hours now, and we haven't made a single decision about what to do next year'!

The leftward lurch of the NUS was halted in 1968 when the radical candidates failed to win any seats on the national committee. An article in *The Guardian* regretted the fact that most British students 'tend to be conservative'. Of the students who took part in a 1969 survey at Leeds University, 86 per cent found politics boring. As a consequence, the disturbances in the UK were mild in comparison to elsewhere. But for Kemp and Bott, the upheavals of 1968 made an indelible imprint on their world view and deepened their conviction that revolution was the only answer to the world's problems.

Once Kemp had overcome his aversion to cannabis and decided it had a part to play in bringing about social change, Solomon suggested he might like to take a crack at solving the THC puzzle. Kemp was intrigued and started work in a crude lab Solomon had furnished with Gerald Thomas' money. Though Kemp made absolutely no progress, Solomon was undeterred. As far as he was concerned, the next step for the young chemist was LSD. Kemp wasn't so sure. Cannabis had proved harmless enough, but LSD? What if it wrecked his mind and ruined his scientific career?

It was an encounter with Francis Crick that tipped the scales. According to a friend of Kemp's, Crick had informed the young chemist that 'some Cambridge academics used LSD in tiny amounts as a thinking tool, to liberate them from preconceptions and let their genius wander freely to new ideas'. More startling was the claim that Crick confided to Kemp that he'd 'perceived the double-helix shape while on LSD'. If this is true, then it's a remarkable revelation, given the world-shifting implications of Crick's work on the structure of DNA. Though Crick was always open about his dalliance with LSD, it is highly unlikely it had anything to do with that miraculous breakthrough. There was almost no LSD in the country when Crick perceived the truth on 17 March 1953 and immediately wrote to his 12-year-old son to share the news that he'd 'found the basic copying mechanism by which life comes from life'. According to his biographer, Crick took LSD in 1967 and got it from Henry Barclay Todd – who would later become a key member of the Microdot Gang. Todd was in his mid-20s, bumming round Cambridge and doing a bit of dealing on the side. However, there is a problem with this version as well. According to police records, Todd spent the period from November 1966 to February 1968 in jail after being convicted of theft by false pretences (fraud).

If so, Todd must have supplied Crick with the LSD in 1968 not 1967, which raises the possibility that the acid belonged to Solomon: the LSD Todd gave to Crick came from Sandoz, the Swiss firm that Solomon had used for years, and Todd was spending a lot of time at the Grantchester cottage because he had developed a serious crush on Solomon's eldest daughter. Whatever the truth, Crick appreciated the acid but decided not to make a habit of it. Even so, Kemp may well have heard Crick being positive about LSD or even spoke to him directly. Soon after, Kemp agreed to make some for Solomon: 'if a man like Crick, who had gone to the heart of existence, had used LSD, then it was worth using it'.

Early in 1969, Solomon was sent some ergotamine tartrate – the raw material of LSD – by Paul Arnaboldi, the Majorcan connection, in a hollowed-out newspaper delivered to an American Express office in the Haymarket. Solomon gave it to Kemp to turn into acid. Kemp retired to his parents' basement and only managed to squeeze out a poor-quality batch of dark syrupy LSD. Solomon gave him a few hundred quid and some marijuana as payment and Gerald Thomas smuggled the inferior product into Canada. Kemp sampled his own wares and was not particularly impressed. However, he was intrigued by the problems posed, the obstacles encountered and the difficulties presented by the process of creating LSD. It was a genuine challenge: a test of his knowledge, skill, judgement and nerve. He continued his experiments over the course of the summer. Late one night he smashed a beaker of concentrated LSD and got a huge dose. This time he was really turned on. He had his LSD awakening. He saw that it was the key to transforming society: 'the answer is to change people's mindsets using acid'. He dropped out and moved to Grantchester Meadows, a decision made easier by the fact that Christine Bott also embraced LSD. She said that 'people would be happier' if they were 'given the chance to use acid' and 'the world would become a better place'.

● ● ●

After Ronald Stark returned to Paris after his summit meeting in Arizona with the Brotherhood of Eternal Love, he ran into an American who was at Cambridge and knew Solomon. Stark liked what he heard. Ever the hustler, he was hoping to piggyback on SOMA's experiments with THC. Perhaps he could kill two birds with one stone. Stark hopped over to London and tracked down Solomon. The inevitable invitation to Grantchester followed and Stark was introduced to Kemp. The Microdot Gang was born.

They had few concerns about manufacturing millions of tabs of LSD for public consumption. During a good trip you were at one with the cosmic chain of being connecting all living matter, in harmony with the universe. They ignored the fact that a bad trip left you totally alienated from that chain of being, isolated in a hostile universe with the cosmos aligned against you. The balance between the two extremes was delicate. Environment and emotional state were crucial. The slightest adjustment of ambience could flip a trip into a nightmare: Leary observed that 'consciousness becomes extremely vulnerable … swung by the slightest pressure. A frown. A gesture. A word.' There was little middle ground.

Kemp was a recent convert and couldn't – or wouldn't – see the negatives. Solomon had travelled too far down the LSD road to turn back. He had little choice but to believe his own rhetoric. Besides, he wanted to change the world and there were bound to be casualties. He could comfort himself with the thought that acid did far less damage than cigarettes or alcohol, not to mention drugs like heroin. Stark didn't care: good or bad made no difference, anything that caused disruption was fine. Whether it was naked people running down the street screaming or thousands too blissed out to go to work, the more the merrier; if things got messy, so be it. A revolution had little hope of success unless society was shaken to its foundations, and Stark wanted their LSD to do a thorough demolition job.

At the beginning of 1970, Stark asked Kemp to join him in Paris and make acid for the Brotherhood to sell. To formalise their arrangement, the three of them gathered at the exclusive Oxford and Cambridge Club in central London, which Stark had wormed his way into with the help of his bogus degree from Harvard. Also present was an associate of Stark and Paul Arnaboldi, who claimed a seat at the table on the basis that he'd supplied the ingredients for Kemp's initial LSD experiments. Aside from his living expenses and some pocket money, Kemp's fee would be finalised once he'd completed the job. Otherwise, the main bone of contention was Solomon's slice of the action. Having talent-spotted Kemp and paid for his first efforts at making LSD, Solomon wanted a share of whatever his protégé manufactured for Stark. He also wanted a guarantee that Kemp would be allowed to return to the UK after fulfilling his contract. It took another meeting – a bad-tempered evening at a Chinese restaurant – to settle the matter. Instead of simply being able to purchase the finished product at a reduced price, Stark agreed to let Solomon have one large consignment free of charge. With the deal done, only one question remained; would Kemp be able to overcome the many difficulties associated with producing premium-quality LSD? Until he did, the future of the Microdot Gang would hang in the balance.

Part Two

THE MICRODOT GANG

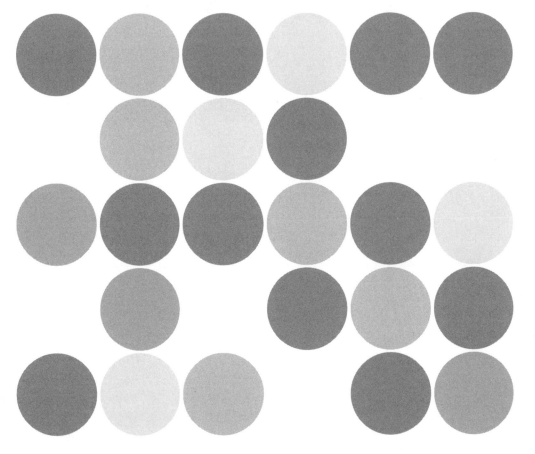

4

The Alchemists

In his book *My Problem Child* (1979), Albert Hofmann – the Swiss chemist who discovered acid's awesome capabilities – recalled the concerns he'd had during the 1960s about the spread of what he called 'black market' LSD. Even though Hofmann believed LSD could help modern society resolve its spiritual crisis, he was worried that 'the huge wave of inebriant mania' sweeping 'the Western world' would inevitably result in unauthorised, unregulated and potentially dangerous acid hitting the streets. Hofmann was convinced that most black-market LSD was 'unreliable when it comes to both quality and dosage' and prone to 'decompose in the course of a week or a few months'. Though detailed information about how to brew your own acid had been widely available since the early 1960s, Hofmann was alarmed by 'claims that LSD might be easily prepared, or that any chemistry student in a half-decent laboratory is capable of producing it'.

Hofmann knew better than most that LSD was an extremely volatile substance to deal with. A fractional shift in atmospheric conditions or clumsy handling could ruin an entire batch. As Hofmann explained, LSD could be 'destroyed by the oxygen in the air and is transformed into an inactive substance under the influence of light'. As a result, synthesising LSD was a delicate balancing act and required the sort of intuitive and instinctive reactions more usually associated with art than science –

a magician's touch. What Hofmann failed to anticipate was the emergence of truly gifted individuals – like Tord Svenson and the Brotherhood's chief chemist Nick Sand – who were capable of mastering these difficulties.

Hofmann was also sceptical about the chances of any aspiring acid-maker being able to source the 'special equipment' required to safely distil and store LSD. But the Swiss sorcerer underestimated the ingenuity and resourcefulness of Sand and his brethren. The alchemists assembled their labs piece by piece, buying from a number of different companies, modifying the component parts and reconditioning their working environment as required. When it came to manufacturing the legendary Orange Sunshine, Sand had the best of both worlds, thanks to the assistance of a respectable middle-aged Professor of Chemistry at Case Western Reserve University who gave Sand access to the college labs. The professor was genuinely curious about Sand's experiments and stood to earn a substantial sum if he lent a hand. While the bulk of the work was done in a DIY lab secreted in an isolated house, the pristine university facilities allowed Sand to concentrate on the fine details, to modify, elaborate and fashion his Orange Sunshine into something distinctive.

Stark's labs in Paris were not quite as sophisticated as this, but were more than adequate for Kemp's requirements. But Kemp had not yet proved that he was capable of making the grade, so Stark called on Sand's expertise to help get him over the line. Sand and his assistant – the helpful chemistry professor – flew to Europe in the spring of 1970 and the four of them met in Switzerland. Over the next few days, Kemp was given a crash course in how to create premium acid, including Sand's own formula for Orange Sunshine scribbled on a piece of paper. Stark thought Sand's notes were so valuable that he put a copy of them in a safety-deposit box in Rome.

All this preparation, however, was useless unless they could lay their hands on the base material of LSD, an alkaloid called ergotamine. Alkaloids are nitrogen-based organic compounds – mostly found in plants and funguses – that possess a remarkable range of pharmaceutical and medicinal properties, and have given rise to a wide range of painkillers and mood-enhancing drugs, including morphine, nicotine, coffee and cocaine. Ergotamine, an alkaloid by-product of the fungus ergot that grows on rotten rye and other cereals, was separated from its host in 1918 by chemists working for the Swiss pharmaceutical company Sandoz. But it wasn't until the 1930s – after staff at the Rockefeller Institute in New York found that lysergic acid could be synthesised from ergotamine – that Sandoz paid closer attention to its various properties.

In 1938, the young Albert Hofmann was assigned the task of examining lysergic acid to see what chemical compounds could be extracted from it. The twenty-fifth substance he found was lysergic acid diethylamide, which he christened LSD-25. For the next five years, he was focused on other tasks, but in the spring of 1943 Hofmann went back to LSD. On 16 April, during 'the purification and crystallisation of lysergic acid diethylamide' his 'work was interrupted by unusual sensations' such as a 'remarkable restlessness, combined with slight dizziness'. Hofmann had accidentally absorbed a tiny trace of LSD through his fingertips. Unsettled, he headed home and lay down in a 'not unpleasant, intoxicated-like condition, characterised by an extremely stimulated imagination' and saw 'an uninterrupted stream of fantastic pictures'. The whole experience lasted about two hours, and afterwards he was determined to repeat it.

Three days later, at 4.20 p.m., Hofmann took a diluted dose of LSD and waited to see what happened next. Forty minutes later, he was disorientated, anxious and overwhelmed by the 'desire to laugh'. The world's first full-blown acid trip had begun, all the more disconcerting because it was so totally unexpected – what on earth was happening to him? Alarmed, Hofmann asked a colleague to escort him on his bicycle ride home, during which 'everything in my field of vision wavered and was distorted as if seen in a fun-house mirror'. Once indoors, he was overwhelmed by a succession of terrifying images. However, once the nightmarish visions had passed and a doctor had been called, he began to relax into it and enjoy some of the sensations: he was treated to a riot of 'unprecedented colours' and swirling 'kaleidoscopic ... images', while every sound, no matter how trivial, took on a unique shape and form, dancing in front of his 'closed eyes'.

Having managed to sleep, Hofmann woke feeling rested, refreshed and without any noticeable hangover from his nocturnal adventure. Pleasantly surprised, Hofmann calculated the amount of LSD he'd ingested and was astounded by how little was needed to trigger such a profound response. What startled him even more was the fact he 'could remember the experience of LSD inebriation in minute detail'. Exhilarated and full of wonder, Hofmann bashed out a report and gave it to his colleagues who couldn't believe what they were reading. Once several of them had tried LSD, 'all doubts' about what Hofmann had described 'were eliminated'. Following standard procedure for testing a new substance, Sandoz went ahead with animal trials. The main difficulty with this approach was the fact that no animal can articulate what is happening in their brains. As a result, Hofmann and his colleagues would only be able to observe LSD's effect on them if it produced 'relatively heavy psychic disturbances'.

But to get anywhere near such an intense state, the different animals had to be subjected to a vastly higher dose than humans. Even then, the results were inconclusive. Mice showed some 'motor disturbance' and 'alterations in licking behaviour'; cats and dogs both displayed signs of 'the existence of hallucinations'; fish adopted 'unusual swimming postures'; on a low dose, spiders weaved 'more precisely built' webs; and a group of chimpanzees reacted very badly when one of them was given LSD and began behaving erratically. Overall, none of the animals suffered damaging physical side-effects. Work on humans could safely continue. Further tests conducted by Hofmann and his colleagues – plus positive feedback from the handful of psychiatrists and psychologists who were the first recipients of Sandoz acid – led to excited company executives authorising production.

From then on, Sandoz supplied governments, universities, medical facilities and private citizens. Everyone from Solomon to the CIA benefited from its stockpiles, until the company stopped making it altogether. On 23 August 1965, one of the firm's directors issued a statement explaining why Sandoz had decided to abandon acid. Though previously 'cases of LSD abuse have occurred from time to time', its widespread use and growing popularity had multiplied the risks to such an extent that in 'some parts of the world' LSD was now 'a serious threat to public health'. As for Hofmann, he spent the rest of his life wrestling with his conflicted feelings about what he'd done and worrying about the fate of his 'problem child'.

● ● ●

Until it shut down its operations, Sandoz had been the main global supplier of the all-important ergotamine tartrate (the industry-standard preparation of the alkaloid ergotamine involved rendering it in the form of a tartrate – a rock salt – which made it easier to manipulate), and the firm's cessation of production caused a collapse in availability. Though there were still some small chemical traders dotted about who were able to exploit loop-holes in the laws governing LSD – and the Czechoslovakian firms manufacturing acid for state-sponsored research programmes continued to export ergotamine tartrate – it was extremely difficult to get enough of it to produce the vast amount of LSD Kemp was expected to make.

The problem was solved by Nick Sand and Billy Hitchcock, who had already addressed this issue when they were putting together the original deal with the Brotherhood. Back then, they'd turned to Charles Druce, an Englishman they'd run across at Millbrook. Druce was a London-based chemical trader who'd established a lucrative arrangement with the UK outlet of a Czechoslovakian company dealing in acid and its component materials. Druce spotted a gap in the market and started an international LSD mail-order business. On a trip to the US in 1965, he appeared at Millbrook and Leary persuaded him to become their supplier. Once LSD was illegal, however, Druce got cold feet and shut up shop.

Next, Druce embarked on a new venture, teaming up with Ron Craze – a British employee of the Czech chemical firm that Druce had patronised – to form Alban Feeds Ltd, with the aim of selling animal feed to developing countries. But to get off the ground, they needed an injection of cash. At the same time, Hitchcock and Sand were wondering where they were going to find the ingredients for the acid production run they'd organised with the Brotherhood. Hitchcock remembered Druce and suggested they give him a try. On 23 June 1968, Druce and his business partner Craze landed in San Francisco and were whisked straight to Hitchcock's luxury pad in Sausalito. Though Craze was nervous about what he might be getting into, Druce had no reservations about taking Hitchcock's money. A $9,000 advance allowed Druce and Craze to set up Alban Feeds Ltd. Sand then placed a $100,000 order for 5 kilos of lysergic acid and around 12 kilos of ergotamine tartrate. Once converted, the resulting LSD would have a street value of $5 million.

To cover his tracks, Hitchcock transferred the funds earmarked for Alban Feeds Ltd from his holdings in the Bahamas to his Swiss bank, then moved them into Sand's Zurich account before depositing them in Druce and Craze's bank in London. Under the Alban Feeds Ltd banner, they purchased what their investors had ordered from a firm in Hamburg, and the ergotamine tartrate was flown straight from there to Canada and smuggled across the border to New York. Everything went reasonably smoothly and, once Kemp was signed on to produce LSD for Stark and his Brotherhood colleagues, the acid consortium contacted Druce and asked for 9 kilos of ergotamine tartrate. But Druce was in no mood to co-operate. An LSD lab in America had been busted and some of the materials found there were traced back to Alban Feeds Ltd. A Scotland Yard detective showed up on Druce's doorstep and advised him to stop playing with fire.

By mid-May 1970, Druce's failure to deliver the goods was beginning to jeopardise Kemp's mission. Stark decided to exert some pressure. He gave Kemp the keys to his brand-new red Ferrari and, with one of Stark's underlings as an escort, Kemp raced off to see Druce in person. When Kemp and his passenger arrived at customs in Dover, Kemp had to admit that the car wasn't his. Stark's man – a UK citizen – immediately took responsibility for the vehicle. Suspicious, the customs officer ran a check on his passport, which showed that he was a registered heroin addict with a criminal record. A team of customs men spent several hours taking the Ferrari apart piece by piece, but their search was fruitless. The car was clean and Kemp and his companion were free to continue their journey. Luckily for them, the officers had ignored Kemp's briefcase, which was full of documents about purchasing ergotamine tartrate. In the end, they returned to Paris from their London meeting with Druce with a piece of essential laboratory equipment and some empty promises: Druce had prevaricated, made excuses and apologetically sent them on their way. But he'd got the message; these people were not going to leave him alone. Unable to take the heat, Druce dropped out of sight, leaving his partner Craze on the hook for the ergotamine tartrate. By now Craze had grasped the true nature of the business he'd been involved in and wanted nothing more to do with it.

Stark had other ideas. He knew that Craze had a big cache of ergotamine tartrate stored in Hamburg. He also knew that Alban Feeds Ltd was in financial difficulties and Craze was looking to sell it all to balance the books. So he set a trap. Stark invented a fictitious company called Inland Alkaloids, contacted Craze through an intermediary and informed him that Inland Alkaloids was interested in buying up his stocks. Given that Alban Feeds Ltd was on the verge of going under, Craze leapt at the offer. But before any money had changed hands, Stark's minion – who'd driven to the UK with Kemp – waltzed into the Hamburg warehouse, told them he was from Inland Alkaloids, handed over the relevant paperwork and walked out with the ergotamine tartrate. When payment still didn't appear and it was obvious Inland Alkaloids didn't exist, Craze started to panic. He wrote to Sand and Hitchcock demanding an explanation. Worried that Craze might betray them, Sand and his assistant confronted Craze in London and suggested that it would be better for him if he forgot the whole thing. Craze was not ready to back off and hinted that he was prepared to go to the police. At which point, he received an invitation from Stark for afternoon coffee and biscuits at the Oxford and Cambridge Club.

One of Stark's many talents was his ability to pinpoint people's strengths and weaknesses, and he quickly realised that hiding behind Craze's indignant rhetoric was a scared man. He also knew exactly what persona to adopt to suit the occasion and his reassuring manner and air of professional competence disarmed Craze. He remembered that Stark was 'polite and pleasant' and willing to 'do everything he could … to help'. Yet Craze left the club none the wiser and resigned to the fact that he would never recover his money. Stark's more subtle approach had done the trick and Craze quietly faded from view.

Meanwhile, Kemp was putting the ergotamine tartrate to good use in Stark's Paris lab, located in a former perfume factory. With Sand's formula as a guide, Kemp worked flat out as he began to master the art of creating acid. Late one night, at the end of another long shift, he decided to put some LSD solution in the fridge rather than leave it at room temperature as he normally would. Next day, Kemp was delighted to discover that refrigerating it had actually sped up the crystallisation process. Here was a safe and easy method of getting to the end product a lot faster, which brought obvious advantages. By the time he finished, Kemp had generated a kilo of pure LSD – a staggering ten million doses worth of Orange Sunshine – half of which went to Stark, the rest to the Brotherhood. Kemp had shown that he was capable of matching the standards set by the other alchemists. Over time, he would surpass them all.

● ● ●

Given the resounding success of their collaboration, Stark was keen to keep Kemp on the payroll. The Paris lab was still ready and available, but Stark decided to relocate operations to a crude, run-down outbuilding on a dismal industrial estate in Orléans, some 80 miles from the capital. Though it is not clear why Stark made this move, various sources suggest that he'd received a tip from the Brotherhood that the Paris lab had come to the attention of the authorities. At first, Stark commissioned Kemp to revert to where he'd started with Solomon a year earlier, trying to synthesise THC – an ultimately frustrating and thankless task. Stark shrugged off the lack of progress on this front and proposed that Kemp return to LSD. But by then Kemp had run out of patience with the primitive working conditions and Stark's high-handed treatment of him.

Neither Kemp nor Stark ever discussed their relationship in any detail and it's hard to imagine them becoming friends. As a rule, Stark didn't do friendship and Kemp was not the most open or sociable character. Yet they had more in common than their wildly different backgrounds – the bespectacled working-class lad from the north of England and the burly hustler from Brooklyn – might suggest. Both had travelled a long way from where they'd come from and neither would ever be able to return to the world they'd left behind. Both were fairly self-contained and self-possessed. Both of them believed that LSD would bring about social revolution. And, though Kemp never called himself an anarchist, his politics were closer to Stark's philosophy than to the more conventional Marxist Left.

Where they differed most significantly was on their attitude to personal relationships. Kemp was not a promiscuous individual. The sexual experimentation and free love ethos of the era held no attraction; Bott was the only woman for him. Stark, on the other hand, didn't have a monogamous bone in his body. There is no evidence Stark ever had a long-term partner, male or female: a diet of no-strings-attached sex was sufficient for him. His voracious appetite and predatory instincts, combined with his open bisexuality, troubled Kemp and he began to worry that he was the object of Stark's desires, especially during a brief excursion to Morocco. This tension undermined their partnership, but in the end it was Kemp's commitment to Christine Bott that broke it apart.

In July 1970, Bott was one of the 483 female students across the UK who completed a degree in medicine. Next came two years of intensive and demanding training to qualify as a doctor, and Bott chose to do it at a hospital on the Isle of Man. Perhaps she opted for such a remote yet beautiful setting – with jagged coastlines, windswept mountains, open plains, undulating hills and wooded valleys – because she was tired of urban life after five years in Liverpool and wanted to rediscover her countryside roots and enjoy the benefits of a more rural environment. Not that the Isle of Man was all peace and quiet. The hospital where Bott was doing her training was in Douglas, the capital city and home to nearly half the island's population. Overlooking the sea, and at the confluence of two rivers, this busy port welcomed thousands of tourists every year. Visitors filled the boarding houses and local resorts, the promenade was lined with fish and chip shops; there were pubs, cinemas, variety shows, dance halls and high-end gambling at the casinos.

Despite the distance between them – and the fact that most of her energy and time would have been consumed by her hospital duties – there was no indication that Bott's relationship with Kemp had cooled off. He was bored of his work, tired of the enforced separation and missing her terribly. Plans were made for a reunion. But Stark was fanatical about security and had refused to let Kemp have any visitors. Kemp ignored his wishes, invited Bott over to stay and, during their time together, she took LSD for the first time. When Stark found out, he was livid. The two of them had an almighty row, which led to Kemp quitting and returning to Britain. Their falling out, however, was only temporary. Stark had no intention of squandering his investment in Kemp or the knowledge the young chemist had acquired. Kemp, on the other hand, wasn't about to abandon the LSD business. He'd found his vocation and felt capable of making the best acid on the planet; he could hardly afford to ignore what Stark had to offer.

In 1970, the Home Office published a report by the Advisory Committee on Drug Dependence, which surveyed all the data it could muster about the LSD trade. According to its findings there was some LSD being produced in the UK, but 'the bulk of it is smuggled from the USA'. The report also noted that 'users preferred the American LSD and regarded the English product as inferior'. Thanks to what Kemp had achieved while under Stark's wing, that was all about to change.

5

Mind Over Matter

Over the course of 1970, Stark spent long stretches of time in the UK, either at the Oxford and Cambridge Club or at Hilton Hall, an elegant seventeenth-century red-brick mansion in Cambridgeshire that belonged to David Garnett, a respected editor and author of several children's books. He'd inherited Hilton Hall from his father – also a writer – who bought it in 1924 and opened its doors to the Bloomsbury Group, an avant-garde clique known for its artistic and sexual experimentation. Though not as unconventional as his father, the current owner created a similarly bohemian atmosphere, with carefully selected guests being given the run of the house in exchange for minimal rent. Stark gained entry thanks to an invitation from Steve Abrams, who had recently moved in with a group of friends. Abrams had founded the legalisation of cannabis pressure group SOMA, collaborated with Francis Crick on his research into THC and written a piece for the UK edition of Solomon's marijuana book. Given that Stark was also keen to crack the THC puzzle, he was hoping to get some answers from Abrams. Any reservations about Stark's arrival at Hilton Hall were quickly banished once the residents were treated to his 'largesse'; Abrams recalled how Stark would take them all out to eat at expensive restaurants and happily paid the electricity and phone bills.

Abrams was fascinated and puzzled by Stark, not knowing whether to fear him or admire him. He was impressed by Stark's scientific expertise, rattled by his habit of talking like a mafia hitman and astounded by the sheer size of his LSD operation. But prolonged exposure to Stark made him increasingly uneasy: although Stark appeared to be 'fairly official and fairly protected', he also 'seemed to be involved in arms trading' and 'buying and selling chemicals which … seemed to have nothing to do with making drugs' and more to do with manufacturing explosives. At the time, however, Abrams and the other residents were more concerned about Solomon's frequent visits and the disruption they caused. In return for letting Kemp team up with Stark and the Brotherhood, Solomon had received around 250 grams of LSD – with a street value of about £1 million. The problem was, he had no idea what to do with it. Solomon's previous drug transactions had been minor affairs, catering for himself and those in his social circle, and he'd only just started taking the first tentative steps towards up-scaling his activities when Kemp transferred to Paris.

Even with the best will in the world, Solomon and his buddies would never be able to consume that much LSD themselves, though Solomon seemed determined to try. Acid-fuelled paranoia took hold as he desperately searched for places to safely hide it all. One option was the grounds of Hilton Hall, and Solomon was spotted prowling round the various barns and out-buildings, and lurking near rows of haystacks. These suspicious comings and goings, combined with his wired demeanour and indiscreet behaviour – according to Abrams, 'Solomon was horribly uncool, and everybody in Cambridge knew what he was doing' – put Stark in a difficult position and he was forced to act. Stark sat down with Solomon and gave him such a thorough talking to that he almost fled the building, never to return.

This showdown between the two New Yorkers had been on the cards for a while. Ever since their first meeting, the differences in their characters and backgrounds made common ground difficult to find. They might share the same core ideas about LSD and its role in ushering in a new dawn, but their approach couldn't have been more different. Solomon was a thinker: Stark was a doer. The intellectual gulf between them need not have been an obstacle, except for the fact that both of them liked to be the dominant personality in any room; much of the friction between them was caused by the clash of two formidable male egos.

Ultimately, Stark had the upperhand. All Solomon's knowledge about acid, his celebrity friends and status as a counter-cultural scholar meant little when he was dealing with Stark and the Brotherhood. Without any experience of international drug trafficking, Solomon was hopelessly out of his depth, while any authority he commanded had been critically undermined when Stark whipped Kemp away from him. From then on, Stark treated Solomon with a mixture of contempt and indifference, culminating in the dressing down at Hilton Hall. Nevertheless, Solomon knew important people and Stark was keen to exploit his address book. It was Solomon who introduced Stark to Abrams, and it was Solomon who could help Stark satisfy an almost obsessive desire to win the confidence of R.D. Laing, the world-famous psychiatrist and advocate of LSD. Solomon had a long-standing interest in the use of acid to treat mental health problems and may well have met Laing when he visited the East Coast in 1964 and 1965. During these trips, Laing partied in New York with Leary and sampled what Millbrook had to offer. Once Solomon was in the UK, he was reunited with Laing through their joint membership of SOMA. According to Laing's son, Solomon was 'a close associate' of his father.

Though there was a degree of confusion, uncertainty and even anxiety about the therapeutic value of LSD, there was general agreement about its ability to mine the subconscious and dredge up deep-seated fears and neuroses, excavating psychic sludge so it could be examined in the clear light of day. During hallucinations, sources of emotional torment and mental anguish were exposed, given character and a visual and aural identity. For the subject, this could be a moment of reckoning, a confrontation with oneself that might open the way to a fresh start. Even if the results were not as dramatic as this, many patients still felt a renewed connection to their environment and sense of their place in the universe. As one leading LSD therapist observed, the subject might realise they are 'part of all things and all things are part of them'.

In the early 1960s, Solomon began investigating the work being done by acid therapists. His LSD anthology featured two pieces by the psychiatrist Humphrey Osmond, who'd guided Aldous Huxley through his first psychedelic adventures; thought LSD could 'help us to explore and fathom our own nature'; and was researching its 'capacity to mimic more or less closely some aspects of grave mental illnesses, particularly of schizophrenia'. In 1964, Solomon reached out to another expert in the field, Duncan Blewett, who was attached to the same Canadian research programme as Osmond and, like the rest of his colleagues, had taken LSD numerous times so he could understand what his patients were going through. According to Blewett, his first trip was 'the most profound experience' he'd ever had, giving him 'direct contact with the infinite' combined with 'tremendous infusions of love' and 'an awareness of very great beauty all about one'.

Blewett shared Solomon's belief that information and knowledge about psychedelics should be disseminated as widely as possible. To advance this cause, Blewett co-authored the *Handbook for the Therapeutic Use of Lysergic Acid Diethylamide-25: Individual and Group Procedures* (1959), a detailed analysis of how to organise sessions and what results to expect from them. Aside from laying down a theoretical framework, Blewett served up practical advice about making the whole experience as easy as possible for the patient. The treatment room needed to be 'comfortable and quiet' and close to a bathroom because having to 'walk through a ward or indeed to walk any distance' under the influence of LSD would be 'a severe strain'. Classical music and walls decorated with paintings would help stimulate the patient. A mirror would promote 'self-understanding'. For nourishment, Blewett recommended fruit, chocolate 'and other candy'.

By the time Solomon got in touch with Blewett, he'd shifted his attention towards developing a science of the soul to compensate for the 'spiritual vacuum' that lay at the heart of contemporary research. Together, Solomon and Blewett planned to establish an Institute for Studies in Normal Psychology, where you could learn how to use your own latent psychic energy to heal yourself. Meanwhile, Solomon contacted William McGlothlin, a Professor of Psychology who was attached to the Logistics Department at the RAND Corporation, based in Santa Monica, California. Formed in the immediate post-war period as a technological and scientific think-tank for the US airforce, by the mid-1950s RAND had become an all-purpose ideas factory exerting tremendous influence over Cold War planning and decision making in Washington and the Pentagon. In 1962, McGlothlin applied for funding from his bosses at RAND to conduct a survey into the long-term effects of LSD on 'normals' – people who had no record of mental illness.

Unfortunately, RAND rejected his proposal because it was not the kind of 'research normally undertaken by the Corporation'.

Forced to turn elsewhere, McGlothlin collaborated with two of his peers on a slim report – *Short-Term Effects of LSD on Anxiety, Attitudes and Performance* (1963) – based on research done at Wadsworth Central Hospital in LA involving 'normal subjects', fifteen of whom had reduced anxiety, a more open mind and unchanged performance levels after completing their acid tests. McGlothlin's next approach to the RAND board was more successful and they commissioned a major study from him – *Hallucinogenic Drugs: A Perspective with Special Reference to Peyote and Cannabis* – which he completed in 1964. As Solomon was putting together his anthology about marijuana, he asked McGlothlin if he could use some of this report. McGlothlin gave his consent and Solomon included a section that featured a brief history of the plant, a comparison with LSD and peyote, an overview of cannabis culture across the globe, an examination of its links to criminal behaviour, both real and imagined, and its relatively benign physical and mental effects.

For all the advances made, doctors like Blewett and McGlothlin realised they'd barely begun to understand LSD and there was still a vast amount of work to be done. But in 1966, the law changed and almost all ongoing studies into LSD ground to a terminal halt. Solomon and Blewett's plan to host a conference as a launch pad for their Institute for Studies in Normal Psychology fell apart. McGlothlin was so outraged by the new federal and state regulations that he issued an eloquent and reasoned challenge to California's anti-acid legislation. In *Toward a Rational View of Hallucinogenic Drugs*, McGlothlin argued that the bill was an example of 'legal repression' and 'poor judgement' based on the nebulous claim that LSD was responsible for 'the increasing incidence of … psychotic reactions' and 'anti-social acts'. Dismissing these charges as over-blown and inaccurate, McGlothlin then pointed out the various harmful consequences of criminalisation: forcing 'students' and other regular citizens to break the law, risking arrest, 'social stigma and other personal harm'; the spread of black-market 'poor quality' acid; and the involvement of 'organised crime as a source of supply'.

● ● ●

Once Solomon arrived in the UK, it was only natural for him to gravitate towards Laing, who had already integrated LSD into his therapeutic practice and world view. Aside from their joint association with SOMA – which led to Laing endorsing the UK edition of Solomon's marijuana anthology – they were both preoccupied by the clinical, philosophical and metaphysical implications of the acid experience. Less easy to explain is why Stark was so fascinated by Laing. The more abstract, spiritual and cosmic aspects of acid culture appeared to be of little concern to somebody like Stark, who followed the revolutionary programme set out by Robert Heinlein's anarchist professor in *The Moon is a Harsh Mistress*. But Stark did mention one other influence on his thinking that might have pushed him in the direction of Laing: the writings of Carlos Castaneda, an anthropologist whose travels to the far side of consciousness – what he called 'states of non-ordinary reality' – had earned him a large and devoted following. In his book *The Teachings of Don Juan: A Yaqui Way of Knowledge* (1968), Castaneda described the time he spent in Arizona and Mexico serving as an apprentice to Don Juan, an old Yaqui Indian shaman. At periodic intervals stretched over the course of four years, Don Juan guided Castaneda through a series of rituals involving a range of specially prepared hallucinogenic plants and herbs – peyote, Jimson Weed and magic mushrooms – that transported Castaneda into a parallel dimension that intersected with our own.

Don Juan was initially reluctant to take on Castaneda as a pupil. But after Castaneda had shown some promise, Don Juan began his education by introducing him to his 'ally', a spirit protector called Mescalito, who was 'capable of carrying a man beyond the boundaries of himself' and would watch over Castaneda in the outer realms. In Castaneda's visions, Mescalito took the form of a giant peyote plant with 'sparkling gold and black' eyes, a head 'pointed like a strawberry' and green skin 'dotted with innumerable warts'. Even with Mescalito looking out for him, Castaneda was often frightened and overwhelmed by what he experienced: during one hallucination, Castaneda felt like he was 'melting' as his whole body dissolved into nothingness. When he wiped his face, all the flesh came off; when he reached out for a solid object, he ended up 'grabbing air'. Desperate to make tangible contact with something, he slammed himself against a wall, but instead of banging against it, he simply sank into it, 'completely suspended in a soft, spongy substance'. He had become the wall. If that wasn't bad enough, Castaneda was also prey to malign spirits intent on devouring him. During his final hallucination, a she-devil tried to steal his soul by pretending to be Don Juan.

Castaneda's psychedelic encounters with evil beings would have been familiar to anyone who'd suffered a 'bad trip', as they often featured the unwanted appearance of demons and devils. This deeply unsettling phenomenon affected people as different as Albert Hofmann – the discoverer of LSD – and Howard Marks, the best-selling author and international hashish smuggling tycoon, who made his fortune by tapping into the Brotherhood's Afghan supply chain. On that historic night in 1943 when Hofmann first grappled with LSD, he arrived home about an hour and a half after taking his dose. Already feeling the effects, he stretched out on the sofa in an effort to stay relaxed. Instead, he was suddenly overcome by terror as 'familiar objects and pieces of furniture assumed grotesque, threatening forms'. Worse was to come. Hofmann remembered how he lost all sense of control over his 'inner being' and was 'seized by a dreadful fear of going insane': it was as if 'a demon had invaded me' and 'taken possession of my body, mind and soul'. Twenty-two years later, Howard Marks was a physics undergraduate at Balliol College, Oxford. Marks was already a fan of cannabis and considered it his duty to sample acid. His first trip was pleasant enough, but on his second outing Marks got 'the horrors'. Instead of 'a state of instant Zen', Marks experienced 'instant psychosis'. Flowers turned into 'werewolves and bats' and his hallucinations were teeming with 'menacing demons'. Haunted by what he'd seen, Marks decided the best way to erase the memory of it was to keep taking LSD. But each attempt to reach nirvana had the same results and left him 'introverted, morose, suicidal, and probably crazy'.

Did Stark suffer from similar acid nightmares? Did he recognise the terrors Castaneda went through during his ordeal? Or was he only concerned with what Castaneda had gained from his apprenticeship? Was Stark seeking to acquire similar magical powers, such as the ability to fly, a supernatural skill that Castaneda mastered after ingesting a hallucinogenic preparation? When this miraculous moment happened, Castaneda's knees had 'felt springy like a vault pole' and his limbs had grown longer and more elasticated. Once in the air, he saw 'Don Juan sitting below me, way below me' as he travelled at 'extraordinary' speed across desert plains, free as a bird. His next flying session took the process a step further. Castaneda was transformed into a crow: he 'had the perception of growing bird's legs' and 'felt a tail coming out the back of my neck and wings out of my cheekbones'. In addition, he saw through crow's eyes and breathed through a beak.

Shape-shifting, the power of flight and an array of paranormal abilities would have seemed very tempting propositions to a man like Stark who always dreamed on a grand scale. With such superhuman talents, he'd be unstoppable. But how could Stark acquire these powers without access to his very own shaman? Stark wasn't about to trek off to the Mexican desert when a perfectly acceptable alternative was near at hand, none other than R.D. Laing, who had been awarded shaman-like status by the LSD truth-seekers: they firmly believed that the solutions to humanity's problems lay waiting to be discovered in the alternate states induced by psychoactive substances and hoped that Laing could point them in the right direction.

● ● ●

Laing's specialist area was schizophrenia and his approach to it rejected much of what had come before. During his psychiatric training – initially as an army doctor, then on the wards at Glasgow Royal Mental Hospital – he became steadily more uncomfortable about the treatment given to schizophrenics, which consisted of a daily diet of medication and bouts of electric shock therapy. Any dialogue or personal contact with the patients was strictly forbidden. But Laing couldn't help talking to them and, as he did, he realised that this failure to take their delusions and manias seriously and acknowledge that their truth was no less valid than anyone else's – and that their phantoms were no less substantial because they did not correspond to any observable reality – was not only counter-productive but also fundamentally cruel. The more Laing engaged with the patients, the further he moved away from the standard line on schizophrenia and began to develop his own theories which came together in *The Divided Self* (1960), the book that established his academic reputation, gained him a wide readership and set him on the road to fame.

That same year, Laing began to explore LSD's potential. Reflecting on this decision, Laing said he was intrigued by the fact it 'seemed to open out very unusual states of consciousness' and was 'identified with and extremely comparable to the experience of schizophrenia'. He got some acid from a friend, had a 'remarkable' trip, and began using small amounts of LSD with his patients at his London clinic, having secured a supply of it from Czechoslovakia. By the mid-1960s, Laing was convinced that the standard doctor–patient model was utterly redundant and there needed to be a total redefinition of this relationship on the basis that schizophrenia might, under the right conditions, be more of a blessing than a curse. In a sick society, where 'alienation awaits us' from the moment we're born, Laing believed that 'madness need not be all break*down*'; it could also be a 'break*through*'.

It was ideas like these that endeared Laing to the younger generation of psychedelic explorers. Laing's embrace of schizophrenia as a kind of state of grace may have alienated many of his supporters and damaged his credibility, but it also won him a whole army of hippy fans, Stark included. At the same time, Laing increasingly spoke in a language that would have been instantly recognisable to Stark and anyone else who was familiar with Castaneda. Laing said that psychosis was like being in a different dimension 'peopled by visions and voices, ghosts, strange shapes and apparitions' and urged his fellow psychiatrists to throw off their white coats and become shamans. In *The Politics of Experience and The Bird of Paradise* (1967) he called for 'guides, who can educt the person from this world and induct him to the other. To guide him in it: and lead him back again'. In a lecture delivered two years earlier – which was published in *The Psychedelic Review* with the title 'Transcendental Experience in Relation to Religion and Psychosis' – Laing deployed almost exactly the same imagery as Don Juan to describe what the shaman called 'the crack between the two worlds', which 'opens and closes like a door in the wind': Laing wrote that entering 'the other world' was like 'breaking a shell': or passing through 'a door'; or slipping 'through a partition'. However, Laing differed from the shaman in one key respect. To Don Juan, the powers he was invoking were so great that only a select few individuals would ever be able to understand them, let alone control them. Laing, however, was an evangelist on a mission to save humanity and wanted us all to 'blast through the solid wall' of reality 'even at the risk of chaos, madness and death'.

● ● ●

Perhaps Stark was looking for a chance to sit at the feet of his chosen shaman and download any wisdom Laing might have to offer about finding that crack between the worlds and returning through it in one piece. Or perhaps there was something deeper at work. Stark had juggled multiple identities, presented a false front to the world and lied and dissimulated for so long that he may have been in danger of losing his grip. Was he frightened that, after years of consuming LSD and other substances, he might fall victim to schizophrenia?

The relationship between LSD and schizophrenia is complex and many-sided. An acid session might leave the patient with a better grasp of the illusory nature of their condition. Equally well, there was always the risk that it might bring on a schizophrenic episode rather than prevent it. Overall, the evidence seemed to suggest that LSD therapy – conducted in a controlled, conducive environment – did not tip schizophrenics over the edge. The largest survey of acid use among psychiatric patients was assembled from forty-four separate studies, and covered 5,000 people who participated in 25,000 LSD sessions. It found that roughly 1 in 1,000 became suicidal or had a psychotic reaction.

Yet vital questions remained unanswered. Given that LSD was circulating in the general population, could it trigger schizophrenia in somebody with no previous history of mental health problems? Equally well, how safe was acid for somebody who had latent schizophrenic tendencies but wasn't aware of them? William McGlothlin paid particular attention to these issues. In 1967, after moving from RAND to UCLA, he began a follow-up study on data collected by three LA psychiatrists between 1959 and 1961, concerning 247 men and women who had LSD therapy. McGlothlin and a colleague approached them all and conducted interviews, questionnaires and tests to assess the long-term impact on them. Although only around 20 per cent tried acid again after they'd finished their sessions, 94 per cent were positive about the outcome and felt they'd gained a deeper 'understanding of self and others'. 63 per cent were less anxious than before. Just seven regretted doing it, of whom 'three regarded it as a painful memory of a horrible experience'. One patient, with a history of mental illness, had a nervous breakdown four years later, which she blamed on the LSD. The most prevalent complaint concerned acid flashbacks; thirty-six people suffered from them, eight quite seriously.

These results confirmed McGlothlin's opinion that it was 'unlikely that LSD can produce more than a temporary anxiety panic in a previously stable and well-integrated person'. He had to concede, however, that it could 'aggravate existing unstable tendencies'. Was Stark among the small percentage of LSD users who were gambling with their mental health every time they dropped a tab? Though Stark never experienced a psychotic break, his sanity was cause for concern during the investigation that led to his conviction for fraud in 1963, and recently declassified FBI documents have provided a clearer picture of the nature of Stark's offence and the circumstances surrounding his arrest.

Between May 1961 and January 1962, Stark worked in government departments that gave him access to classified material. Initially based at the Bureau of Ships in Washington, where he was head of Technical Analysis and Operational Research, he was then loaned out to the Defence Department where he worked in Research and Engineering. This placement ended in February 1962 when Stark resigned from the Bureau of Ships. A month later, he was pulled in for questioning by the FBI. Its agents were interested in Stark's association with an art dealer from Georgetown who they were keeping an eye on because of his suspect political activities, which included attending rallies and meetings related to nuclear disarmament. The agents wanted to know if Stark had ever spotted the man's name on any FBI documents and had then told him about it. Stark – who'd known the art dealer for a few months and was contemplating going into business with him – flatly denied the accusation and stated that he had 'never informed anyone he had seen an FBI report or their name on an FBI list'. The agents took him at his word, gave him a stern warning and let him go, not completely convinced that he was innocent and concerned about his 'mental condition', which they found 'questionable'.

Stark was then investigated by the Office of Naval Intelligence after he made a false application for another government position. Stark had changed his name to Clark and included 'misrepresentations concerning his true age, educational background, and relations to prior employers'. Stark was arrested, pleaded guilty, and in May 1963 a New York judge delivered his verdict: Stark was sentenced to five years and put on probation. Soon after, he violated the terms of this agreement and was hauled before the judge. At this point, Stark exhibited symptoms of mental illness that were serious enough to convince the judge to send him for observation at Bellevue Hospital rather than straight to jail. Once again, Stark ignored the conditions set out by the judge and found himself back in court. The judge took pity on him. He extended Stark's probation, sent him for treatment at the New York Psychiatric Institute, and allowed him to work as a janitor at Cornell University Medical Center, where he occasionally posed as a medical student. In April 1964, after breaking the rules again, the judge did not hesitate and Stark was dispatched to Lewisburg State Penitentiary, where he completed the rest of his sentence.

In 1966, as his release became imminent, there was no recommendation that Stark undergo further treatment: he was considered safe and well enough to be let back into society. Stark immediately headed to Europe. After that, there was no recurrence of the symptoms that had given the judge pause for thought. But unless it was all just a performance designed to keep him out of jail, Stark did appear to go through some sort of identity crisis at the time of his arrest, alarming enough to suggest that he might be prone to further bouts of instability. For somebody in Stark's position, this whole episode had the potential to tarnish his image. It's no surprise that he rarely referred to this period in his life. When asked about it, Stark told people that he'd been engaged in top secret government work at the time, but couldn't go into details.

Whatever his motives for pursuing Laing, Stark's persistence paid off and he secured an audience with him. After Stark's showdown with Solomon at Hilton Hall, that avenue to Laing was closed, so Stark pestered Abrams instead. According to Abrams, Stark 'was interested in what Laing would do with him and also what he could get out of Laing'. He passed on Stark's request and Laing agreed to a meeting at his north London home. But rather than take control of proceedings as he normally would, Stark acted like a starry-eyed overexcited fan who meets their idol and is suddenly deprived of their senses. With every passing minute, the opportunity to bond with Laing was slipping through his fingers. Desperate, Stark went for broke and insisted they take a large amount of LSD together. Laing grudgingly obliged and, as he and Stark were hitting the high-point of the trip, Stark launched into an extraordinary monologue about the crisis facing LSD culture and how a lack of leadership was fatally compromising its revolutionary aspirations.

Up to then, Leary had been the focal point of the acid corporation: if Stark was chief executive and the Brotherhood were company directors, then Leary was the visionary founder. But Leary was finished with. Yesterday's man. And the only person who could replace him was Laing. If Laing agreed to become their guru and guiding light, then everything he and the Brotherhood had accumulated was at Laing's disposal: assets totalling around $50 million. Stark's fantastic scenario – in which Laing assumed the characteristics of a medieval mystic, a James Bond villain and a super-intelligent being from outer space – stunned and bewildered Laing. Thrown off course by Laing's failure to respond to his plan, Stark tried to get some indication that Laing was on board by demanding to know what his orders were.

Something in Laing snapped. He flew into a rage, grabbed Stark and threw him out onto the street. Unable to comprehend what just happened – and still reeling from the acid – Stark sought out Abrams and confessed that Laing had 'fucked my head'. Soon after, Stark passed out. When he awoke the next day, the whole embarrassing incident was like a nightmare he could barely remember having. He'd had a bad trip, that's all. Nothing to worry about. His meltdown in front of Laing was a temporary aberration, quickly forgotten and never mentioned again. He quit Hilton Hall, ended his association with Abrams, left the country and spent Christmas and New Year 1970–71 in the US with the Brotherhood, celebrating the success of their Paris operation and planning their next venture. Arrangements made, Stark headed back to Europe, landed in Belgium, hooked up with his former chemist Tord Svenson – the Swede had recently reappeared on the scene after time away travelling – and began looking for a suitable spot where they could safely install some new acid labs.

6

New Faces and Old Faces

Back in London, Kemp was looking to make use of the knowledge he'd gained in Paris and build an LSD network that followed the blueprint designed by Stark, Billy Hitchcock, Nick Sand and the Brotherhood. Solomon, though bruised from his encounters with Stark, had learnt from him as well and was thinking along the same lines as Kemp. Their partnership was back on, but this time the roles were reversed. Kemp was no longer Solomon's pupil; now he was behind the wheel, with Solomon in the passenger seat. To lay their hands on the required amounts of the all-important ergotamine tartrate, Solomon invented a company called Inter-Dominion Associates, gave it a postal address in central London and wrote to various chemical traders under an assumed name. A major West German supplier – Dr Rentschler of Lampheim – agreed to his request and in June 1971 Solomon drove there, picked up a kilo of ergotamine tartrate and took it across the border into Switzerland, where he handed it over to Kemp.

Like their former associates, Kemp and Solomon took advantage of the Swiss banking system to protect their assets. Both of them signed up with the Swiss Bank Corporation, a syndicate of privately owned banks with branches across the country. Established in the nineteenth century, it slowly expanded the number of outlets it owned and managed to prosper during the Second World War thanks to its willingness to handle

Nazi gold. By 1971, it had quadrupled in size with dozens of branches in Switzerland and a significant presence in the US. At the Swiss Bank Corporation's Geneva branch, Kemp acquired safety-deposit box no. 4079 and stored all the ergotamine tartrate in it, while Solomon opened an account at the corporation's Fribourg branch. In November 1971, Kemp and Bott got themselves a safety-deposit box at the Kantonel Bank – a state-owned conglomerate – where she kept the key to Kemp's other treasure chest.

Having nailed down this end of the operation, Kemp was left to decide where best to install his acid labs. With Bott still in the Isle of Man completing her medical training, Kemp was in no hurry to settle down anywhere permanently. In May of that year, he was officially registered as living at an address in Bristol with a friend of Solomon, but he was also renting out a number of small flats in Ladbroke Grove, west London, on short leases, setting up temporary labs for quick production runs, then packing away all his kit and leaving it in storage, ready for the next location.

As Kemp's first batches of LSD began to appear, all that was missing was somebody to deal with tableting and distribution. Solomon had just the man: an old acquaintance from Cambridge, Henry Barclay Todd, a solidly built, physically imposing man who'd given LSD to the geneticist Francis Crick and had a crush on Solomon's daughter. Solomon had turned to Todd for assistance when he was trying to offload the bulk consignment of Kemp's Paris-made LSD that was his share of the deal with Stark and the Brotherhood. Freaked out by having so much acid in his possession and thwarted in his attempts to conceal it in the grounds of Hilton Hall, Solomon ended up burying it in the gardens of his Grantchester cottage. This was only meant to be a temporary measure, however, as the thought of all that LSD resting on his property did little to ease his frayed nerves. Yet if it wasn't going to sit there indefinitely, he had to find a route to market. Solomon was well aware that Todd had done a reasonable bit of dealing – hashish mainly – and seemed to know what he was doing. More importantly, Todd had a thick skin, survivor's instinct and feral cunning that made him well suited for the task ahead. When Solomon approached him, Todd was at a loose end and happy to lend a hand. Their first move was to shift the acid a safe distance from the cottage. They rented the ground floor flat in the old vicarage of a sleepy Hertfordshire village under the name Robert Greenwood-High, and hid the LSD under the floorboards. The next step was to get it measured out into doses. Unable to obtain any degree of precision with basic kitchen scales, Solomon persuaded a student he knew to use the university science department's weighing machine instead.

Once the acid had been measured out, they had to convert it into tablet form. At first Solomon did it by hand, inserting the LSD into capsules one at a time. Aside from being a painstakingly slow process, Solomon kept spilling the contents and triggering hallucinations that persisted for days on end. Todd intervened and they started adding calcium lactate, a white powder, to the acid after it was dissolved in a bowl of water, stirring the ingredients together with a glass rod to form a doughy paste that was much easier to get into the capsules. As time went on and the funds available to him increased, Todd was able to procure a factory-standard pharmaceutical industry tableting machine that dramatically increased productivity. The LSD paste was squeezed into a mould that compressed it into the shape of a flat tile, which was then placed on the base plate of the tableting machine and sliced into twenty equal strips by its nineteen parallel razor blades. After adjusting the angle of the operating lever, the action was repeated and repeated until each slab was subdivided into hundreds of tabs.

Though he was pleased with the results, Todd had no intention of wasting his time on this laborious job, so he hired a friend from Reading to manage the tableting, who then brought in several others to lighten the load. With his Reading associate, Todd also recruited a handful of dealers to help with distribution. From the start, he was extremely security conscious, insisting on strict rules of engagement similar to those employed by secret agents. One of Todd's tableting team remembered him giving instructions about 'hiding places, precautionary procedures, handovers, fall-back arrangements' and 'emergency signals'. There was to be no chatting on the phone except in code. If Todd needed to see any of them in person, they always met at the Maids of Honour Teashop opposite Kew Gardens, which according to him had 'amazing cakes and scones'.

Once Solomon's legacy had finally been dispersed, he and Todd had netted £50,000. In the process, Todd had developed a network capable of shifting as much acid as Kemp could make. He'd more than proved his worth, yet Kemp had reservations about involving Todd in the new operation because his commitment to the LSD trade was not driven by a desire for revolution. Todd did not share any of the ideological, philosophical or spiritual ideas that animated the counter-culture; he harboured no illusions about LSD leading humanity into the promised land and had zero interest in politics. To him, drugs were fun, and dealing them seemed an easy way to make money.

What Todd did share with his counterparts was the same sense of rootlessness and restlessness and a desire to reject the values and habits of their parents' generation and throw off the dull monochrome world they'd inhabited for something more colourful and exciting. Todd's hunger for travel and adventure may have been more urgent than others because of his experience of growing up in South East Asia. Though Todd was born in Dundee in 1945, his father was an RAF squadron leader stationed in Malaysia and Singapore during the last days of empire and Todd was out there until the mid-1950s when the family returned to Scotland. This dramatic change of environment – from jungle heat to slate grey skies – must have been a shock to Todd's system, and left him with lingering memories of the different world he'd inhabited during his formative years.

Todd then attended Dundee Grammar School, where he was an able, if not exceptional, pupil and performed well on the rugby field. Cut loose at 18, he passed up the opportunity to go to university and worked as a hospital porter until he'd scraped together enough funds to escape to Paris and become a fashion photographer. Exactly what that amounted to is unclear; there is no surviving evidence to suggest he spent any time behind a camera. After two years sampling the city's delights, Todd landed back in the UK with no plan and no prospects. Settling near Oxford – which by then had a thriving drug culture – Todd was arrested in November 1966 for theft and false pretences after he was caught using dodgy cheques. Todd was convicted and did over a year inside. After being released in February 1968, he somehow talked himself into a job at an accountancy firm, where he knuckled down for six months before hitting the road again. This time he headed for Prague to stay with friends.

At first glance, Todd's choice of destination seems odd given the situation in Czechoslovakia at the time, only a matter of months after the Prague Spring, when the outburst of optimism and democratic energy that greeted a new administration determined to find an alternative to the restrictions of Stalinism and the excesses of capitalism was extinguished by the Soviet army. When the smoke cleared, its leaders were replaced by stooges hand-picked by Moscow who proceeded to purge any remnants of resistance and smother any murmurs of dissent. Yet the country did still have one major attraction for somebody like Todd: its state-sponsored LSD factories. Whether or not Todd returned to the UK in January 1969 with a suitcase laden with acid is impossible to say, but he did immediately drift towards Cambridge and into Solomon's orbit. While doing some light dealing, Todd took on another regular job, this time as a systems analyst at a London firm. As before, the luxury of a steady salary lost its appeal fairly quickly and Todd made a definitive break from 9–5 wage labour when he and eight others were arrested in Cheltenham for possession of cannabis. Though they were all acquitted, the whole incident marked the point at which Todd committed to an outlaw existence, and soon after this he teamed up with Solomon.

Given how efficiently Todd took the reins from Solomon and steered their enterprise to a satisfactory conclusion, Kemp was impressed enough to put his doubts about Todd's character to one side and bring him into the Microdot Gang. Nevertheless, Kemp remained wary of Todd and kept a close eye on him: Todd's foreign travels and petty criminal mind-set, allied to his background and temperament, gave him the air of one of those refugees from the British class system who lurked on the fringes of spy novels. Useful but not to be trusted.

When Stark settled on Belgium as the next location for an acid lab he embarked on a project that surpassed anything he'd attempted before in terms of ambition and sophistication. Instead of occupying a disused factory space or dingy warehouse, Stark inserted his new venture into the heart of an extremely prestigious, high-profile experiment in urban planning and design. In 1968, one of Belgium's oldest and most venerable universities became caught up in a wider dispute over national identity and language that pitted Flemish speakers against French speakers. The previously mixed University of Leuven split in two; the

Flemish contingent stayed put while the French faculty decided to relaunch itself as the Louvaine-la-Neuve University, and drew up plans for a new campus that would include a railway station and a shopping mall. The aim was to realise a utopian vision of integrated living in a harmonious environment that featured futuristic concrete and glass structures arranged around open plazas and perfectly groomed lawns, linked by pedestrian pathways lined with symmetrically arranged trees; like something out of a sci-fi novel.

The university purchased a plot of farmland nearly 20 miles south-east of Brussels and work began in 1970. The first area completed was the Science Park. Built to encourage co-operation between industry and academia, it was a large zone where innovative tech companies could rent out premises. It was the perfect spot for Stark's new enterprise; nobody would be paying much attention to what Stark was doing tucked away in the Science Park while the rest of the campus was still under construction. Stark took possession of a villa there in the spring of 1971 and christened it the Laboratoire Le Clocheton. To pull off this coup, Stark applied everything he knew about blurring the line between his legitimate businesses and his acid assembly lines, and exploited connections he'd been nurturing ever since he'd begun building a portfolio of companies – real and fake. Back when he was preparing the ground for his very first Paris lab – set up in 1968 – Stark created the Inter-Biochemical Company, a legit firm based in Ghana. During his stay there, Stark befriended an economic advisor at the US embassy in Accra. By the time Stark was moving into Belgium, the diplomat was based in London and did everything in his power to grease the wheels and ensure that his colleagues in Brussels lent Stark their support.

Another US expat seduced by Stark was the head of an electrical goods company, who had a son who was employed by a New York law firm, Surrey, Karasik and Morse. If Stark was going to push through the Belgian deal he needed proper representation and the East Coast lawyers recommended their man in Paris, Sam Goekjian, who, like the rest of them, was totally in the dark about Stark's illegal activities. Aside from using Goekjian to launder LSD money by investing it in a Panamanian paper company, Stark got him to process all the contracts and paperwork relating to the Laboratoire Le Clocheton and make a $300,000 downpayment to cover the associated costs.

From the start, Stark ran the lab as a commercial concern, exporting small amounts of chemicals to Switzerland, and hired the necessary staff by advertising in a local trade magazine. They occupied Le Clocheton during normal working hours, but once they'd gone home Tord Svenson moved in. With the labs all to himself, the Swedish alchemist would work straight through the night, clocking off before the day shift arrived. To make sure that Tord could take full advantage of the facilities, Stark amassed an unprecedented 30 kilos of ergotamine tartrate via his string of existing businesses and contacts. Nevertheless, by the summer of 1972, and a year into production, stocks of it were running low and his supply lines were exhausted. So Stark turned to the same West German company that Solomon and Kemp had recently done business with.

This may have been no more than a coincidence, except for the fact that when Stark ordered the ergotamine tartrate he masqueraded as the English owner of an English outfit – the Amalgamated Pharmaceutical Company. This was registered at two London postal addresses: one in Holborn, which was identical to the one Solomon adopted when he dealt with the West German supplier; the other in Holland Park, just 500 yards away from one of the flats Kemp was renting. Though Kemp had previously declined an offer from Stark to work for him in Belgium, it seems that Stark had not completely lost touch with his former colleagues. Stark went on to buy 8 kilos of ergotamine tartrate from the West Germans, plenty to keep Tord busy until Laboratoire Le Clocheton was wound down later that year. Over the course of its existence, it had churned out a mind-boggling 20 kilos of LSD, enough for fifty million doses. It was the largest illegal acid operation ever mounted. It dwarfed the competition and put its predecessors in the shade: Stark had truly become the acid king.

● ● ●

On his regular trips to Switzerland, Solomon was reunited with his former sparring partner Dr Timothy Leary. Once the law caught up with the acid guru and he'd been dubbed America's 'most dangerous man' by President Nixon, Leary was convicted on charges related to his two earlier drug arrests and in March 1970 he was sentenced to twenty years. After being shunted through the system, Leary wound up at California

Men's Colony, a minimum-security jail surrounded by wire fencing and home to mostly aging career criminals. Treated with kid gloves by the staff and generally respected by his fellow inmates, Leary took music classes every afternoon – the electric organ and the flute – had access to a typewriter, got sacks of fan mail and received visitors who slipped him LSD. Life was pretty congenial, but Leary thought it was his duty to escape, and the Brotherhood – who'd already contributed to his defence fund – thought it was their duty to free their high priest. Though the Brotherhood had plenty of experience forging passports and other forms of ID, their area of expertise was moving contraband, not people, especially not ones as famous as Leary. So they turned to a group with the necessary know-how: America's most famous left-wing terrorists, the Weathermen.

In the late autumn of 1969, with the country ablaze, the war in Vietnam a bloody open wound and the state resorting to ever more ruthless repression, a core of around a dozen prominent radicals, with a history of student activism behind them, came to the conclusion that mass protest was redundant – a blunt weapon – and the movement they'd helped construct was incapable of delivering on its revolutionary promise. It was time to go underground, adopt guerrilla tactics and start planning a campaign of bomb and arson attacks. Given that most of the Weathermen were well-educated, solidly middle-class citizens and not urban warriors, the group embarked on a programme of reconditioning in an effort to dismantle learned behaviours and bourgeois attitudes, to harden their hearts and sacrifice their identities to the collective will. The group was all, the individual nothing. Egos were to be left outside the door. Everybody was encouraged to have sex with everybody else; long-term partnerships wilted in the heat generated by orchestrated free love. Looking back, one senior member concluded that this process had transformed them into 'a classic cult'.

During these rituals, the Weathermen used LSD to break down the barriers between them. Acid was also employed during intense sessions of self-criticism as a way of weeding out weak candidates and exposing FBI undercover agents looking to infiltrate the group. The only FBI mole who ever managed to join the Weathermen remembered them subjecting him to a harrowing cross-examination, which he only survived because he concealed the LSD tab they'd given him in his hand rather than swallow it. Given the importance of acid to the group, it was essential to have a reliable source and the Weathermen relied on their connections to prominent members of the Brotherhood to keep them supplied with Nick Sand's Orange Sunshine. This meant that when the Brotherhood contacted them about Leary – via a radical lawyer who knew both parties – they were guaranteed a sympathetic hearing.

By then, the Weathermen had become national celebrities thanks to a devastating accident: on 6 March 1970, the Greenwich Village townhouse that some of them were staying in was flattened when the stockpile of explosives in the basement spontaneously detonated, reducing the building to rubble and leaving three of them dead. Though the remnants of the New York chapter managed to pull off one spectacular attack that June – igniting a dozen sticks of dynamite in the New York City Police HQ and injuring seven people – most of the nationwide network evaporated. The founding members regrouped in San Francisco and were licking their wounds and pondering their next move when the Brotherhood – who were still supplying LSD to at least one of the group – offered them $25,000 to liberate Leary. The Weathermen took the job: not only would the cash come in useful, it was a chance to raise their profile and make the US government look stupid.

At around 9 p.m. on Saturday 12 September, Leary crept out onto the floodlit prison yard, scampered across it, scaled a telegraph pole, clasped the wires between his gloved hands and bare feet, and dragged himself along, pausing to rest his aching limbs and wait for what seemed like an eternity as a patrol car idled nearby. Finally over the outer fence, he dropped down, sprained his ankle and hobbled about a quarter of a mile to the highway, where he was picked up by two young women, who deposited him in the backseat of their car and handed him new identity papers, a change of clothing and some hair dye. About 150 miles south of San Luis Obispo, the car pulled in at a gas station and Leary was transferred to a camper van being driven by a veteran Bay Area communist, accompanied by a single mother and her 8-year-old son. Joined by several other vehicles, they proceeded in convoy to an apartment in San Jose, where Leary spent the night. Forty-eight hours later, following another change-over at a campsite near Sacramento, Leary finally arrived at his destination – a secluded farmhouse near Seattle – where he was greeted by senior Weathermen.

Together they issued a communiqué in which the Weathermen defended their actions on the basis that Leary 'was held against his will and against the will of millions of kids in this country' and the substances he promoted were 'like the herbs and cactus and mushrooms of the American Indians' and would 'help us make a future world where it will be possible to live in peace'. Leary adopted a more aggressive tone as he accused the US government of being 'an instrument of total lethal evil' and warned that 'the hour is late' and the only option remaining was violent rebellion: 'fight to live or you'll die'.

A few days later, a heavily disguised Leary flew from Chicago airport via Spain to Algeria, which had already given sanctuary to a prominent Black Power activist. In typical fashion, Leary ignored the sensitivities of his hosts and potential allies; instead, he offended everyone with his demented behaviour. Handed his marching orders, Leary travelled incognito to Switzerland. Once across its border, he was whisked away by Michel Hauchard, a jet-setting playboy who'd been convicted of fraud, sold weapons to the Palestine Liberation Organization (PLO), and spent his winters skiing and his summers racing speedboats. Within hours of settling into his new luxury hide-out, Leary was arrested and spent a couple of months in prison before he was released into the care of Hauchard. Soon after, Leary was visited by two Brothers, who brought him a briefcase full of cash, two blocks of hashish and a container of pure LSD.

For the next eighteen months, Leary was untroubled by the Swiss authorities as he engaged in a never-ending social whirl, entertaining rock stars, film directors, writers and intellectuals, while consuming copious quantities of acid, peyote, coke, cannabis and even heroin. It was in this decadent environment that Solomon saw Leary for the first time since their Millbrook days. But his visit wasn't entirely social. Solomon had been persuaded to help Leary get a UK publisher for the book he was trying to write about his imprisonment and escape. To help him finish the manuscript, Leary hired a 37-year-old English author and artist, a representative of the Beat generation, who'd done four years in a UK jail for drug offences; was interested in black magic; and sought out Leary in Algeria where they took LSD in the desert and tried to summon up demonic spirits.

While he and Leary laboured fitfully on the book, their host Michel Hauchard focused on finding a publisher, encouraged by the fact that he'd convinced Leary to give him the rights to his written works for the next twelve years and 50 per cent of his earnings from them. As Hauchard tried to land a deal in the US, it appears Solomon was asked to do the same in London, and he may well have smuggled portions of the text back from Switzerland to shop around town. How far Solomon got with his efforts to pitch the book is hard to say, but among his private papers was a bank statement dated September 1972 that belonged to Leary's co-author, issued by a bank in Berne. Why this document came into his possession is a mystery, but the very fact he had it at all suggests that, whatever his exact role, Solomon was privy to the behind-the-scenes machinations and secretive negotiations that surrounded Leary's manuscript. As it was, Hauchard managed to secure a $25,000 advance from Bantam Books, a mass market paperback imprint based in New York. Unfortunately for all concerned, Leary's *Confessions of a Hope Fiend* (1973) failed to register on the bestseller lists despite a big print run and a lot of publicity.

By then, it was clear that the Swiss government, which was under unrelenting pressure from the Americans, was about to extradite him. Leary made for Afghanistan, but was seized at Kabul airport and carted back to the US. Leary was charged, taken to Folsom maximum-security prison and dumped in the cell next to Charles Manson. The infamous cult leader thought Leary was a genuine prophet and welcomed him with a gift of four books, one of which was Castaneda's *The Teachings of Don Juan*.

Claims that LSD played a crucial role in the Manson murders surfaced almost immediately. Once Manson and his gang were on trial, LSD featured so frequently in the courtroom that it might as well have been in the dock alongside the other defendants, charged as an accessory. Focusing on LSD was a key part of the prosecution's strategy as it attempted to overcome the main obstacle to convicting Manson; he'd not harmed any of the victims and was nowhere near the scene when the slaughter took place. To tackle this, the prosecution tried to prove that Manson used LSD to gain complete control over his followers' minds and turn them into robots programmed to carry out his orders; acid had wiped their brains clean and convinced them that Manson's fantasy world was more real than the one outside their compound. This highly tenuous proposition went unchallenged by the defence because it was hoping to get the actual killers off the hook by following the same line of argument: they were not responsible for their actions because Manson had brainwashed them with LSD. In the end, the acid theory worked for the prosecution but failed the defence. The accused were all found guilty of the charges against them, while media coverage of the trial constantly emphasised the fact that LSD was an evil substance and a source of satanic power.

Leary spent six months in Folsom prison enjoying lengthy discussions with Manson about the nature of Good and Evil before being moved to another facility. In the spring of 1974, Leary was paid a visit by DEA agents who laid out his future for him. He was 53. He would grow old and probably die in jail. Leary may have aspired to be a famous guru and the leader of a global spiritual awakening, but he had no interest in becoming a martyr. He wrote a long and elaborate confession about his involvement with the Brotherhood and the drug culture in general. The DEA was delighted, largely due to the propaganda value of Leary's admission of defeat. The story was leaked to the press and Leary's betrayal of everything he'd stood for was greeted with dismay and anger by his old colleagues, fellow travellers and even his son. Nicknamed 'Charlie Thrush' by the DEA – because he sang like a bird – Leary was released on 21 April 1976 and entered the witness protection programme. Soon after, he was recognised by a member of the public and forced into the open. Free at last, Leary quickly discovered that nobody really gave a damn about what he had to say about anything anymore: he was, as Stark predicted, yesterday's man.

7

Into the Grove

The majority of the LSD manufactured by Tord Svenson at Stark's Laboratoire Le Clocheton was intended for the Brotherhood. One huge consignment was concealed in a brand-new Jaguar sports car and shipped to Canada, from there to New York, then on to California and into the possession of one of the original Brotherhood members. Since Stark appeared at their Arizona ranch in the summer of 1969, the Brotherhood had changed beyond all recognition. Shortly after Stark's visit – and the sudden death of their inspirational leader, John Griggs – the key personnel abandoned their base and went in separate directions. Several headed to Hawaii with the aim of constructing their ideal community and growing tons of weed. One went to Oregon, some stayed in southern California, and a few others were constantly on the move from continent to continent and country to country, overseeing the global movement of their goods and capital. While the senior Brothers still controlled and coordinated the flow of international traffic and the output from various production centres, they had almost nothing to do with the street-level supply chain. The Brotherhood had become a franchise: anyone who could claim any kind of association with them could set up as an independent wholesaler, while making use of their brand name and guarantee of quality merchandise.

As a result, the Brotherhood swelled in size; at its peak there were around 750 members with identifiable ties to the early days of the gang, and as many as 3,000 affiliates. Such rapid growth meant it was impossible for the leaders to track what was happening on the ground and made the network hard to control, yet this lack of central planning had its advantages and the Brotherhood's management system was flexible enough to allow plenty of room for improvisation and innovation, especially when it came to adding new items to their product range. During 1970, Stark managed to score a small amount of THC dimethylheptyl – a synthetic derivative of THC that is far stronger than LSD – from the only Swiss chemical company that made it for experimental purposes. Stark was blown away by its hallucinogenic properties, but put off by the expense and difficulty associated with producing it. However, he had a reasonably good alternative in mind: hashish oil. Though not as brain twisting as THC dimethylheptyl, hashish oil is considerably more psychoactive than its source material. While standard hashish has about 20 per cent THC content, hashish oil contains 85 per cent.

Hashish comes from the resin secreted by the female cannabis plant and is gathered by putting dried buds and leaves through a sieve. The recovered resin is then gently heated until it begins to melt, at which point it's pressed into blocks and sealed with either cloth or cellophane. Hashish oil, a concentrated liquid, is obtained by mixing the resin with a chemical solvent – such as acetone or petrol – to produce a greasy, sticky residue that can be smoked in a glass pipe or by smearing some on a cigarette paper. To make sure he had everything properly in place before approaching the Brotherhood, Stark went to Afghanistan, met with their main hashish brokers and discussed the practicalities of manufacturing hash oil. Fact-finding mission complete, Stark brought in the Brotherhood, who were easily won over by hashish oil's potency and retail value. Using Stark's instruction manual, a lab was set up in Michigan that could churn out 40,000 doses a day: within a year, there were six others up and running.

By 1972, the Brotherhood accounted for 50 per cent of all the weed and acid sold in the US. It had roughly $1.8 million in cash sitting in Swiss banks, and an estimated total turnover of around $200 million. But the Brotherhood's phenomenal expansion did not go unnoticed. Since

1970, a multi-agency task force had been conducting a major operation against them. Spearheading the investigation – alongside the FBI, the IRS and local police forces – was the Bureau of Narcotics and Dangerous Drugs (BNDD, the immediate forerunner of the DEA), which had been formed in 1968 out of several drug-related government agencies. Chief among these was the Federal Bureau of Narcotics, which had policed the legal and illegal trade in drugs both nationally and globally since 1930, dictating policy to other countries and manipulating treaties and agreements made by international bodies like the UN: the war on drugs was very much its creation. Building on this legacy, the BNDD had 1,361 agents – of whom 86 were overseas – at its disposal and a substantial war chest filled to the brim by the Nixon administration. Beginning by concentrating on the Brotherhood's continued presence in Laguna Beach, the BNDD slowly assembled a detailed picture of the whole network and, bit by bit, they got a clearer picture of where Stark fitted into the Brotherhood's empire.

In December 1971, BNDD agents uncovered a hashish oil lab along with 86,000 doses of Stark's European-made LSD. From then until next spring, there were three further raids in Laguna Beach and 228,000 hits of his acid were seized. Meanwhile, the IRS was following the money trail and realised that high-ranking Brothers owned 546 acres of land in southern California. When they examined the purchase records they discovered that the real estate had been bought by a Panamanian paper company – the same one that Sam Goekjian, Stark's Paris-based lawyer, had invested in – and that the titles and deeds to the land were held by a front company in Lichtenstein originally set up by Billy Hitchcock. Determined to get to the bottom of this, IRS officials showed up at Goekjian's office in March 1972 and quizzed him about Stark's role in the money-laundering operation. Goekjian pleaded ignorance and the IRS left empty-handed. Nevertheless, by that summer, the BNDD's chief investigators were certain that Stark was the mastermind behind the Belgian acid lab and responsible for introducing hashish oil to the Brotherhood. According to them, he was near the very top of the organisation: Stark had made it onto the most wanted list.

● ● ●

During 1972, Stark's ex-partners in crime were settling into their new homes in north-west London. Kemp and Bott were now officially renting a flat at 8 Westbourne Grove Terrace, a four-storey white stucco Georgian villa with an attic and basement, located at the heart of an area synonymous with the counter-culture. Mixing a shabby bohemian grandeur with inner-city grime, and enlivened by its large African Caribbean community, it attracted writers, musicians, artists, radicals and drug dealers. Within a ten-minute radius of their home was Notting Hill Gate, Bayswater and Ladbroke Grove, which was bisected by Portobello Road, the spine that held the whole alternative scene together. Ladbroke Grove played host to a variety of grassroots organisations: there were tenants' groups fighting for squatters' rights and against venal landlords; free schools; food co-ops; drug counselling; and community clinics where Bott, who was now a qualified GP, could put her training to good use. Acting as a focal point for all these initiatives was the Notting Hill People's Association, which had a meeting room and coffee bar, and was just around the corner from Kemp and Bott at 90 Talbot Road.

A typical example of the sort of projects that were springing up in the area was the West London Claimants Union, which accused the current welfare system of keeping people trapped in 'poverty, undernourishment, depression, boredom, despondency and anxiety', and demanded 'an adequate income for all without condition' on the basis that any humane 'welfare system should feed, clothe and provide for *all* its citizens … with no strings attached'. The union was brought into being by a young activist living in a squat at 25 Powis Square – right next to Portobello Road – who'd been a student in Cambridge at the same time as Kemp and had organised the anti-exam protests. In December 1970, he and some of his flat-mates moved north-east to Islington to pursue a different route to revolution. Seeing themselves as part of an international struggle that stretched from the battlefields of Vietnam to the ghettos of inner-city America and the capitals of Europe, they decided it was time to shake the masses out of their apathy and inspire them to rise up against their masters.

After much debate, they named themselves the Angry Brigade and their first move – firing a machine-gun at the Spanish embassy in London – was intended to demonstrate their solidarity with the First of

May Group, who were busy terrorising representatives of Franco's right-wing dictatorship in Spain, and had given the Brigade access to weapons. From then on, the Angry Brigade pursued a campaign focused on individuals and institutions involved in industrial relations. At the time, the Conservative government was trying to subdue the trade unions and bring workers to heel by managing pay disputes and preventing employees from going on strike. Bitter conflict ensued and the Angry Brigade were determined to exploit these tensions and further aggravate the situation with a string of bomb attacks, each one accompanied by a communiqué sent to the mainstream press explaining their motives and calling on others to follow their example.

On 9 December 1970, they exploded a bomb at the Department of Employment and Productivity. On 12 January 1971, they targeted the home of Robert Carr, the Employment Minister, announcing in the accompanying communiqué that they had 'started to fight back' and were confident of victory: 'the war will be won by the organised working class, with bombs'. This attack thrust the Brigade into the spotlight and whipped the media into a frenzy. Just two weeks after it occurred, the *Daily Mirror* offered a £10,000 reward to anybody providing information that led to a conviction. Over the next seven months, the Angry Brigade hit the offices of the Ford motor company and the home of its managing director, and the residence of the Minister for Trade and Industry. In a slight deviation from this pattern, they detonated a device outside the trendy Biba fashion store in Kensington, (Communiqué 8: 'the only thing to do with modern slave-houses – called boutiques – IS WRECK THEM'), and one inside the Metropolitan Police computer room (Communiqué 9: 'we are slowly destroying the long tentacles of the oppressive State machine').

By that summer, however, the authorities were closing in on the main Angry Brigade unit. Their hunt had gained momentum at the beginning of the year when an associate of the group – who'd lived with them in the Powis Square squat – was stopped on Talbot Road by two coppers. They went through his pockets and found a tiny amount of cannabis and three stolen cheque books. Held on remand, he couldn't resist bragging to his cell mates about his connections to the notorious Angry Brigade. Unfortunately, one of the prisoners was a police informer. From February onwards, the police descended on anybody even vaguely connected to this big-mouthed revolutionary, and Ladbroke Grove was badly affected. Two properties in Talbot Road were given a thorough going over. The one in Powis Square was searched from top to bottom, and another four addresses in the area received the same treatment. But it wasn't until 20 August, when the police hit a house in Stoke Newington, that they caught the alleged ring-leaders. Eight arrests were made and an automatic pistol, two machine-guns and a stock of dynamite and detonators were found at the scene.

In January 1972, four men and four women – dubbed the Stoke Newington Eight by their supporters – were indicted under Section 3(a) of the Explosive Substances Act 1883 and charged with plotting to blow things up. During their lengthy trial, which started on 30 May 1972, a benefit gig for the Stoke Newington Eight was held not far from Kemp and Bott's flat. The headline act was the local band Hawkwind, a free-wheeling motley crew who'd placed LSD at the heart of their music from conception to rehearsal to performance: combining long free-wheeling jazz influenced improvisation with heavy rock rhythms, they reached levels of intensity that either propelled them into orbit or degenerated into noisy chaos. Lyrics came from the acid-saturated brain of another Ladbroke Grove resident, a South African poet who regularly contributed to the experimental and ground-breaking sci-fi magazine *New Worlds*, whose long-term editor was the author Michael Moorcock. In *New Worlds*, Moorcock hoped to steer the genre towards 'the strange new countries of the mind which will exist tomorrow' and build 'a new mythology' by exploring the frontiers of inner-space rather than the frontiers of outer space.

When Kemp and Bott moved to Ladbroke Grove, Moorcock had already been living there for nearly a decade – first in Colville Terrace and then at 51 Blenheim Crescent – and used the area in his fiction; a series of books about Jerry Cornelius, a time-travelling, ultra-hip, rock star secret agent, were set in the streets and squares near Moorcock's home. With his thick mane of unkempt hair and flowing beard, Moorcock looked like an urban druid, and his friend and fellow writer J.G. Ballard called him 'the resident guru of Ladbroke Grove'. Moorcock could be seen in any of the area's popular pubs or cafes; or selling copies of *New Worlds* from a Portobello market stall; or on stage with Hawkwind, who were big fans of his work and had formed an alliance with him after he'd organised a gig for them under the Westway flyover. Moorcock would occasionally appear during Hawkwind's shows dressed in outlandish robes and recite his poetry, dance and bang percussion.

As a young anarchist, Moorcock had enthusiastically embraced the counter-culture and began experimenting with LSD in the early 1960s. Its impact on his work was considerable, and in the years that followed these experiences he almost single-handedly reinvented fantasy fiction and dragged it into the psychedelic era. Yet Moorcock was no wide-eyed convert. He understood that hallucinogens had the power to rewire society, but not necessarily for the better. In his 1963 novella *The Deep Fix*, Moorcock envisioned an apocalyptic near future in which the well-meaning efforts of psychiatrists 'to help with the work of curing mental disorders of all kinds' ends in disaster. While the previous generation used 'the old hallucinogenic drugs such as … Mescaline and Lysergic acid' to achieve insights into their patients' suffering, clinicians at Hampton Research go a step further and design a machine – the Hallucinomat – which can produce the same results but much more efficiently and effectively. The Hallucinomats are called into service when the world is seized by an epidemic of mental illness, 'a dark tide of madness'. Hoping to reverse this disturbing trend, leaders position the Hallucinomats around the globe and turn them full on. But instead of soothing nerves, the machines reduce 'the greater part of the human race' to a catatonic state and cause 'a great many others, who were potentially inclined to melancholia, manic depression and certain kinds of schizophrenia' to commit suicide.

The corner of north-west London Moorcock called home had its fair share of acid casualties: a music journalist remembered seeing people 'in the Ladbroke Grove underground community who'd just taken too much LSD and were just floating around and not making much sense' and were 'headed for self-destruction'. Exactly how much of the acid swilling round the neighbourhood was coming from Kemp's labs is hard to gauge. The Microdot Gang's distributors took in London, but at some remove from them personally. Kemp never sold any directly to customers, though he may have shared some with friends. Solomon, on the other hand, was in the habit of dishing it out wherever he went, and he was now living only fifteen minutes' walk away at 39b Randolph Avenue, Maida Vale, in a similar style house to Kemp and Bott.

One of Solomon's regular hang-outs on Portobello Road was the offices of the alternative magazine *Frendz*. Launched in 1969 as *Friends* – it became *Frendz* in May 1971 – its editor wanted it to have a more political agenda than main competitors *The International Times* and *OZ*, so alongside the sex and drugs and rock 'n' roll were issues dedicated to gay liberation; women's rights; the green movement; the 1926 General Strike; and the Angry Brigade, whose aims and methods the *Frendz* team endorsed and supported from beginning to end. Solomon killed many hours soaking up the atmosphere at their HQ and may well have crossed paths with Moorcock and Hawkwind, who were heavily involved with the magazine. The November 1971 edition included a two-page comic strip written by Moorcock and starring Hawkwind as the Sonic Assassins, a 'band of dedicated men' who are called into action when Void City comes under attack from a deadly onslaught of mainstream pop. Recognising the seriousness of the situation, they fly their Omnipod to Void City. On landing, they find a discarded 'plastic grin' belonging to their sworn enemy – a BBC radio DJ – who suddenly appears in a flying machine that resembles a cross between a submarine and an antique gramophone, leading a fleet of similar vessels that are blasting out waves of easy listening music. Before it's too late, our heroes deploy their Sonic Wall, repel the invaders and save Void City from destruction.

In the end, even the Sonic Assassins couldn't stop *Frendz* from collapsing. Dwindling sales and the constant strain of having to beg, borrow and steal just to get from one edition to the next had taken its toll, and the magazine folded in August 1972; the last issue featured Hawkwind and William Burroughs. Its demise added to the feeling of defeat and disappointment that hung in the air after the numerous arrests, constant raids and police harassment that were inflicted on this tight-knit community because of its links to the Angry Brigade. On 2 December 1972, the trial of the Stoke Newington Eight finally finished. Two days later, a divided jury delivered its verdict. Four of them were found guilty of conspiracy to cause explosions and possession of the means to do so, and were sentenced to ten years. The other four were acquitted. Summing up, the judge regretted the fact that 'such educated people' had ended up in his courtroom, and blamed their 'warped understanding of sociology' for leading them down such a dangerous path.

● ● ●

On 5 August 1972, agents from the BNDD dealt the Brotherhood an almost fatal blow. In dozens of raids across America, fifty-three arrests were made. Of those detained, sixteen were prominent Brotherhood figures. Over the subsequent months, another forty-seven Brothers were seized, along with four LSD labs and over a million tabs; 30 gallons of hashish oil and 6,000 pounds of hashish; plus 104 grams of peyote, 8 pounds of amphetamines and nearly 14 pounds of cocaine. Yet, some of the main players were still at large, including Stark. That November, his Paris lawyer, Sam Goekjian, got another visit from the IRS, this time with the BNDD in tow, and they removed a stack of documents relating to the Laboratoire Le Clocheton. Then, on 13 August, the same team appeared on the campus of Louvaine-la-Neuve University, headed for the Science Park and entered Stark's lab, only to find the regular staff still there but no sign of their boss or his mystery chemist or any LSD-making equipment. Further enquiries went nowhere. Stark had slipped the net.

Ever since, those familiar with Stark's career have claimed that he evaded capture because he'd been tipped off by his contact at the US embassy in London – who'd helped him secure the site for his Belgian lab. More significantly, the suspicion remains that the diplomat was actually working for the CIA, whose agents were always given innocuous embassy job titles as cover for their clandestine activities. If so, Stark's ally would have been privy to the BNDD's investigations, as the CIA liked to keep track of what they were up to. According to an internal memo, BNDD operations were a source of 'valuable information to the agency' and 'for this reason, they will be followed closely'.

Of course, there is another possibility: Stark was protected because he was on the CIA's payroll. Many who encountered Stark over the years were convinced he was working for them; at one point, Stark openly declared that he was a CIA asset. Yet nothing he said can be taken at face value. Implying he was CIA only added to his legend, while the paranoia that circulated among his LSD-addled counter-cultural comrades meant they saw its agents hiding round every corner. But even if Stark's claim was true, the question remains as to why the CIA would deliberately sabotage such a large-scale anti-narcotics operation involving various arms of its own government so that Stark could walk free? The area of espionage most suited to Stark's talents and way of life was counter-intelligence; one CIA veteran called it a 'highly complex and devious activity' that 'depends on cunning entrapments, agent provocateur, spies, and counter-spies' and 'double and triple crosses'. Much of the CIA's counter-intelligence machine rested on many dozens of informal sources who, in exchange for money and protection, fed them information – anything from inconsequential scraps to more meaty offerings – during a casual drink in a bar or a walk in the park. In this shadowy world, Stark could have performed the same sort of function as a Paris-based agent – code name QRPHONE-1 – who was hired in 1965 and paid $900 a month to spy on 'his extensive contacts among leftist, radical, and communist movements in Europe and Africa'.

Since the 1950s, CIA stations on foreign soil had monitored resident and visiting Americans with left-leaning views and/or connections to Communist bloc countries. On the domestic front, the FBI kept its eyes and ears on any potential subversives and tracked their movements in and out of the US. In 1967, faced with what intelligence mandarins feared was an escalating threat from the radical movement, discussions were held about how best to confront it. The immediate priority was to assess the scale of the problem, especially its international dimension. In the autumn of that year, two reports were commissioned; one studied 'Overseas Coverage of Subversive Student and Related Activities', the other examined the 'International Connections of the United States Peace Movement'. Their contents convinced the CIA that there needed to be a coordinated effort to collect together in one place all the data 'concerning foreign contacts with US individuals and organisations of the radical left' such as 'students, anti-Vietnam war activists, Draft resisters and deserters, Black nationalists, Anarchists, and assorted new Leftists'. On 25 June 1968, all the CIA's European stations received a cable about this 'sensitive high priority program', which was called Operation Chaos.

A small team was secreted away in a suite of windowless rooms in the basement at Langley, hidden behind a steel door. Here, they began collating the information streaming in from their CIA brethren round the world, the FBI, and from intercepted mail and cable communications – a voluminous amount of material that was stored in HYDRA, an IBM System/360 mainframe computer. Over the course of the next six years,

HYDRA consumed the details of 300,000 people, organisations and publications, out of which the Operation Chaos analysts created 13,000 files on 7,200 US citizens. Of particular interest were the young men dodging the Vietnam War draft and seeking refuge in Europe and, even more worrying, the increasing number of deserters fleeing the killing fields of south-east Asia. For many of them, Sweden was the destination of choice, where the American Deserters Committee was ready to greet them. Paris was the next most popular port of call. Two groups, both sponsored by luminaries from the city's cultural elite, ran safe houses for the runaways to shelter in. Resisters Inside the Army owned several properties, while the French Union of American Deserters and Draft Resisters had one in Pantin, a suburb on the north-eastern fringe of Paris.

For all the goodwill shown by their hosts, the deserters were a constant source of grief. Cut off from home, often hooked on drugs, and lacking any clear direction, many of them simply fell apart. The local CIA station were given an insight into this strange world by one of its informers – code name PETUNIA – who mixed with the deserter crowd. At 5.30 p.m. on 8 July 1969, PETUNIA met his handler in the Café Bavaria near Dupleix Metro station and briefed him about the latest developments at the Pantin safe house. According to PETUNIA, most of the fugitives living there were 'apolitical bums', though one had written to Chairman Mao to tell him that there were '1,000 men in Canada, 15,000 in Alaska and others in France who were preparing to take over the US'. Otherwise, there was one ex-soldier who regularly pulled a knife on visitors, one who went on starvation diet and another who 'got thrown out because he was an acid-head'.

There's no doubt that Stark was at home in these kinds of environments, and if he had been employed at any time to spy on US citizens abroad – whether it was a radical intellectual or a desperate deserter – then it's conceivable that the CIA would have thought it necessary to intervene on his behalf. Whatever the truth, Stark was still a marked man. The US was out of bounds. Paris was no longer safe. Nor Belgium. For the rest of that year and most of 1973, Stark flew under the radar, almost invisible, leaving only the faintest traces of his movements. One of the places his footprints made a discernible imprint was London, where his compatriots in the Microdot Gang were proving more than capable of filling his shoes.

8

The Band Breaks Up

When Kemp and Bott occupied 8 Westbourne Grove Terrace, the original plan was to install a lab there, but it quickly became clear that the premises weren't suitable. So Kemp rented nearby flats on short leases instead. He looked for ground-floor apartments with covered drains that discharged straight into the mains, thereby preventing the noxious smells – which came from the lab's chemical waste – leaking out and alerting the neighbours. Before moving in his equipment, Kemp would wait two weeks to make sure the site was secure and the other residents weren't too nosey. Then he'd set up in the kitchen, leaving the window permanently open to release fumes and a fan on to keep the air circulating. Once the production run began – and it normally took Kemp around two months to complete one – either he or Bott were always on duty. Conditions were not ideal, and Kemp grew increasingly frustrated with cramped spaces and run-down fixtures and fittings; at one point, he rented an entire house in Liverpool and went to work there. Nevertheless, between 1972 and 1974, Kemp made enough LSD for at least seventy-five million doses.

By now, Todd had several machines to convert the acid into tablets and hired-help to operate them. To distinguish their merchandise from the other brands, Kemp and Todd perfected a unique tab: the microdot. With more sophisticated tableting equipment available to them, manufacturers were offering distinctive products, but Kemp and Todd had a monopoly on the microdot, which was much smaller and neater than the alternatives; no larger than a pinhead, you could conceal hundreds in a matchbox. To keep things interesting, Kemp introduced different colours, using a technique pioneered by the original alchemist, Owsley Stanley the Third, mixing food dye into the LSD before tableting. At the same time, Todd varied the shape and the design imprinted on the surface, which often featured pyramids or other psychedelic imagery. At the gang's height, there were as many as sixty different types in circulation, and as their microdots spread across the globe, they became the gold standard for acid-heads everywhere. Overall, Todd's distribution network accounted for between 80 and 90 per cent of the UK market. Though some of his dealers also exported their microdots to faraway places like Australia, the main route to the outside world was via contacts in Amsterdam and West Germany. As far as the US was concerned, what evidence there is suggests that surviving members of the Brotherhood were responsible for offloading the acid in America and probably in other territories as well. In total, the gang's microdots were found in a hundred countries. Of the acid consumed around the world, 60–70 per cent came from Kemp's labs.

Watching enviously from the sidelines was Solomon's old compatriot Gerald Thomas, who'd been drifting ever since he quit Majorca, shifting minor amounts of cannabis into the US – with Solomon's help – and bouncing from one short-term base to another. Given he was the one who originally introduced Kemp to Solomon, Thomas felt he deserved to be part of their LSD empire. Having settled in St John's Wood, just a short walk from Solomon in Maida Vale, Thomas pestered his friend until he introduced him to Kemp and Bott in June 1972. Reluctantly they agreed to bring Thomas on board in a limited capacity, concerned that he was an accident waiting to happen. To get the ball rolling, Kemp gave Thomas some LSD to tablet and sell but Thomas got greedy, paid them £7,000 less than he should have for the amount he'd shifted, and was promptly sacked.

Irritated with Solomon for foisting Thomas on him, and growing tired of his antics, Kemp began to edge Solomon out of the gang. He got Todd to source ergotamine tartrate from a Swiss firm rather than rely on Solomon's West German connection. Yet, as time went on, the financial arrangement between Kemp and Todd became a bone of contention.

At the beginning, Todd agreed to pay Kemp £300 per 5,000 doses. This dropped to £200 as Kemp increased his output, and then down to £137 as Todd started offering his dealers discounts. Even with these reductions, Kemp was making around £50,000 a year, while Todd and the network were racking up between £300,000 and £1,500,000. What troubled Kemp was what Todd's approach to business revealed about his character: a hustler only interested in the bottom line. Money was all that mattered to him.

Kemp and Bott were thoroughly anti-materialistic and disinterested in the accumulation of wealth for its own sake. He and Bott donated substantial sums to small radical groups and publications, and to the organisers of the various free festivals held every summer. According to Kemp, he'd also 'loaned money' to 'friends' who'd 'run into debt' without expecting any of it back. Their only major indulgence was their motor cars, which they took on occasional excursions to the continent. Unfortunately, they were terrible drivers and kept having accidents. In April 1971, Kemp bought a Daimler. Two months later, Bott wrecked it while on a trip to Scotland. The following May, Kemp paid £2,000 in cash for a red Range Rover. In August, he crashed it in Norway, and then again in London that October. But aside from the cost of running these ill-fated vehicles, no other aspect of their lifestyle was going to make much of a dent in their acid fortune.

Todd, on the other hand, ate through his profits fast. He lived at 29 Fitzgeorge Avenue in the ground-floor flat of a classic red-brick mansion block in Earl's Court, a slightly more upmarket area than Ladbroke Grove. He had a common-law wife and child to support – about whom almost nothing is known. Aside from these basic expenses, Todd revelled in life's luxuries; he liked fine dining – Harrods and the Savoy Grill – and tailored clothes. He collected rare stamps and speculated in stocks and shares. He also loved to travel and did so in style. No backpacking along the hippy trail or slumming it in downbeat hotels; only the best was good enough. From 1970 to the end of 1974, Todd visited France, Germany, Denmark, Spain, Greece, Malta, the US, India, Nepal, Senegal, Sierra Leone, Barbados and the Bahamas.

Not all these trips were vacations. Some catered for Todd's one overriding passion: mountaineering. Todd caught the climbing bug when he was 13, and in the early 1970s he joined a new generation of mountaineers who were part of a rapid rise in the sport's popularity: an article in the 1973 edition of the *Alpine Journal* stated that mountaineering was no longer a 'minority' pastime but one 'suitable … for the masses' (who were attracted to it by their need 'to escape suburbia and find an antidote to twentieth-century city living'), and calculated that there were roughly 50,000 dedicated climbers and another 250,000 casual climbers in the UK alone. Todd fell into the former category and was especially fond of rock climbing – the sea cliffs of north Wales were a favourite spot – and in 1974 he went to Switzerland to scale the peaks with friends from the International Mountaineering School, an elite training camp high in the Alps. When they weren't hanging off the sides of cliffs, Todd and his fellow climbers enjoyed what one of his contemporaries described as 'a vibrant social scene' with 'wild partying' and 'drugs'.

With all these outgoings, Todd was always looking for ways to increase his turnover. Due to the unparalleled strength of Kemp's LSD – government experts said it was the purest acid they'd ever seen – Todd would be able to dilute it and increase the number of microdots he produced without there being a noticeable drop in quality. Todd roped in a young chemist he and Kemp knew from their Cambridge days, and they set about reducing the potency of each consignment from the agreed 200 micrograms per dose to 100. Some sixth sense alerted Kemp to what was going on. He bought some of his own acid at a festival, tried it out and immediately noticed the difference. As Kemp's overriding goal was to make LSD powerful enough to accelerate the fall of capitalism, any attempt to undermine that was the equivalent of a counter-revolutionary act. Furious, Kemp confronted Todd. Todd admitted he was short-changing Kemp and doubling his take. There was an almighty row, but Todd apologised in the end and promised it wouldn't happen again. Kemp was not so easily placated. The next time he needed some ergotamine tartrate he bypassed Todd and went back to Solomon, who still had plenty left from his numerous trips to West Germany.

● ● ●

When he wasn't running the odd errand for Kemp or plotting with Gerald Thomas, Solomon was labouring over his latest anthology. Like the previous two, it honed in on a hot topic that was the subject of widespread controversy and media attention: Solomon's new project looked at sex and, befitting his credentials, its relationship to drugs. By tackling this subject, Solomon was giving himself every chance of reviving his flagging fortunes and rebooting his literary career. Self-help sex manuals and guides to the ultimate orgasm topped the bestseller charts, ate up column inches and were discussed on TV chat shows. Soho was packed with row upon row of triple X cinemas showing blue movies next to sex shops groaning with hardcore European imports. Low-core sex comedies jostled for space in the regular cinemas with soft-porn offerings dressed up as art, like *Last Tango in Paris* (1972) and *Emmanuelle* (1974). Glossy airbrushed *Playboy* centrefolds sat next to readers' wives on the magazine racks.

Unlike his earlier efforts, this book was a collaboration with another editor, a fellow American expat, George Andrews. Given that his previous anthologies had done well, it's not clear why Andrews was brought in – whether it was because Solomon requested help from a kindred spirit or because Panther had lost confidence in him and thought he needed the assistance. Those close to Solomon noted how he'd become less focused and more erratic, lacking drive and ambition. Solomon was knocking on 50. He'd been systematically taking LSD and other psychedelics for nearly twenty years and smoking cannabis on an almost daily basis for decades. It's possible he was no longer capable of sustained periods of concentrated work.

As it was, Andrews was the perfect fit. The same generation as Solomon, he'd arrived in post-war New York and immersed himself in the counter-culture. During the 1950s, Andrews became a Beat poet and, like Solomon, was an early adopter of mescaline and LSD. Towards the end of the decade, Andrews migrated to Tangier, where William Burroughs was one of a coterie of expat writers and artists, and it was here that Andrews met Leary when he passed through town in the summer of 1961. This led to Leary including a poem by Andrews in the very first issue of his journal *The Psychedelic Review*, June 1963. The poem, entitled 'Annihilating Illumination', tries to capture the avalanche of sensations Andrews experienced during a hallucination:

I am alive with the living God
I throb unique among the infinite variations

and so what if all the evolution of consciousness only leads to the
knowledge
that I am a germ in the guts of a greater being
I am older than creation older than all beings
the stars revolve within me
I voyage through the inner space between my atoms
I take space ships to the different parts of my body
each organ becomes a constellation as I spread across the sky.

In 1965, Andrews made for London and straight for the World
Psychedelic Centre (WPC), a bookshop and meeting place in Belgravia
that had been opened by Leary's emissary to the UK, who'd shown up
in the capital armed with 5,000 doses worth of Czech LSD and several
hundred copies of *The Tibetan Book of the Dead.* The mutual connection to Leary meant that George Andrews was always welcome at the
WPC and its owner invited him to speak at a workshop in consciousness
expansion at the ICA on 14 February 1966, alongside Burroughs and
R.D. Laing.

Seeking to make London his permanent home, Andrews rented a
room in a ground-floor flat at 101 Cromwell Road, West Kensington, an
address that was notorious on the London LSD circuit because a poet
from New Zealand – nicknamed the Spider – had hidden 1,000 doses of
acid there, with another 4,000 concealed a few streets away. The house
also accommodated several members of Pink Floyd, who were at the
vanguard of acid rock. In 1965, Roger Waters and Syd Barrett came down
to London from Cambridge, where they'd both grown up. In his teens,
Waters was the chairman of the local youth branch of CND, while Syd
'the Beat' Barrett loved Kerouac's *On the Road,* smoked his first joint
in 1962 and, three years later, took LSD by the banks of the Cam. Soon
after moving to London, Waters and his girlfriend took the top-floor
flat at 101 Cromwell Road and, when they moved out, Barrett moved in.
By then, he was taking acid in his coffee every morning. In July 1967, he
suffered a nervous breakdown and was diagnosed with schizophrenia.

In the midst of this chaos, Andrews managed to get a collection of
eight poems published – *Burning Joy* (1966) – and finished compiling
an anthology about India's thousands-of-years-old cannabis culture, *The
Book of Grass: An Anthology of Indian Hemp* (1967). Released by a small

imprint, there was a French translation, a US edition, and then, in 1972, a reissue in paperback by Penguin Books. This wider exposure got the book some attention and good reviews and put Andrews at the front of the line for the job with Solomon. What clinched the deal, however, was their long history together; though it's difficult to know exactly when and where they were first introduced, it could have been at any time during the previous twenty years.

To lure as many readers as possible, Panther launched Solomon and Andrews' *Drugs and Sexuality* (1973) as a mass-market paperback with a marine-blue cover that featured a naked, bejewelled woman sprawling seductively on an exotic divan, lazily cradling a hookah pipe, with a large joint in an ashtray beside her. On the back cover, the blurb boasted that the book contained 'an unsurpassed wealth of revelations, ecstasies, warnings and entertainment': on the inside, it promised the reader that they were about to enjoy 'one of those all too rare books capable of opening one's mind's eye on vistas of feeling and experience previously undreamed of'.

Unfortunately, *Drugs and Sexuality* did not live up to its billing. What followed was a dated, almost half-hearted, effort to throw together a bunch of texts, some of which barely mentioned sex or drugs. Organised chronologically, the text meandered across the centuries, beginning with erotic poetry and sacred texts from ancient Greece, Rome, China and India, then a procession of writers and thinkers – Boccaccio, Shakespeare, the Marquis de Sade and Baudelaire – mixed in with long extracts from obscure studies on aphrodisiacs, and several essays on yoga and tantric sex. More contemporary content included a short description of sex on amphetamines by Burroughs; a review of a survey of cannabis users and their generally positive attitude to sex; and a short story by Andrews, which first appeared in *Frendz* magazine, set in a café in Tangier, where nine people eat, smoke hashish, and have a simultaneous collective hallucination during which their bodies merge together in an act of sexual union that transforms them into 'a naked hermaphroditic giant nine times larger than an ordinary human'.

The relationship between sex and LSD was explored in a reprint of Leary's 1966 *Playboy* interview. In it, Leary explained how 'sex under LSD becomes miraculously enhanced and intensified' as 'every cell in your body ... is making love with every cell in her body' and your senses reach fever pitch. Leary also claimed that LSD could 'cure' frigidity, impotence and homosexuality, because it unearthed childhood traumas, the root of all sexual dysfunction. Leary's retrograde views – which reflected the reactionary attitudes of a society where homosexuality was illegal and considered by many to be a crime against nature – were repeated in another piece in the anthology, an essay entitled 'Marital Problems'. Having analysed numerous first-person accounts about the impact of acid on intimate relationships, the authors concluded that LSD ought to be 'regarded as a strong asset to marriage counsellors'. As far as treating cases of frigidity and impotence was concerned, acid seemed 'to first define the problem, then dissolve it'. It also proved 'successful in homosexual problems because it can reveal early traumas, which underlie the condition'. However, they were slightly more enlightened than Leary and happily accepted the fact that, after taking acid, some would 'want to stay that way', and believed that 'a continuance of homosexuality' should be viewed as a positive affirmation of self rather than 'a relapse'.

It was ideas like these that made the book feel, even in 1973, seriously out of step with the times, as if Solomon and Andrews were still clinging to the attitudes of the era they'd felt most comfortable in. Perhaps unsurprisingly the book flopped; there were no reviews and sales remained flat. Though Andrews would edit another anthology for Panther – *Drugs and Magic* (1975) – and the publisher reissued Solomon's cannabis book in a new paperback edition, the failure of *Drugs and Sexuality* brought his relationship with Panther to an end; for now, Solomon's literary career was at a standstill.

● ● ●

The disappointing response to his anthology pushed Solomon closer to Gerald Thomas, who was still hoping to hit the big time. Convinced he could replicate Kemp's LSD formula, Thomas was proposing they go into production for themselves. Equipment was bought and capital raised, largely through selling cannabis in the US, which Thomas smuggled in from India via Canada. Before flying off to complete the transfer of 15 pounds of hashish from a locker at Montreal airport to Boston, Thomas stored all his drug-manufacturing paraphernalia – including material for making cocaine – and most of his clothes and belongings in a warehouse at Blake's Wharf by the London docks. On 3 June 1973, Thomas landed in Canada, picked up the dope, went to get his connecting flight, was stopped and searched by customs officials, and arrested. Out on bail, with nothing but a long cold Canadian winter to look forward to, Thomas began considering his narrowing options. About the only bargaining chip he possessed was his insider knowledge of the Microdot Gang's operation and, though he had no particular loyalty to Kemp or Todd, selling them out would also mean betraying Solomon.

Yet his supposed friend didn't seem interested in helping Thomas with his predicament. Thomas was very worried because among his luggage was a business card with the address of the warehouse in London where he'd stashed his stuff, and it'd only be a matter of time before the Canadian authorities informed their British counterparts. Desperate to limit the damage, Thomas repeatedly called Solomon and asked him to retrieve his possessions. Solomon reluctantly agreed, but instead of keeping them safe as Thomas requested, he simply burnt the lot. Incensed, Thomas demanded compensation. Solomon refused. Thomas threatened him. Solomon threatened him back. Angry, resentful and scared, Thomas spoke with his lawyer and arranged to sit down with the Canadians. In January 1974, Thomas told them everything he knew about the gang. Yet because Kemp and Todd had done their best to keep him at arm's length, his grasp of the intricacies of their network was hazy. Crucially, he couldn't remember Todd's surname, and wasn't sure if he was called 'Harry' or 'Henry' or another name beginning with 'H'. However, he didn't hesitate to put Solomon, Stark, Kemp and Bott squarely in the frame.

Rightly convinced that Thomas would crack under pressure, Solomon decided to cut his losses; without a book commission to distract him and with day-to-day life slipping through his fingers, he returned to New York. The others were relieved to see him go. Solomon's cavalier approach to the drug trade and loose tongue had already made him a liability and, with Thomas behind bars, he'd become a significant security risk. Like Leary, Solomon had never adjusted to the new reality that came with the criminalisation of LSD. He simply couldn't grasp the fact that they were the 'bad guys' and the culture they'd inspired had moved beyond its early 1960s optimism to a much darker place or that the majority of people remained fearful of what LSD was capable of.

For the others, Thomas' incarceration was a problem, but not a disaster. Though Kemp and Bott now owned a caravan and were contemplating leaving London for somewhere more rural, they didn't seem in any hurry to leave. A clear indication that they were planning to extend their stay was the fact that Bott – who'd been doing shifts at local surgeries – started working at Charing Cross Hospital on 1 April 1974. But at virtually the same time as Bott assumed her new role, two officers from Scotland Yard's Central Drugs Intelligence Unit (CDIU) were spending a couple of days in Canada interrogating Thomas. Then on 24 April, Bott suddenly quit her job at Charing Cross. She and Kemp unhitched their caravan and hit the road: by that summer they were camped in north-west Wales.

It's difficult to believe that these events were unconnected, and that it was merely a coincidence that Kemp and Bott high-tailed it out of London immediately after Thomas confessed to the CDIU detectives. The timing and manner of their hasty departure raises the possibility that they were warned that they were no longer invisible. The Metropolitan Police were certainly corrupt enough for this to be true. If this was the case, it seems more likely that Todd received the tip-off and passed it onto Kemp, rather than the other way round. Kemp was not the type to cultivate friends on the force. Todd, however, in his role as head of sales and distribution, was in prime position to reach out to the boys in blue and come to a mutually beneficial arrangement. And if Todd was indeed privy to the Thomas file, it meant he knew that even though his associates had been named, he'd escaped identification and therefore could afford to be more relaxed about the whole thing.

So while Kemp and Bott headed for the hills, Todd stayed put. He had plentiful reserves of Kemp's LSD to draw on and a smoothly functioning, well-oiled supply chain that practically ran itself. There was no reason to stop now. Equally well, Kemp was not about to abandon his dreams of overturning the social order. The Microdot Gang may have split, but it was a long way from going out of business.

● ● ●

During 1973, Stark's past caught up with him: specifically, his dealings with Billy Hitchcock and Nick Sand. Hitchcock was in the cross hairs of the IRS and the FBI for money laundering and tax evasion. The IRS had finally reconstructed the intricate nature of Hitchcock's investments in Resorts International, the mafia-run casino-hotel complex in the Bahamas. Its agents also managed to prise open the accounts in Switzerland that Hitchcock held at the Paravicini Bank. Between these, his holdings in Resorts International and other funds secreted in the Bahamas, Hitchcock was facing a tax bill of $1 million. If this wasn't bad enough, the IRS also found proof of the illegal trading in stocks and shares that Mr Paravicini, the president of the bank, had engaged in on behalf of Hitchcock and a former Lehman Brothers colleague. Mr Paravicini bought stocks and shares in major corporations like IBM and Polaroid – with a total value of $67 million – and deposited them in Hitchcock and his partners' secret accounts, thereby violating stock market regulations and breaking a number of federal laws in the process.

As the investigators examined the books at Paravicini, they uncovered Hitchcock's role as the acid banker and the fact that Stark, Sand and several other Brothers had accounts there as well. Though there were no immediate consequences for Stark, this discovery meant trouble for Sand, and the IRS began digging into his financial affairs. On his return from Europe – where he'd helped Stark and Kemp with their Paris lab – Sand had kept a low profile, aware that the BNDD had the Brotherhood in their sights. But Sand was not only on a mission to spread the psychedelic message, he was also an artist who could not stay away from his studio for too long. In April 1972, he moved to St Louis, Missouri, established a front company – Signet Research and Development – bought a building downtown and set up a major lab there, and put a smaller one in the basement of the house he was renting in the nearby suburb of Fenton. Sand's main facility was the largest LSD production centre of his career and within six months he'd tableted 50,000 doses of Orange Sunshine and had the ingredients ready for another 14 million.

With everything progressing nicely, Sand and his girlfriend went on vacation at the end of the year. Unfortunately, they forgot to cancel the post. Before long, their mailbox was overflowing. Worried, the postman called the police. They came and noticed water seeping out from under the front door. Inside, a water pipe had frozen and burst. The cops entered the house, found cannabis in the bedroom, the drug lab in the basement and information about Signet Research and Development. Its downtown address was raided and the contents of Sand's LSD factory were seized.

On 19 January 1973, Sand and his partner returned from holiday and were arrested, but the charges were dropped on a technicality relating to the initial search. This lucky escape was only a temporary reprieve: Hitchcock had decided to do a deal with the government and was ready to tell the authorities everything he knew about the acid business. In exchange for Hitchcock's co-operation, the IRS settled for a payment of $543,800 and his part in the Paravicini stocks and shares scam was quietly forgotten, leaving his Lehman Brothers colleague to carry the can, as the bank had closed its doors and Mr Paravicini was nowhere to be found.

Next came the LSD conspiracy case. On 26 April 1973, at a federal court in San Francisco, a grand jury indicted Hitchcock, Stark, Sand and four others for the manufacture, possession, distribution and sale of LSD. In the course of the proceedings, Stark got a special mention: 'the Grand Jury specifically charges that … Ronald Hadley Stark managed and operated a laboratory under the name Laboratoire Le Clocheton … at Parc Scientifique De Louvain La Neuve … from approximately September, 1971, through August, 1972.' These charges, plus the ongoing investigation by the BNDD, which had just become the DEA and was still after him for his involvement with the Brotherhood's hash oil business, put Stark in a perilous position. For years he'd been hiding in plain sight. Flaunting his wealth. Jumping from continent to continent. Causing ripples wherever he went. That way of life was over. It was time to go underground.

Stark always had a fondness for aliases – he was Gordon Simpson in Switzerland and Jean Claude Van Der Leuwe in Belgium and Holland – but in 1972 he went a step further and acquired a new identity. In New York, he was issued a US passport under the name John Clarence Dillon, born on 4 September 1938, the same year as Stark. For further protection, he went to London in the spring of 1973 and got a UK passport with the name Terrence William Abbott, born on 4 December 1942. Furnished with these documents, Stark was temporarily beyond the reach of the FBI and the DEA.

As a result, Stark wasn't in the dock when the LSD conspiracy trial started on 12 November 1973. He wasn't present for the verdicts, or for the sentencing on 8 March 1974. Hitchcock, who'd been the prosecution's star witness, was given a five-year suspended sentence and a $20,000 fine.

Sand, on the other hand, got fifteen years. This harsh punishment was justified by the judge on the basis that 'the psychedelic movement' was responsible for 'the degradation of mankind and society', and if left unchecked would cause 'anarchy in this country'.

Meanwhile, one of the men intent on creating 'anarchy' was still very much at large. Sometime that year, Stark resurfaced in Italy, ready to seize any new opportunities that might come his way. He was about to enter a treacherous world where drug dealers mingled with mobsters, political extremists, terrorists and spies, leaving a blood-stained trail behind them.

David Solomon in a relaxed mood

The 1966 US paperback edition of David
Solomon's LSD anthology

Timothy Leary preaches to his followers at the Human Be-In, San Francisco, 1967 (Shutterstock)

Billy Hitchcock outside the main house at Millbrook (Getty Images)

A rare photograph of the elusive
Ronald Stark

Christine Bott and her prize-winning goat

Richard Kemp, the alchemist

Henry Barclay Todd caught on camera by the
Julie team

Renowned psychiatrist R.D. Laing addresses a captive audience (Alamy)

A poster in support of the Angry Brigade members arrested for possession of explosives

Police break up the party at the Windsor Festival, 1974 (PA Images)

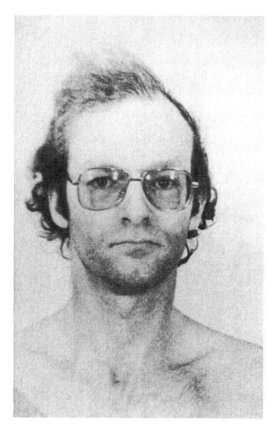

The PhD chemist Andy Munro who made acid for Henry Barclay Todd

Kemp and Bott's farmhouse in Wales (Shutterstock)

# of Martyn the hippie cop

OPERATION JULIE

MIRROR COMMENT

Julie's Angels

TWENTY-SIX weary coppers were out on the town celebrating last night. And the rest of the country should be celebrating too.

The twenty-six were the police team who, over two years, pulled off the biggest drug investigation in the world.

The drug squad was drawn from ten different forces and "Operation Julie" took them all over the world.

Their success was spectacular. A year ago one microdot of LSD cost £1. Now it is so scarce that the price has shot up to £5.

Pity

The twenty-six were away from their families for weeks on end. Eighteen were based in a three-bedroomed house which was so crowded that even a cupboard under the stairs was used as a bedroom.

They shivered during observations in the Welsh mountains. During the 1976 heatwave they fried in temperatures of up to 118 in the back of surveillance vans. It was total commitment.

Sadly the squad has now broken up. Six have left the police. The rest have returned to their separate forces.

What a pity their tremendous experience couldn't have been put to use in a national drug squad.

HART: Martyn the uniformed cop. Pictures: PETER STONE.   SCRUFFY: Martyn the hippie as he dressed for Operation Julie

d, having just finished prosecution run. He sized terrible — but a think of the revenue.

Work on a run of a llion tablets would last ee weeks. To set it up d them, say, £20,000.

million tablets were eria to them £300,000, d at the end of the only line £2 million Such and legitimate

business with returns like that? No wonder this lot lived so well.

They were very efficient, too, especially with their cut-off system to keep various members of the gang apart.

When some of the key plotters—Kemp, Munro, Todd, Fielding and Spencetey—were arrested and taken to Operation

Julie headquarters in Swindon, it was the first time they had all met.

We pieced it all together for them, and when they realised how much we knew they coughed it all.

Richard Kemp, the brilliant chemist, was busy telling us how great LSD would be for everyone. And how he

wanted to turn on the world.

When we asked him about the deaths and the terrible injuries to some acid trippers, he told us coolly: "Every revolution has its casualties."

There were times when I could easily have ended up as a casualty myself.

Like the time I had to go to court to give evidence after we bust

a cannabis rocket in 1975.

The Daily Mirror published a rear-view picture of me so that it wouldn't blow my cover.

A couple of years later I went into another commune while I was working on the Operation Julie job, and found they were using the picture as a dartboard. Charming!

DEFIANT SMILE FOR THE JUDGE

GUILTY: Henry Todd

A BURLY drug baron swaggered off to begin a thirteen-year jail sentence yesterday . . . with a smile.

Henry Barclay Todd, one of three "directors" of an LSD syndicate which manufactured two-thirds of the world's supplies, told the judge sardonically: "Thank you, my lord."

Todd and fourteen others received sentences totalling 120 years for their part in the drug ring.

The sentences were the final chapter in the bizarre story of the gang, many of them university graduates, who thought they could turn on the world with LSD.

Todd, 33, chemist Richard Kemp, 34, and American author David Solomon, 51, were described by Mr. Justice Park at Bristol

Crown Court as equally responsible for the beginning of the highly successful conspiracy.

Kemp, he said, was a man of considerable talent and one of the world's top experts on the manufacture of LSD.

The judge told him, as he jailed him for 13 years: "This was done in pursuit of the ideal that LSD liberated people's minds and therefore in your words would be beneficial to mankind.

False

"That, I think, was a false ideal."

Solomon, who has written books on drugs and sex, was jailed for ten years.

Kemp's lover, Dr. Christine Bott, 32, was jailed for nine

years after the judge said he did not believe her claim that she co-operated in the conspiracy only because of her love for Kemp.

Among the other plotters jailed yesterday were:

Chemist Andrew Munro, 29, who was jailed for 10 years.

Brian Cuthbertson, 29, a top man in the distribution network. He was sentenced to 11 years. He had amassed assets totalling £160,000.

Two women, who pleaded guilty to conspiracy were given two-year suspended sentences.

Janine Spenceley, 28, said she had joined the plot to help her husband Russell, who was jailed for 13 years.

Monica Kenyon, 22, helped mass on tablets at the flat she shared with a boyfriend.

TOMORROW: Piranha peril

Spot on value!

Cassette players really come to life with BASF Chromdioxid cassettes. And, together with the BASF Super Cassettes, they represent fantastic value at Currys.

BASF

	Rec. Price	Currys price
BASF Super		
C60	£1.57	£1.15
C90	£2.09	£1.55
BASF Chrome		
C60	£2.09	£1.45
C90	£2.61	£1.85
C120	£3.39	£2.25

Prices subject to availability.

Currys

OVER 480 BRANCHES NATIONWIDE Look in your phone book.

The two faces of undercover cop Martyn Pritchard (Mirrorpix)

'Doctor Chick' found guilty in drugs trial

FACTORY No. 1: The Welsh mansion house at Tregaron where Kemp lived with his sweetheart, Dr. Christine Bolt.

A WOMAN doctor described as "the banker" for an international drugs ring was found guilty yesterday of taking part in a plot which produced LSD worth an estimated £8 million.

One showed her as a responsible doctor, proud of her profession.

The other, Bristol Crown Court was told during the eight-day trial, was a drug-taking revolutionary who thought LSD would make the world a better place.

Bott, of Tregaron, Wales, was found guilty of possessing LSD and aiding and abetting others to possess the drug.

The court had heard how Bott, an army officer's daughter, had opened a safe deposit box in a Swiss bank.

It was, said prosecuting counsel Ian Kennedy, a "nest egg or bust fund" which would have been used if police had got onto them.

At one time the box contained £45,000 in cash and bonds.

She admitted in court that she knew her lover, 33-year-old chemist Richard Kemp, was making LSD while they lived together in Wales.

And she told the court she knew that money she put into the safe deposit box came from the sale of the hallucinatory drug.

But she claimed she played no part in the production or distribution of the drug.

THE court heard how she and Kemp fell in love when they met at Liverpool University and according to Bott, Kemp "turned her on" to cannabis and LSD.

And she told police that while the LSD was being made it had been "great, we were high all the time."

But she claimed she had been a prisoner of love who did things against her better judgment because of her emotional involvement with Kemp, who is not before the court.

Bott, nicknamed "Dr. Chick" because she told police she had been a "chick", living in a house with two men, admitted taking expensive foreign holidays with Kemp even though he was unemployed and she had only worked for short periods.

The money came from

THE FACTORIES OF DEADLY DREAMS

FACTORY No. 2: The house at Hampton Wick

the sale of LSD.

She said she thought that LSD, if used properly, helped people to reach unexplored areas of the mind.

It was a way to create the "alternative society." It lifted the veil to show takers the world as it could be, she claimed.

But in evidence she denied saying she saw herself as a revolutionary.

Her alternative society, she said in her soft, well-spoken way, was a chance to bring people closer to nature, to live

close to the earth.

The court had been told the gang bought eight kilos of the base material for making LSD. It was capable of producing at least 16 million tablets.

These, Mr. Justice Park told the jury, were selling on the streets for 80p each.

Bott challenged court room evidence about huge amounts of money being made from the plot.

She said some of it was "almost given away" at pop festivals.

But she could not dis-

pute evidence that she had withdrawn money from the Swiss safe deposit box to buy their £26,000 home in Wales.

When pressed, she admitted that the money being made from the drug was an embarrassment.

In the words of the prosecution, the gang "had money coming out of its ears."

Bott showed no emotion when the jury returned their guilty verdict after an absence of five hours, but she did allow a fleeting smile when she was led down to the cells.

Cuthbertson, who pleaded not guilty to the same charges as Dr. Bott, was cleared of the plot charge.

Both were arrested as part of a huge police investigation codenamed "Operation Julie."

The investigation closed down two big LSD factories, the Welsh one and another in Hampton Wick, London.

Both used a new production method which crystallised the drug in a big way and make it into handy tablets which could be handled easily.

A vital ingredient in the new process was calcium lactate, a chemical commonly used to combat disease of the bones.

Forty pounds of calcium lactate is enough for 1,800,000 microdots. Police found mountains of calcium lactate bottles outside the London factory.

The chemical was ground down in a meat mincer, mixed with pure LSD and scraped into the tiny holes of a transistor radio circuit board to make 1,000 tablets per board.

The extra eight were

The horrors of LSD

ONE of the deadliest of drugs, LSD is harmless enough to look at — a clear, colourless, odourless, tasteless liquid. LSD takers—"acid heads"—used to put a drop on a lump of sugar to swallow. Now the drug is available in tablet form.

Users say it enhances reality—but it doesn't. It only creates a false, dream-like state in which takers have been known to leap off buildings believing they could fly . . . chew a hand to the bone, believing it to be an orange . . . or truss and prepare a baby for roasting, believing it to be an oven-ready chicken.

Three Operation Julie detectives had frightening accidental "trips" on LSD when they were left to guard the drugs "factory" at Hampton Wick.

They took special precautions and

known in the drugs trade as "a baker's dozen."

From May 1970 until March 1977, the two factories fed the world's drugs market with LSD.

According to official police estimates, enough base material has been recovered to make more than 20 million tablets.

No one will ever know how many were sold before the ring was smashed.

The factories provided about 60 per cent of the world's supplies.

AT the moment when police were beginning to nail their operation, they became "flash." They produced a pack of three tablets — red, white and blue, to celebrate the American bi-Centennial.

There were plans for a similar run for the home market, in appreciation of the Queen's Silver Jubilee.

But "Operation Julie" foiled the conspirators' plans . . . and they spent the best part of Jubilee Year in prison, awaiting trial and sentence.

opened all the curtains because it was then thought that LSD deteriorated in daylight.

But then strange things began happening . . .

Two of the detectives found themselves laughing uproariously when watching "Jesus of Nazareth" on TV. The third, taking a bath, thought he could feel every drop of water dripping from his hair to his back.

Flowers

As the three walked back to the house they thought the pavement was covered with filled carpet. Trees seemed to be sprouting multi-coloured flowers.

And one detective, looking at a pile of logs, saw instead a herd of deer at rest, watching him.

Back at the house they called for medical help. Doctors found they had been on an unwitting LSD "trip" due to absorbing drug dust with which the house was impregnated.

KAYS SPRING & SUMMER 1978

Kays new BIGGER Catalogue

...it makes fashion sense

Shopping from Kays new bigger catalogue saves you time, trouble and money. It also brings you goods on 14 days' approval, with free credit on 20 and 38 weeks — with 10% commission on all your purchases.

Best of all, it offers you the pick of today's fashion – from summery dresses, to the prettiest casuals.

Kays-for those who expect the best

KAY & CO. LTD., FREEPOST, WORCESTER WR1 1JF
Please send me, without obligation, my free catalogue and details of how to earn a Kays agency.   PLEASE USE BLOCK LETTERS

Name

Address

County   Postcode

I am over 18. The right to refuse any application is reserved.
Applications from the Channel Islands, Northern Ireland and Forces at home and overseas are most welcome.   J41749

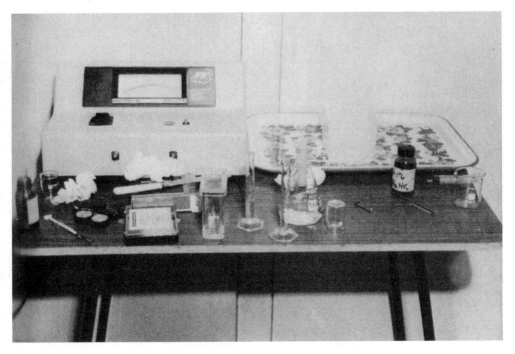

Laboratory equipment and moulds for tableting found at 23 Seymour Road, Hampton Wick

Detective Inspector Dick Lee and members of the Julie team pose next to some of the acid they seized (Gloucestershire Police Archives)

DAILY Mirror

MIRROR EXCLUSIVE

Roddy's playboy brother, a lover of fast cars and gorgeous girls

THE CAD

See Centre Pages

BRITAIN'S BIGGEST DAILY SALE   7p   Thursday, March 9, 1978

Jail for the LSD plotters who planned to drug a city

WE'LL BLOW A MILLION MINDS!

JULIE: Life switched off.

THE BRAINS: Top chemist Richard Kemp and his mistress Christine Bott.

Hope is born as a little girl dies

By STANLEY VAUGHAN

ONE ray of hope lightened the grief of a couple whose daughter lost her fight for life.

They had agreed that her kidneys could be used in transplant operations. And when doctors switched off seven-year-old Julie Pettinger's life-support machine, her parents knew that she was not dying entirely in vain.

Julie was knocked down as she was crossing the road near her home in Radford Street, Worksop, Notts. When her case was judged to be hopeless, it was decided that her kidneys could help two youngsters in need of transplants.

Mrs. Hazel Pettinger, 31, said last night:

❝ The doctors told us tests had shown Julie's brain was dead. They asked us to consent to the machine being switched off and Julie's kidneys removed for transplanting.

We thought of what the parents of the other children were going through.

And we knew that Julie would never again be able ❞ to do anything.

Doctors at Sheffield Royal Infirmary switched the life-support machine off on Tuesday.

One of Julie's kidneys went to a hospital in the London area. The other was flown to Holland.

Mrs. Pettinger added: "We may never know who the children are.

"But Julie might have helped someone else to have a happy normal life."

Her husband Peter said: "It was a terribly hard decision to take. But perhaps we have spared other parents some of our agony."

AN ENTIRE CITY stoned on a nightmare drug — that was the crazy ambition of the masterminds behind the world's biggest LSD factory.

They planned to blow a million minds simultaneously by pouring pure LSD into the reservoirs serving Birmingham.

Detectives were horrified when they heard what the drug barons had in mind.

By SYDNEY YOUNG and EDWARD LAXION

But the ghastly plan was cut short last March when police arrested the plotters and shut down their two production plants in Wales and London.

And their dream was finally smashed yesterday when the plotters and their aides were given jail sentences totalling 120 years.

Elite

They were trapped by a team of undercover "hippie" detectives in a vast investigation codenamed Operation Julie after the woman police sergeant who helped to co-ordinate the inquiry.

The police in this elite squad outwitted one of the most educated teams of criminals the world has ever known.

One of them brilliant chemist Richard Kemp, 34, perfected a new way of processing LSD.

But instead of bringing him academic honours, his brilliance earned him

the shame of a thirteen-year jail sentence. His mistress, Dr. Christine Bott, 32, was jailed for nine years for her part in the drug ring.

She had pleaded for a lighter sentence so that she would still be well within child-bearing age when she was released.

But Mr. Justice Park said at Bristol Crown Court that the sentences were intended to serve as a deterrent.

Patience

The scale of the plotters' operations was enormous.

The LSD shortage caused by the closure of their "factories" has sent the street price of a microdot tablet soaring from £1 to £8.

Last year the gang's turnover reached an estimated £200 million—equal to that of British Home Stores.

At that time, dazzled by their own brilliance, their immense profits and their dreams of "turning on" the world, the gang seemed unstoppable.

But they reckoned without the patience, tenacity and sheer guts of the Operation Julie team — the handful of shabby supercops who took them on in a battle of wits—and won.

GANNEX TYCOON UNDER PROBE

KAGAN: Wilson's friend

A BIG inquiry was going on last night into the textile empire of Gannex raincoat tycoon Lord Kagan, friend of Sir Harold Wilson.

Customs and Treasury officials were examining documents, including invoices and bank statements, seized in raids on Lord Kagan's homes and offices.

For the past six months the Customs have been investigating claims of

By RICHARD STOTT and ROGER BEAM

irregularities over textile exports — particularly denim.

They have looked into allegations about discrepancies between the face value of textile exports, invoices and cash returns for the goods back into Britain.

Checks have been made on connections with a firm in Brussels and on links with at least one

Swiss bank. The raids on Lord Kagan's premises in Yorkshire, Lancashire and London were carried out by a team of twelve men acting on Treasury authority.

They were granted search warrants by magistrates.

Lord Kagan, 63, could not be contacted last night.

A staff member at his luxury flat in Bayswater said: "I think he's gone back to his factory headquarters in Yorkshire because that's where all his documents and files are."

● Supermock!—Page Nine

JUNKIE PATROL

Pages 2 & 3

The Microdot Gang are accused by the press of plotting to poison Birmingham's water supply (Mirrorpix)

Police attend the scene of the Aldo Moro kidnapping (Shutterstock)

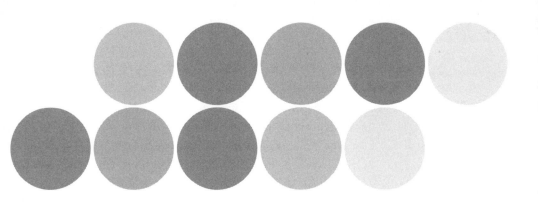

Part Three

BUSINESS AS UNUSUAL

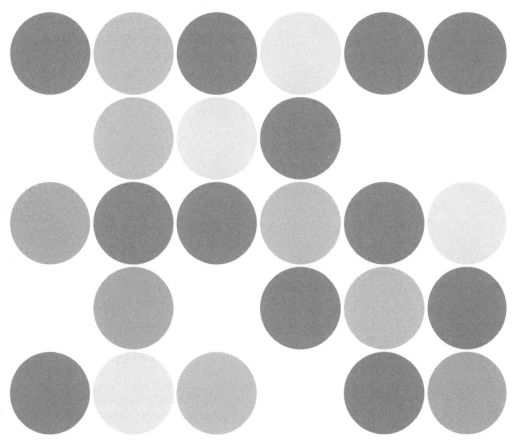

9

The Network

In any business, the quality of your merchandise is irrelevant if you can't get it to your customers. With drugs like heroin and cocaine – and to a lesser extent cannabis – producers relied on their existing ties to organised crime to get their goods to market. In the case of LSD, systems of distribution had to be created from scratch; the one assembled by Todd linked seller and consumer in unique and unprecedented ways, more of a college fraternity than a criminal enterprise. The starting point on the acid's journey was Reading, 40 miles from London, where Todd's two-man team tableted it all. Once their work was complete, they bought regular household products – cereal, teabags, dog biscuits, baby food – opened the packets, tins and jars they came in, removed the contents and filled them with small bags containing around 1,000 microdots each. These were then buried in obscure countryside locations – near a tree in the woods, by a hedgerow, in a field – where they could be safely retrieved by a trusted associate who would farm out the microdots to their connections. Some of these caches were intended for the owner of the Last Resort restaurant in Fulham, who supplied a contact in Amsterdam, who distributed the acid across Europe; the rest radiated out from Reading and across the south of the country.

Reading boasted a large student community that provided a pool of customers and ready-made dealers. From 1971, the town was also home to the National Jazz, Blues and Rock Festival, a fairly professional well-organised event where punters paid £5–6 to see major bands on a number of stages, while a free festival sprung up in its slipstream and colonised Windsor Great Park, a massive chunk of well-tended royal real estate 28 miles from Reading. The presence of these two events in the heartlands of Thames Valley, both taking place towards the end of August, sucked thousands into the area, all keen to have their own festival experience: and for many that meant taking LSD. Anticipating this surge in demand, Kemp and Todd coordinated their production schedule so that their microdots were ready to launch at the beginning of each festival season. As a result, the majority of the LSD consumed by the intrepid festival-goers was Kemp's handiwork. Though his acid was readily available at the Reading Festival, the 1973 and 1974 Windsor free festivals were like trade conventions for the low-level links in the Microdot Gang's supply chain; you could do business before them, during them and after them.

For Kemp, however, the free festivals were not just commercially important. They were also an opportunity for the various strands of the counter-culture to congregate, intermingle and achieve a deeper sense of shared purpose, and his acid would encourage that process. Kemp said he donated thousands of pounds to the organisers of free festivals and declared that it was 'a marvellous moment of unity when so many heads gather together'. Many of the individuals and groups behind the events at Windsor were part of the Ladbroke Grove scene and brought their anarchic agenda with them, like the Albion Free State, which represented the 2,000–3,000 squatters who lived in the area and wanted to apply the right of common ownership to the whole country. Occupying a disused bingo hall close to Portobello Road, members of the Albion Free State were extremely active at Windsor '74, the same year they issued their manifesto, which called for liberation from 'dead-end jobs'; an end to the mass production of 'non-essential consumer items'; the introduction of 'neighbourhood and workers' control of local factories, businesses, banks and supermarkets'; and the foundation of 'permanent free festival sites, collectives and cities of life and love, maybe one every fifty miles or so'.

At Windsor '74, their vision for a new England must have seemed within their grasp, as lines of battered cars and all manner of vans daubed in every colour of the rainbow clogged nearby roads; rows of makeshift tents, dwellings and authentic-looking tepees formed a hippy encampment; unruly hair, headbands and wristbands, patched-up denim and shaggy coats, topless women and face paint were everywhere to be seen; and all the while Kemp's premium-grade LSD was circulating through the crowds, adding to the already otherworldly atmosphere. One festival veteran remembered that 'there was a vast amount of acid at Windsor in 1974. Everyone was talking about it and it was obvious it was the focus of the festival'. For the dealers it was open season. Some charged 50p a microdot. Some were giving them away for free. Some advertised their wares by fixing signs on their tents – 'I want to Destroy your Brain Cells' – others pinned notices on trees – 'Green acid – third tent on the left behind Stage B'.

Inevitably, Kemp's mind-blowing LSD – a festival newsletter warned punters not to take more than one microdot – was too much for some to handle. The drug charity Release, which tended to the casualties, was overwhelmed by lost souls suffering from bad trips, freak-outs, accidental injuries and self-harm. There was also the risk of running into the ever-present Hells Angels, who preyed on the vulnerable and punished anyone who caused them offence. However, the main concern for the majority of festival-goers was the constant threat of arrest. The hostile attitude of many senior police officers to the festival scene was forcefully expressed by the chief constable of Hampshire. He thought these events were 'evil' because they allowed 'drop-outs and anarchists' to 'influence … weaker characters' and encouraged 'amorality, perversion, drug addiction and contempt for all forms of law'.

To control and intimidate the crowds arriving for the perfectly legal Reading Festival, Thames Valley Police employed tactics that would have made your average dictatorship proud. At Reading Station plain-clothes officers met London trains and ushered any likely candidates into a side room full of cops. Drugs seized were sent to a forensic lab especially set up for the occasion. Magistrates' courts stayed open to ten at night and council workers put in overtime to clear the paperwork; cells at the local stations were bursting at the seams and the overflow was transported in coaches to a nearby army barracks.

This heavy-handed approach was applied with even more vigour at the Windsor gatherings. In 1972 – when there was a small, less publicised event – the cops outnumbered punters four to one. In 1973, the festival had been granted permission by the Home Office, so the police maintained a relatively low profile. At Windsor '74, however, the gloves were off. Over the first four days of the festival there were 280 drug-related arrests, then on the morning of 29 August, the decision was made to break up the festivities and send everyone packing. At 8 a.m., the police announced their intention to terminate proceedings. Three hours later, 800 officers – with truncheons at the ready – invaded the site: an undercover cop, who'd pitched his tent in the midst of the hippy tribes, recalled with some relish the moment 'a great line-up of uniforms like Colonel Custer's cavalry descended on the savages' encampment'. Mayhem ensued – 'there were tents and sleeping bags going up in the air and full tins of beans and vegetables being hurled at coppers' – as the boys in blue kicked pregnant women, punched small children and generally put the boot in wherever possible; 220 people were arrested, many of whom were strip-searched at a local army base. When the dust settled, there were 255 allegations of police brutality.

The following year, neither the government nor the organisers wanted a repeat performance. A compromise was hammered out and the festival relocated to an abandoned air-base at Watchfield, half-way between Reading and Oxford. This may have seemed like neutral territory, but the 600 residents of the nearby village felt differently. They held a protest meeting and organised a petition; one journalist observed that 'some of the villagers are frightened. Most of them are worried and anxious'. A few even cancelled their holidays because they didn't want to leave their homes unattended. In the end, the nine-day event passed off reasonably peacefully. Red and green microdots were on the menu, Hawkwind were the headline act, and the police were less visible. Nevertheless, there were still teams of undercover officers patrolling the scene; seven officers masqueraded as hippies, while two carried cameras and sound equipment and pretended to be a freelance TV crew.

● ● ●

The next stop on the LSD trail was Oxford, 26 miles north-west of Reading. Like its historic rival Cambridge, the university drug scene there was up and running by the mid-1960s and demand for LSD remained constant from then on. If the students needed any further encouragement to move acid in and out of the various colleges, they got it from the university statutes, which effectively placed them outside the law. Infractions of the rules were dealt with internally and the police were only called in when absolutely necessary, much to the frustration of the Oxford Drug Squad.

At the same time, the non-student part of the town was large and diverse enough to offer room for expansion beyond the cloistered college grounds. The Victoria Arms – a pub by the river on the north-eastern fringe of Oxford – had psychedelic posters on the walls, a jukebox selection that featured Hendrix, Pink Floyd and Led Zeppelin, and catered for the inhabitants of an area of town that was home to a dense concentration of hippies living in squats, communes and bedsits, many of them on Plantation Road: no. 20 was something of a drug storehouse. Around forty squatters lived three or four to a room without gas, heat or electricity and virtually no furniture except the odd mattress. In the bathroom upstairs, thousands of pounds worth of drugs of all kinds were hidden in a plinth under a raised bath.

From Oxford, the microdot expressway branched south-west towards the county of Wiltshire and its neighbour Somerset. The West Country was a particularly popular destination for followers of the Age of Aquarius, and much of this gravitational pull was down to the works of John Michell, an Old Etonian amateur polymath who studied archaeology, anthropology and philosophy, and was fascinated by UFOs. Having moved to 11 Powis Gardens in Ladbroke Grove in the mid-1960s and sampled LSD and other hallucinogens, Michell had a series of revelations about the true origins of human civilisation, which he believed began thousands of years ago when our species encountered a race of alien super-beings who passed onto us their knowledge and wisdom, out of which we gained agriculture, medicine and art.

Over the centuries, humanity had forgotten this critical phase in its evolution – until now. According to Michell, all 'the signs' pointed to 'some form of encounter with an alien force'. As far as he was concerned, this transformative moment could not come soon enough. Given that 'the earth is slowly dying of poison' and humanity was incapable of reversing this process, Michell believed our survival depended on 'the achievement of a new higher vision'. Luckily, this crisis coincided with 'the increasingly wide interest in the use of drugs', which was 'opening the way to what may be an entirely new series of concepts'. This development was so 'remarkably opportune' that Michell found it hard to believe that it was 'a matter of pure chance' and suspected 'the influence of an external force'.

In his first book – *The Flying Saucer Vision* (1967) – Michell conducted a global survey of pre-historic places of worship, identified them as contact points for our meetings with the aliens from outer space, and investigated how our memory of them was preserved through the images, symbols and stories of ancient mythology that depicted the extra-terrestrial visitors as gods who arrived in circular, disc-shaped objects; how burial mounds and giant earthworks were landing platforms for their spaceships; and how these awesome vehicles and their owners were represented by dragons and giant serpents in the myths and folk-tales of antiquity. Michell's next publication – *The View Over Atlantis* (1969) – focused on the UK and was a big bestseller, going through three editions in the next four years and garnering a legion of fans. For those whose idea of Britain's mystical past was largely informed by King Arthur and the works of Tolkien, Michell provided an apparently coherent explanation for the many legends and mysteries attached to it, grounded in the tangible physical reality of the country's ancient monuments – 'the old sites of sacrifice to the sky-gods' – that viewed together formed a cosmic grid joined by a 'vast number … of regular geometrical lines' much like the ones used by 'flying saucers'.

These ley lines radiated out from key centres of worship, of which Stonehenge was the most important. According to Michell, Stonehenge was 'a holy city compiled by the philosophers of the ancient world' and served as 'an instrument' for studying 'the patterns of the universe', as well as being a place to meet 'with people of the divine race'. When the aliens stopped coming, the 'occult' rituals they performed at Stonehenge were kept alive by the druids, who possessed a range of powers similar to those that the shaman Don Juan passed onto Carlos Castaneda: the 'ability to fly'; 'to raise the dead'; 'to travel in a state of invisibility'; and 'to pass through the barrier of time'.

The summer solstice at Stonehenge had been drawing crowds since the end of the nineteenth century and their often-rowdy celebrations were a persistent cause of conflict with local villagers, the authorities and the druids – who'd been paying homage there since the late 1700s. The situation had got so serious that by 1966 the stones were surrounded by barbed-wire fences and guarded by military police. From 1970, however, bands of hippies began joining the druids and, having demonstrated that they intended to grant Stonehenge and its custodians the respect they deserved, they were able to forge a spirit of peaceful co-existence. In 1975, nearly 3,000 people showed up for a free festival where Hawkwind performed and one reveller remembered 'Tolkien-esque wanderings through woods' and seeing 'hundreds of people, sitting cross-legged in meditation, as the sun came over the horizon'.

Meanwhile, 50 miles to the west, and linked to Stonehenge by a ley line, was Glastonbury Tor, with its ancient abbey rising up from its sacred roof, from where Michell claimed 'men left earth to join the gods'. Located in the Vale of Avalon, the whole area around it was 'laid out to a sacred plan' that reproduced 'exactly the same numbers and patterns as those that determined the form of Stonehenge'. Glastonbury's unique place in Michell's cosmic scheme was celebrated in 1971 at the legendary Glastonbury Fayre, which coincided with the summer solstice and was located at Worthy Farm, 110 acres of pastoral land, 7 miles from Glastonbury.

The impetus for holding a free festival there came from Revelation Enterprises, an events company whose office was at 307 Portobello Road (next door to *Frendz* magazine, which had promoted a 'People's Free Carnival' in Ladbroke Grove), and was co-owned by the granddaughter of Winston Churchill. Her business partner was a devotee of Michell's theories and told *The Observer* that he was utilising 'pre-historic science' and 'spiritual engineering' to help plan the festival. When it came to divining the right spot for the stage, he was looking to tap into 'the planet's life force' and locate the ley line that ran through the site from Glastonbury Tor to Stonehenge. At the same time, the idea to make the stage the same shape as a pyramid came to the set designer in a dream; once on site, he called Michell for advice about how to construct it. According to the designer, Michell 'said it should be based on the dimensions of Stonehenge'. Working from that model, and applying 'sacred geometrics', he ended up with a stage that was equivalent to 'a hundredth part of the Great Pyramid'.

Between them, these two citadels of the space gods – Stonehenge and Glastonbury – accounted for the establishment of hippy communes and out-posts across Somerset and its neighbour Wiltshire, as well as attracting curious tourists and pilgrims seeking enlightenment. Consequently, there was a healthy demand for Kemp and Todd's microdots, and the network had a distributor in the village of Frome who supplied a dealer based in the small market town of Chippenham, both around 30 miles from Glastonbury and Stonehenge. Todd's man in Frome was an old acquaintance and operated from a flat above a shop on the high street. His contact was a builder from Chippenham who could be found in the back bar of the Bear Hotel selling hundreds of microdots a night. Their activities were made a lot easier by the fact that Wiltshire didn't even have a drug squad. A Thames Valley undercover cop who'd been sent to scout out the area recalled how easy it was to get 'any amount of pills, cannabis and acid' in these 'quiet country towns', where the 'dealing, smoking and tripping were all out in the open'.

● ● ●

The final destination on the microdot's journey was Llanddewi Brefi, a small Welsh village with two pubs, a hall, a store, a police house and St David's Church, named after the patron saint of Wales and allegedly built on the spot where he was said to have preached at some point during the sixth century. Llanddewi Brefi sat quietly in a region known as the Green Desert, a relatively unspoilt landscape that gave the impression that the past co-existed with the present. All around were traces of Celtic legends, woven into the fabric of hills and ancient stones, not merely relics but living and breathing entities, as if supernatural beings lived side by side with the human inhabitants, visible to those who looked hard enough.

The Microdot Gang's contact in Llanddewi Brefi was known to everybody as Smiles. He passed through the village in 1971 before returning with his partner and her two kids in 1973 to buy a terraced cottage near the centre of the village that was called Y Glyn (The Hollow). Working class and ex-army, Smiles had lived in Birmingham, Manchester and London – his accent bore the imprint of all three cities – and he was perfectly at home in a world of pubs, clubs, after-hours poker games, betting shops and racetracks, where wages were blown on Friday and Saturday nights, you expected to rub shoulders with the criminal fraternity and nobody batted an eye if you bought and sold stolen goods or did some dealing on the side for a bit of extra cash. In March 1970, Smiles was convicted of conspiracy to steal and given a three-year conditional discharge. Two years later, he was fined £50 for possession of cannabis. Though he'd briefly been employed as a social worker in the late 1960s, by the time he moved to Llanddewi Brefi drugs were his sole source of income. But for Smiles, LSD was not merely about raking in the cash or having a bit of fun at the weekend; he'd had his own acid awakening. Years later, he remembered how LSD had opened his mind and helped him understand 'that everything is ultimately connected'. Searching 'for the divine spark within', Smiles took up meditation, travelled to India, studied Buddhism and encouraged everybody in the village 'to experience' the same 'one-ness' that he had: 'I turned the bread-man onto acid, the milkman onto acid, even the man who sold me the house'.

The residents of Llanddewi Brefi were unfazed by Smiles' presence in their midst. He wasn't the first LSD evangelist to fall for the village's charms. Since the late 1960s that part of Wales held a magnetic attraction for those in the counter-culture looking for an alternative to hard-edged urbanised modernity. Part of the appeal was due to its remoteness and rugged beauty, separated from the border with England by a central rib of mountains, interspersed with deep valleys, and close to stunning coast-line. Even more tempting was the fact that, due to the steady decline of the local rural population, there were dozens of empty farmhouses and acres of land available to buy or rent relatively cheaply. This was particularly appealing to those seeking a communal way of life. One colonist, who arrived in the area in 1973 with a dozen or so brethren, recalled that their 'aim was to establish a self-sufficient rural community, run according to ecological/organic principles'. It was a daunting task, especially as the farm they'd purchased was 'unbelievably run-down' with 'ramshackle build-ings, soggy fields and a road that was impassable in winter'. In these sorts of conditions, many struggled to survive much longer than a year or two. An exception were the Tepee People. Assembled in 1975 at Stonehenge, they'd been drifting from festival to festival until they landed in a valley 10 miles from Llanddewi Brefi, erected their tepees and decided to stay, slowly buying up the land around them.

These hippy migrants were well served by a number of free festivals, the largest of which was Meigan Fayre, held in a field rented from a farmer, not far from Tepee Valley, and 700ft above sea level. The first event in 1973 was organised by a local commune and attended by 400 blissed-out revellers. In 1974, the site was flooded, but in late August 1975 thousands of people were treated to three days of hot weather. The site had taken a fortnight to get ready. There were two stages and a lighting rig, an observation tower, a sauna, a range of organic food tents and some stalls run by artisans and craftspeople. Every effort was made to respect the environment; the poster for the 1975 festival welcomed visitors with open arms – 'we are here together to celebrate this wonderful summer in the spirit of love' – but reminded them to dispose of their rubbish responsibly; keep any pets, especially dogs, under control; stay off private land; use the toilets provided; peel back turf before starting any fires and refrain from stealing wood to light them with. The organisers also put up a sanctuary tent for acid casualties to take refuge in, which proved a wise decision: on the first day, one punter remembered how most of the crowd 'were incapable due to the huge consumption of psychedelics', while another remarked that 'it was the only event I ever went to where it seemed as if the lysergic state was the normal state'.

With so many hippy settlers and visitors passing through, there was no shortage of customers for what Smiles was selling. But he also funnelled some of his stock of LSD back into England, where it was picked up in Wiltshire, Somerset and Reading. This loop effect – reversing the westward trajectory of the acid – had been dreamt up by Todd as a way of confusing any police investigation, sending it in several directions at once and further obscuring the true origin of the microdots. Once he and Kemp split up, Todd saw no need to tamper with this carefully constructed network. It stayed in place, as did the personnel associated with it. As long as Todd could fill the gap left by Kemp, Smiles and his fellow microdot suppliers would continue to prosper.

● ● ●

On 3 November 1974, Detective Inspector Dick Lee, the middle-aged head of the Thames Valley Drug Squad, was sitting in his second-floor office at the police HQ in Kidlington, Oxfordshire, going over the information gathered by his undercover officers at that year's Windsor Festival and the figures for arrests and drug seizures. Struck by the prevalence of LSD, he checked the files on Windsor 1973 and noticed the same trend. Put together, the evidence contradicted the national crime statistics, which calculated that there were roughly 20,000 hits of acid in circulation each year. But the festival data indicated that almost that amount had changed hands during Windsor '74. Clearly, somebody somewhere was either manufacturing or importing LSD on a vast scale.

Before joining the drug squad, Lee – nicknamed 'Leapy' by his colleagues – had been working his way to retirement as a crown court officer in Reading. Married with three children, Lee was an old-school copper. He drank whiskey, wore waistcoats and smoked a pipe. He had zero experience of drugs but learnt fast and was liked and respected by his team. Though he considered LSD to be uniquely capable of pushing a 'sad number of wasted individuals ... to the fringes of society' and leaving them stranded there, unable to return, it barely figured on his list of priorities, an attitude shared by the majority of his peers. Compared to the growth in heroin use and the continual spread of cannabis, acid was a minor problem, an esoteric oddity that had peaked during the Summer of Love before receding into the background. Yet the media kept reminding the authorities and the public that acid remained a menace by running a string of tragic stories. These tales of death and madness were given a fresh twist by the emergence of Kemp's super-strong microdots. Dubbed the 'pinhead killer' by the press, the microdot was allegedly behind a new wave of horrific incidents: one senior drug squad officer told *The Guardian* that they were 'the pusher's latest weapon in the drug war', not least because they were 'so tiny' and could be 'disposed of at a moment's notice'.

Confronted by the possibility that there was a microdot network doing business on his patch, Lee visited the CDIU on the fourth floor of Scotland Yard to see if they had any information about a major LSD organisation operating across the south of England. Given the CDIU's remit was to monitor drug trafficking at a national level, it was the obvious place for Lee to go looking for answers. However, despite the fact that the CDIU had the Gerald Thomas file and two of its detectives had gone to Canada to grill him, they told Lee there was no evidence at all to support his hunch.

As a result, Lee was left to wait for some intelligence from his undercover officers that would confirm his suspicions. It eventually came from Martyn Pritchard, who was one of a new breed of 'hippy' cop. Since the mid-1960s, the police had struggled to get a handle on the hippy movement, so far removed from their experience as to be almost incomprehensible. Faced with such an unfamiliar phenomenon, a million miles away from their own hard-drinking culture, the police struggled to gain any meaningful traction. Informers were less easy to recruit. Undercover officers would wander into clubs and venues wearing white shirts with black suits, shoes and ties, and wondered why nobody wanted to talk to them. By the early 1970s, it was obvious that a more subtle approach was needed if the police were going to get anywhere with the citizens of the drug culture, and new undercover recruits like Pritchard were required to blend in with them, adopting their habits and lifestyles.

Born in 1947, Pritchard grew up in Reading, trained as an apprentice engineer, spent a year in Norway with an oil company, then joined the Thames Valley Police aged 21. In early 1972, after two years on the beat and nine months with CID, he volunteered for the Oxford Drug Squad, which consisted of five men and one woman. Once undercover, his chances of going undetected depended on his ability to tune into the same wavelength as his prey, an act of deception that was made easier by his interest in the same kinds of music – he used to play bass in a band – and party-loving nature. Like many other operatives who spent long periods undercover, he began to forget where the hippy ended and the cop began, and admitted that he got 'the two characters muddled up'. Nevertheless, Pritchard had no doubts about where he stood on LSD: 'I hate acid. You will find ninety per cent, if not more, of all drug squad coppers put it top of the hate list. They see the results of bad trips.'

Before hitting the Oxford scene, Pritchard learnt how to roll a joint and smoke it without inhaling, familiarised himself with the relevant slang and assumed the identity of an itinerant painter-decorator called Martin Poole. He grew his hair and added a moustache and chunky sideburns. He wore the hippy uniform, blessed with a touch of petula oil as 'it gave off the scent of cannabis'. However, according to Pritchard, it was 'not enough to just look like a hippie'. You had to have 'dirt under your finger-nails, holes in your socks and tatty old underwear': a clean pair would be an instant give-away. In his pockets, he always carried ticket stubs from recent gigs and letters containing drug references. In his car, he kept packets of Rizla papers, a half-full tin of Old Holborn rolling tobacco, a guitar, some LPs and the mouthpiece of a hookah pipe. To complete the picture, he was given a criminal history, logged at the Criminal Records Office, which consisted of three previous convictions, the most recent for possession with intent to supply 500 tabs of acid.

Once he'd done a stint in Oxford, Pritchard moved onto Reading. One of his hunting grounds was the Star pub on the outskirts of town, where a major local dealer called the Count plied his trade. In the spring of 1975, Pritchard was trying to get the inside track on a gang who were smuggling Moroccan hashish into the country and offloading it in the Let-it-Be commune near Reading. Pritchard thought the Count was involved and arranged a meeting with one of his minions at the Star. After a few pints, the minion and Pritchard came to an arrangement. Pritchard would pay £6,000 for 20 pounds of hash that he'd collect once he'd made a down-payment of £2,000. Deal done, the Count's minion then mentioned that he could throw in a thousand microdots for £150, if he wanted. Pritchard said he did, and went straight to his boss to give him the news. Lee was intrigued; did this mean the Count had access to the LSD network that he was trying to locate?

On Saturday 12 April, Lee waited for Pritchard in the Traveller's Friend pub as other officers lurked in cars and flats close to the Count's terraced house on Westfield Road. Pritchard showed up as agreed and was introduced to the Count. During a brief discussion, the Count told Pritchard he could get him up to 10,000 microdots a week. Having dropped the Count and his minion off at a nearby car park, Pritchard drove to the Traveller's Friend and told Lee what had happened. Excited by what he heard, Lee authorised a bust. At 3 p.m., Pritchard returned to Westfield Road, picked up the Count and his minion, and headed towards the Reading suburbs and a semi-detached house where they were greeted by a tall blond Australian who led them into the kitchen, opened the fridge and pulled out 20 pounds of hashish and 1,008 microdots. Satisfied with the merchandise, Pritchard and his companions left to get the money. As they stepped out the front door, Pritchard lit a cigarette, signalling to the waiting coppers that drugs were inside the building. Within a matter of minutes it was all over. Pritchard's car was stopped 200 yards down the road and all three of the occupants arrested. Officers swarmed into the house and took the Australian and his stash away with them.

Back at Reading police station, the Count and the Australian were held in custody to await a court hearing. The minion was cut loose and immediately put under surveillance, only to disappear twenty-four hours later, skipping town and going to ground in the Tepee Valley commune in Wales, not far from where Kemp and Bott were beginning their new life.

10

There'll Be a Welcome
in the Valleys

Kemp and Bott's hasty departure from London to Wales in the late spring of 1974 left them temporarily homeless and subsisting in a caravan until they found a suitable property to buy. The place they chose was a square, two-storey dark-stone cottage with a slate roof called Penlleinau (Headlands) that rested on the upper slopes of the Blaencaron Valley. The cottage came with two acres of land, some of it meadow, and backed onto a narrow track that led into the mountains. It was 6 miles from Llanddewi Brefi, a mile or so from the market town of Tregaron and roughly 19 miles from the coastal town of Aberystwyth. Inside the cottage, conditions were basic: there was no central heating, the furnishing was rudimentary, the plain walls were coated with white cement paint and the toilet was outside. The only change Kemp and Bott made to this sparse interior was to install a Victorian spiral staircase they'd bought in London.

Kemp and Bott had chosen to adopt a self-sufficient lifestyle – based on organic farming techniques – that was particularly prevalent among other migrants from the capital who'd been arriving in ever-greater numbers since 1972. Though most of them lacked any agricultural training, they were determined to succeed. One of those who did spoke for many when he summed up what drove so many young people to go back to the land: 'like so many of our generation, we were swept up with the dream to find a relevance to our lives away from the rat race … a dream to get back to basics ... and produce our own food ... away from the endless materialism of town life'. A couple from London who moved to the area in 1975 remembered they 'were desperate to move out of the city and grow vegetables', while another wanted to be where the 'air was clean and pure and the land relatively cheap'. For Kemp and Bott it was a question of leading by example: the more people who took this course of action, the more pressure there'd be for others to follow – as Kemp put it, 'I'd have everyone out in two-acre plots like ours, being self-sufficient'.

The shift that Kemp and Bott made from the radical Left towards the Green movement was not a hard one to make. There was no need to abandon their commitment to revolutionary change. Ecological politics dovetailed neatly with their pre-existing ideals, which were anti-capitalist and anti-materialist and in favour of the decentralisation of power, local communal and collective organisations, and autonomous self-government. This new form of society was almost identical to the one championed by the Greens, who argued that a profound transformation was necessary to tackle the threat to the planet posed by rampant industrialisation, urbanisation, intensive monocrop agriculture, sky-rocketing fuel consumption, depletion of natural resources and raw materials, environmental destruction, species extinction, pollution and over population.

At a time of rising awareness about the damage being done to the eco-system and the dire consequences of pursuing unlimited growth, there was a chorus of voices sounding the alarm and calling for immediate action. One of those predicting imminent disaster was G.R. Taylor, the author of *The Doomsday Book* (1970), who claimed that unless we fundamentally altered course, humanity would soon be condemned to an existence 'which would be scarcely worth living'; we might be able to 'detoxify the soil', 'clean the air enough to breathe' and 'purify at least some of the water', but much of the planet would be uninhabitable, forcing us to crowd together 'like battery hens' in underground tunnels. Similar prophesies of apocalyptic doom were made by the small pool of activists behind *The Ecologist* magazine, some of whom would go on to form Friends of the Earth. In *A Blueprint for Survival* (1972), they plainly stated that 'the industrial life with its ethos of expansion ... is not sustainable' and 'its termination within the lifetime of someone born today is inevitable'. The total collapse of the current economic system would come about either 'against our will, in a succession of famines, epidemics, social crises and wars' or 'because we want it to'. The only effective way out of our self-inflicted predicament was to make small communities 'the basic unit of society' and ensure that each one was 'as self-regulating as possible'.

Their vision of a scaled-down and mutually harmonious social structure was conveyed to a wide audience by two friends and colleagues, E.F. Schumacher and John Seymour. Schumacher concentrated on moral issues, Seymour on more practical ones. Over the course of a long and distinguished career – including twenty years as the National Coal Board's Chief Economic Advisor – Schumacher tried to make large organisations function better, only to realise their inherent limitations: soulless, inflexible, wasteful monoliths resistant to reform and adaptation. Out of these experiences came his hugely influential *Small is Beautiful: A Study of Economics as if People Mattered* (1973), a penetrating analysis of the forces driving us to destruction and of the alternatives that might halt our headlong rush to oblivion.

Schumacher declared that 'the task of our generation' was 'one of metaphysical reconstruction' and proposed that we reorientate our mode of being away from the purely functional and reprioritise spirituality and creativity. For him, the cardinal error of our age was allowing narrow economic thinking to dominate decisions about how to live as 'it takes the sacredness out of life, because there can be nothing sacred in something that has a price'. Worse still, it produces a society that is driven by our basest instincts: 'the modern economy is propelled by a frenzy of greed and indulges in an orgy of envy'. Though wealth may 'rise rapidly' as 'measured by statisticians', most people were 'oppressed by increasing frustration, alienation' and 'insecurity'. This woefully misguided approach had to be replaced by one built on 'the traditional wisdom of mankind'. Emphasising the ethical foundations underpinning the major world religions – which were supported by virtues such as 'love' and 'temperance' – Schumacher advocated 'the development of a lifestyle which accords material things their proper, legitimate place, which is secondary, not primary'.

To achieve this goal, Schumacher wanted us to abandon gargantuan factories, stop the onward march of mechanisation and assembly-line manufacturing, and restore the dignity of labour – the intimate connection between workers and what they made – by adopting 'technology with a human face'. The end result would be a society composed of a mass of producers rather than one governed by mass production. This stripped-down approach would also apply to agriculture, encouraging a society of growers where as many as possible had access to enough land to feed themselves. For those choosing the same path as Kemp and Bott, Schumacher's words lit the way. One aspiring organic farmer – who called Schumacher 'a huge inspiration' and his book a 'seminal' work – set up the Mid-Wales Soil Association, which counted Kemp and Bott as members. Other newcomers to the area who felt the same way about Schumacher grouped together to establish the Centre for Alternative Technology and began to experiment with ways to implement his theories.

Of equal importance to these intrepid hippy migrants was John Seymour's series of books on self-sufficiency; they provided some of the basic knowledge required to put Schumacher's ideas into practice. Seymour had spent eleven years in Africa as a young man, observing how small tribal communities sustained themselves by carefully controlling the resources available to them. Eager to apply what he learnt, he took up organic farming. In 1964 – after a period in Sussex – he relocated to Wales and occupied some land on the edge of a mountain close to the Meigan Fayre festival site. In the opening pages of his bestselling *The Complete Book of Self-Sufficiency* (1976), Seymour reassures his readers that 'self-sufficiency is not "going back" to some idealised past in which people grubbed for their food with primitive instruments and burned each other for witchcraft. It is going *forward* to a new and better sort of life.' Seymour recommended using 'a carefully worked out balance between animals and plants, so that each fed the other: the plants feeding the animals directly, the animals feeding the soil with their manure and the land feeding the plants'. On their patch of land, Kemp and Bott established a large vegetable garden, kept half a dozen chickens and two goats. Kemp took charge of growing the food and applied Seymour's ground plan, which involved separate areas for different types of crop – potatoes, peas and beans, cabbages, and root vegetables – to be rotated every four years.

Compost to nourish the soil would come from the goats, who were Bott's responsibility. According to Seymour, goats are 'the perfect dairy animal' for 'the self-supporting smallholder'. They're very efficient at 'converting roughage into milk' that is 'as good' as cow's milk and doesn't cause allergic reactions. Equally well, goat's milk makes 'magnificent cheese because its fat globules are much smaller'. Goats also helped manage the land by chomping their way through thickets, brambles, weeds, bushes and piles of fallen leaves. But for all the advantages of having goats, they still needed a lot of work. In the early stages, Bott would have had to make sure that her kids got 1.1 litres of milk per day for two months, while to feed a doe during winter required 2 pounds of good hay a day, 1–2 pounds of roots and succulents, and 1–2 pounds of grain. As they were sensitive to cold and rain, Bott would have needed to provide them with shelter and had to ensure the outbuilding they were housed in was kept dry, airy and draught proof. Their habit of stripping bark from trees had to be contained and they had to be kept away from Kemp's vegetables. Following Seymour's instructions, she erected fences consisting of three electric wires strung from poles.

Bott took her goats – Stella and Petra – very seriously, intent on raising the best animals she could in what were ideal surroundings, close to heather- and gorse-covered mountainside. To underline her commitment, Bott joined the British Goat Society, which benefited greatly from people like her: according to its official history, the 1970s were 'a period when self-sufficiency and the need for unpolluted foods became the rage' and the British Goat Society had to 'adjust to new situations' as 'membership increased rapidly' due to 'increased public awareness'. Among this fresh herd of goat enthusiasts, Bott distinguished herself by winning first prize at the annual Aberystwyth Agricultural Show in July 1975. Her moment of triumph was captured in a photograph that appeared in *The Cambrian News* and showed her standing next to Petra wearing a white knee-length smock with jeans poking out underneath, her hair back in a bun, squinting and smiling shyly at the camera.

Though Kemp did not breed any first-rate animals, he did make first-rate LSD, perhaps the best ever. Since childhood Kemp had been convinced that he was special, carrying a sense of his own superior intellect, which seemed justified given his academic success. Having applied his exceptional gifts to acid, the end results were proof of his genius. Once his ego had experienced that degree of gratification, it was almost impossible for him to go on indefinitely without yearning to feel that thrill again; he admitted that he got 'a great feeling' from 'turning people on'. Other than satisfying Kemp's psychological and emotional needs, there was another key reason why he and Bott decided to carry on manufacturing LSD; they believed it could help the Green movement capture people's imaginations. Not only could acid reorder your whole view of reality and your relationship to it in a matter of hours, a good trip often led to an almost cellular awareness of the essential unity of all organisms as the distinctions between living entities dissolved and you merged with your surroundings. According to Bott, 'you feel as one with the world. You begin to appreciate everything surrounding you. The trees, the stones, everything becomes beautiful. It really helps you see the truth.' Kemp thought LSD could 'catalyse' change by making people understand that 'happiness' did not come from 'buying things' or accumulating possessions; once this happened 'the problems resulting from consumerism would be to a large extent solved'.

Soon after quitting London, Kemp was reunited with Solomon's old comrade Paul Arnaboldi. Solomon had befriended Arnaboldi at Millbrook, hung out with him in Majorca, and involved him in Kemp's very first attempts to make LSD. Always elusive, with his Spanish island retreat acting as a safe haven and his boat ready to sail him away from trouble, Arnaboldi's movements are impossible to reconstruct with any accuracy. One indication of the extent of his smuggling activities occurred during May 1974, just before he partnered with Kemp: the yacht he was on, which had dropped anchor in the Malaysian port of Penang, was searched by the Australian authorities who were convinced drugs were on board. Though the boat was clean, the whole experience may well have prompted Arnaboldi to embark on a new business venture thousands of miles away. He and Kemp weren't close and had little in common – Arnaboldi had sworn off LSD after an especially harrowing trip – but the alchemist knew that Arnaboldi was a professional who could be relied upon not to make waves. Essentially a marriage of convenience, it was an arrangement that Kemp hoped would enable him to put together his biggest LSD production run yet.

Over the course of early summer 1974, Kemp and Arnaboldi toured mid-Wales looking for a suitable site and found one on the outskirts of the village of Carno – about half an hour away from Kemp and Bott's cottage. Plas Llysyn was a grand but dilapidated early eighteenth-century manor house with thirty rooms and substantial grounds, surrounded by high walls and accessible via a long driveway. Crucially, it had a large basement, ideal for Kemp's lab. Arnaboldi bought it outright for around £25,000. Kemp contributed £8,000; Arnaboldi covered the rest by selling a stack of shares. To silence any local gossip about the strange American who'd moved into Plas Llysyn, Arnaboldi spread the word that he'd purchased the manor for his mother in Florida and would only be staying there temporarily while working on a biography of John F. Kennedy.

With Arnaboldi coming and going, Kemp spent much of the latter part of the year refurbishing and renovating the basement, focusing on two rooms in its maze of cellars. Starting from scratch, he put in a new concrete floor, replastered the walls and washed them with lime. A hole was made in the ceiling to create better ventilation, and in January 1975, Arnaboldi came and installed a new drainage system. Having put the basic infrastructure in place, Kemp began fitting out his lab and sourcing the chemical agents he needed. Some of the equipment he'd accumulated in London – and kept in a rented garage in Bristol – was removed from storage, the rest he ordered from a bunch of legitimate firms such as Baird and Tatlock in Chadwell Heath, Ferris in Bristol, Mersey Chemicals in Liverpool, and Orme Scientific in Manchester. According to Kemp, he'd 'buy a little here and a little there', working through his 'big shopping list … in bits and pieces'. When he placed his orders, he invariably 'bought a complete set of spare parts with it and extra parts of vulnerable pieces' as he preferred to have 'two of everything so that any breakage wouldn't cause delay'. But what Kemp couldn't get in the UK was ergotamine tartrate. For that, he turned to his former colleague, David Solomon.

Determined to dodge any nasty fall-out from Gerald Thomas' arrest, David Solomon had returned to New York, nearly a decade after he last set foot in the US. Despite having been absent for so long, Solomon was still able to get another book deal, and with George Andrews once again acting as co-editor, he put together an anthology about the coca leaf and its synthetic derivative cocaine – *The Coca Leaf and Cocaine Papers* (1975) – for yet another heavyweight publisher, Harcourt Brace Jovanovich. As the title suggests, the book was as much about the coca plant as it was about cocaine: almost two-thirds of the text is given over to densely academic studies of the biological properties of the plant and its role in indigenous Peruvian culture, where it was used for its medicinal properties, as a stimulant to moderate the strain of a hard day's labour and as an intoxicant to enhance religious ritual. Dominating this part of the anthology is a 150-page extract – entitled 'The Divine Plant of the Incas' – taken from an early twentieth-century history of coca written by an American pharmacologist.

This emphasis was deliberate as the aim of the anthology was to rehabilitate and promote the coca leaf, and explain its value as a plant – 'the various alkaloids present in coca leaf … are both harmless and life-enhancing if taken orally and in moderation' – while clearly distinguishing it from cocaine, which had done nothing but damage its image and criminalise its users. In their introduction, Solomon and Andrews acknowledged the benefits of cocaine ('it temporarily makes the user feel stronger and happier' and has 'almost magical energizing qualities'), but took pains to stress the downsides of over-use, such as depression, paranoia and loss of libido. They also point out that habitually 'slamming concentrated cocaine rapidly into the bloodstream by snorting it into the delicate mucous membranes lining the nasal passages' could 'burn a hole right through the nose'.

This negative view of cocaine is evident in the handful of selections about it that appear in the book's final section: a long article by a journalist based on his experiences shadowing a Harlem dealer; a 1971 piece from *Rolling Stone* that charts the appearance of coke on the LA music scene, locates references to it in songs by various bands and describes how it became fashionable among the East and West Coast elites; and part of the Consumers Union Report on *Licit and Illicit Drugs* (1972), which underlined the dangers of cocaine and warned that it was entering the country through Miami in ever-increasing quantities. These last few extracts pointed to the future, suggesting the direction cocaine was going in, yet neither Solomon nor Andrews were that interested in exploring its upward trajectory. To them it was a passing phase. Given what came next, this could be seen as a bad error of judgement and meant their book was almost immediately out of date. This was not entirely their fault. In 1975 – when *The Coca Leaf and Cocaine Papers* was published – almost nobody could have foreseen the unholy alliance of forces that combined to fuel the cocaine boom that exploded across the US over the next decade as the white powder and its more lethal cousin crack cocaine tore through society from Main Street to Wall Street, from the suburbs to the inner cities.

Ultimately, the book's failure to win a large audience – it was the only one of Solomon's anthologies not to appear in paperback – was down to the overwhelming amount of scholarly material about the coca leaf. Solomon's career as an editor suffered a fatal blow. Another income stream had dried up. This disappointing outcome, combined with the expense of trying to maintain a trans-Atlantic existence, meant that when Kemp requested his assistance with another LSD operation, he was in no position to refuse. In total, Solomon was able to lay his hands on 9 kilos of ergotamine tartrate. Three of them were left over from when Kemp and Todd were working together, the rest came from the same West German company Solomon had previously ordered from, via the fake firm he'd set up with a London address. As before, Solomon collected the ergotamine tartrate personally, then transported it to Switzerland where it was lodged in Kemp and Bott's safety-deposit boxes.

Having assembled all the elements, Kemp was ready to proceed when disaster struck. While he and Bott were making the short journey from their cottage to the manor, he skidded on a wet slippery road, lost control of their Range Rover and collided with a Mini Estate being driven by the Reverend Eurwyn Hughes, who had his pregnant wife next to him in the passenger seat. He was badly injured; she was killed instantly. Charged with causing death by dangerous driving, Kemp appeared at Welshpool Magistrates' Court a few months later. He was fined and had his licence suspended for a year. This lenient sentence must have come as some relief to Kemp and Bott and was symptomatic of a justice system that treated murder by motor vehicle less seriously than possession of a few ounces of weed. Yet the judgement was clear; it was Kemp's fault. He was responsible, and he and Bott couldn't simply write it off as just another accident like all the others they'd been involved in, beginning with his motorbike crash eleven years earlier. This was different. They'd taken two lives – a mother and her unborn child – and by any estimation it was spectacularly bad karma, especially as they considered themselves to be on the side of the angels. As a result, the emotional impact was considerable. According to a reliable source, they were 'extremely distressed by the accident and mourned the death of the woman for some time'.

As well as being the cause of sleepless nights and existential doubts, the crash had also been a major breach of security. The case had earned Kemp unwanted publicity – there was coverage in the local press – and a criminal record. He and Arnaboldi decided to err on the side of caution. They sealed the lab, closed up the manor and agreed to wait nine months before opening them up again. With everything on hold, Arnaboldi slipped back to Majorca and Kemp went back to tending his vegetables.

● ● ●

On the day before Kemp's Range Rover careered into the reverend's car, Detective Inspector Dick 'Leapy' Lee was on the phone to the head of the Dyfed Powys Drug Squad. After the recent Reading bust that netted the Count and his microdot supplier, Lee's men had been given the slip by the Count's minion; out on bail, he'd skipped Reading and taken refuge in the Tepee Valley commune. Concerned by the sheer volume of acid being traded and consumed on his turf, the Dyfed Powys commander was eager to give Lee a hand. Then Lee got word from an informer that the microdots originally offered to Pritchard by the Count's minion had come from the small village of Llanddewi Brefi and a house known as Y Glyn, which is where Smiles lived. Eager to act on this tip, Lee asked his counterpart in Dyfed Powys to organise a raid.

What happened next would not have been out of place in an Ealing comedy. On Wednesday 16 April 1975, a bevy of drug squad officers – including two from Thames Valley – and the constable in charge of Llanddewi Brefi, set off from Aberystwyth, a thirty-minute drive from Smiles' cottage. In the meantime, one of the constable's men called the police house in the village with a routine question for him. On hearing that his superior was en route to Y Glyn, he called the constable's wife and asked her to intercept him and give him the message. Figuring it was urgent, she walked down the road to Smiles' house and knocked on the door. Smiles answered, and she enquired whether her husband was there. Surprised by her question, Smiles said he wasn't and agreed to tell him to contact her as soon as he arrived. As Smiles watched her go, he rapidly put two and two together. Unable to believe his good fortune, he removed all the drugs from hidden compartments in the house and buried them in a nearby quarry. When the raiding party arrived, it searched the premises from top to bottom but found nothing.

Despite this fiasco, Lee's men did not leave Wales empty-handed. The following day, the Count's minion was caught by Dyfed Powys police after a high-speed car chase. By then, Lee had managed to extract Kemp and Bott's names from two Scotland Yard detectives who'd shown up at Lee's office to discourage him from collaborating with the Dyfed Powys Drug Squad, claiming it would compromise their own acid investigation. Ignoring their wishes, Lee dropped Kemp's name to his helpful Welsh colleague. It rang a bell. The Dyfed Powys officer had heard about the fatal car accident. He sent two of his men to check over Kemp's Range Rover, which had been seized and was sitting in a police compound in Aberystwyth. They went over every inch of the vehicle and found some torn scraps of paper. Put together, they bore the words 'hydrazine hydrate' – one of the chemicals used to synthesise LSD.

Between the end of April and the end of July, Lee made three attempts to get the head of the CDIU to authorise a joint operation involving a number of different forces. Each time he was turned down. The result was the same when Lee went to his own boss and pleaded for the resources to cripple the network's activities in the Thames Valley. At this point, Lee could have decided to forget the whole thing, but his resolve was stiffened when he heard about the death of a teenager in Preston from asphyxia, brought on by a massive panic attack, triggered by one of Kemp's microdots, which had been bought at the Star pub in Reading from the Count's minion.

Determined to keep those responsible in his sights, Lee was happy to oblige the Wiltshire police when they asked for help with their out-of-control drug problem, and sent them Pritchard and another undercover officer. During November 1975, Pritchard and his colleague familiarised themselves with the local scene. By Christmas, they had got a fix on the builder from Chippenham, whose supplier in Frome was part of Todd's microdot distribution chain, and on Friday 11 January 1976 they found him in a convivial mood in his favourite pub, chatting with two young French guys who had a large block of good-quality hashish they were hoping to sell to a nearby commune consisting of about a dozen members who called themselves the Wombles. As it happened, they were having a party that night. Pritchard, his partner, the builder and the French duo showed up and had a good time, during which Pritchard persuaded the builder to meet him in the morning at the Bear Hotel to discuss business.

At their 11 a.m. rendezvous, the builder explained that his contact in Frome was extremely cautious and any arrangement he and Pritchard made was strictly provisional. That said, he offered Pritchard a starting price of £300 for 1,000 microdots with the promise of up to 80,000 a week if all went well. But as the builder predicted, things moved very slowly. When Pritchard was finally introduced to the man from Frome he immediately realised he'd be a tough nut to crack; Pritchard thought he was 'heavy', probably 'a Londoner' and 'very shrewd'. Pritchard's first impression proved correct. The supplier had three previous convictions relating to cannabis and acid. Aware that he was tangling with a big fish, Pritchard redoubled his efforts to gain his target's confidence, arranging to run into him whenever possible. The moment of truth came when Pritchard was invited back to the supplier's flat. As he sat with him and his girlfriend, Pritchard was told to roll a joint. Knowing full well that this was a trap designed to ensnare and expose any inexperienced undercover cop who hadn't perfected his technique yet, Pritchard rose to the challenge. Instead of the standard three Rizla papers, he used five: 'I had one paper long-ways, joined three going across, then another long-ways on the end. A five-skin.' Impressed and reassured, the man from Frome intimated that he was ready to trade and invited Pritchard to a party that weekend. Though 'the party was a knock-out', everything went wrong at 3 a.m. when a new arrival recognised him: Pritchard remembered that he 'looked straight at me' and kept looking. Pritchard had been made. A few days later, the supplier called off the deal.

While Pritchard was hitting a dead end, Lee was making headway with the stubbornly secretive CDIU. Lee had approached them hoping they'd stop the Wiltshire police from interfering with Pritchard's investigation – they wanted a quick result and were pressing for arrests – and found himself in a room with one of the CDIU detectives who'd interviewed Gerald Thomas in Canada. Reluctantly, and without going into details, he confirmed that Kemp and Bott were involved in acid trafficking, along with an American called David Solomon and an unidentified Englishman known as 'Henry'.

By now, Lee's persistence had made it impossible for senior figures within the police – and at the Home Office – to ignore his demands any longer. Lee was given a chance to state his case on the 12 February 1976 at a conference in Swindon, attended by representatives of five provincial forces, Scotland Yard, the CDIU and the Home Office. Having heard what Lee had to say, they agreed that there was clearly a big LSD operation out there and that the only way of tackling it was by forming a joint task-force. Unfortunately, nobody present had the power to put one together. Five days later, however, at a secret four-hour meeting held in Brecon, the Chief Constable of Dyfed Powys – who also happened to be Chairman of the Association of Chief Police Officers – the Chief Constable of North Wales, the CDIU officer who'd questioned Thomas and a Home Office mandarin decided to give Lee what he needed to bring down the Microdot Gang.

11

Home and Away

In July 1975, Henry Barclay Todd became the owner of 23 Seymour Road, a three-storey detached Edwardian townhouse with off-street parking, which he bought for £33,000 using the name J.J. Ross. This imposing, substantial house was in Hampton Wick, a leafy suburban enclave on the south-western fringes of London that hugged the Thames on one side and bordered a royal deer park on the other. Mixing period architecture with commuter-belt housing, it was solidly Conservative voting and family orientated, a largely middle-class haven: it was the last place anybody would think to look for an LSD factory.

From the moment Kemp left for Wales, Todd knew that at some point the reserves of his LSD would run dry and he'd have to start manufacturing it himself. Deploying an array of aliases, Todd ordered lab equipment from Farley & Sons and the D. Bewhay Company, and chemical agents from Hopkins & Williams and British Drug Houses, Enfield Branch. To get hold of ergotamine tartrate, he set up a front company – Fine Organics Ltd. Through it, he ordered ergotamine tartrate from Dolder AG in Basel, which was then routed through Inter-Saint Philippe, a Paris-based firm that collected its clients' mail and sent it wherever they wanted it to go. Todd would have them forward the packages of ergotamine tartrate to drop-off points in London to pick up at his convenience. At the same time, he stored a large amount of it –

enough for thirty million tabs – in a safety-deposit box at the Kantonel Bank in Switzerland – the same branch that Kemp and Bott used – and lodged some of his funds in the Vontobel Bank, which also counted Ronald Stark as a customer.

With the infrastructure in place, Todd was ready to install his chemist. Born in 1947, Andy Munro was from a solidly lower-middle-class background – his father had been a policeman – and attended grammar school before doing chemistry at Cambridge, where he met Kemp and Solomon. Yet another brilliant student with a restless, enquiring mind, Munro went on to do a masters at the University of East Anglia. While there, he participated in the lengthy student sit-ins that paralysed college life for weeks on end; Munro's role was to make sure the protestors did not run out of cannabis. In 1972, having successfully completed his course, Munro moved to London and lived at 4 Hanover Road, Kensal Rise, ten minutes' walk from Ladbroke Grove.

Munro moved in the same radical circles as Kemp and Bott, and was especially close to a veteran anarchist who'd been part of King Mob, an artists' collective that staged subversive spectacles. In the summer of 1968, King Mob gave out flyers inviting 'the damned, the rich, the screwed, the despised, the thugs, the drop outs, the scared, the witches, the workers, the demons' and 'the old' to a 'Devil's Party' in 'Notting Hell' on 15 June, during which they intended to break into the private gardens in Powis Square that were for the exclusive use of wealthy residents. Wearing a gorilla costume, and with a pantomime horse at his side, Munro's friend and mentor – along with his other King Mob comrades and a parade of excited kids – removed the wire-fencing round the gardens with bolt-cutters and poured in. The police came. King Mob were arrested and fined, but three months later the local council opened the gardens to the public.

Munro also hung out with the Microdot Gang and spent time observing Kemp at work in his makeshift labs. Though Kemp was careful not to reveal all his secrets to Munro, he did trust his judgement and asked Munro to check whether Todd was meddling with the strength of the microdots to increase his profits. Munro did as requested – thereby contributing to the falling out between Todd and Kemp – yet he was still uppermost in Todd's mind when it came to recruiting a chemist. By then, Munro was based south of the river at 71a Webbs Road, close to

Clapham Common, in a flat above a shop. While his skills as a chemist were not in doubt, Munro struggled to cope with the strenuous demands of manufacturing acid on a massive scale. Munro lacked Kemp's stamina and powers of concentration, his ability to remain focused for long stretches of time. One of Todd's associates thought Munro had an 'encyclopaedic' brain that was 'full of fascinating ideas', but had to concede that he was wilfully eccentric and disorganised, wandering round with 'his head in the clouds'. Munro's interest in Kemp's approach to synthesising LSD sprang more from intellectual curiosity than any desire to be locked up in a small room immersed in noxious fumes for weeks on end. Nor did he experience the same thrill or sense of achievement; he would later claim that he was acting under duress and the £50,000 Todd paid him was insufficient compensation for being treated like a prisoner on a chain gang.

He was also extremely clumsy and accident-prone. Perhaps the most serious of several incidents occurred at the end of a long day in the lab. Lying down for a momentary rest, Munro shut his eyes and fell completely asleep. Waking in the middle of the night, he realised that he'd neglected to put his phial of acid in the fridge before taking his unscheduled nap. To make sure his forgetfulness hadn't done any damage to his delicate creation, Munro decided to take its temperature with a thermometer. Still dozy and not fully alert, he shoved it into the phial so hard that it went right through, cracking the glass. 150,000 tabs worth of pure LSD poured out, soaking a small patch of carpet. Fearful of Todd's reaction, Munro kept quiet about the spillage, hoping he wouldn't notice the loss. He didn't: the wasted acid was merely a drop in the ocean.

Tableting was the responsibility of Todd's closest colleague, Brian Cuthbertson. Todd had turned to Cuthbertson back in 1971 when he was preparing to offload the LSD Solomon had received from Kemp's production run in Stark's Parisian lab. Cuthbertson was a middle-class grammar school boy, who'd gone to Reading University but dropped out in 1970 after failing his mathematics exams. Not long after, he arrived in London and was introduced to Todd. They instantly hit it off and Todd put him in charge of tableting, an arrangement that would continue throughout the Kemp years, right up to the split. At the same time, Cuthbertson communicated with key suppliers in the microdot distribution network. Like Todd, he was fond of fine living and disinterested in left-wing politics and hippy culture. For him, the acid enterprise was a business and his main source of income: he used his earnings to dabble in antiques and property development, renovating aging houses; in 1974 he purchased a dilapidated chateau in the Dordogne that overlooked a wooded valley.

Cuthbertson set up his tableting operation on the first floor of Seymour Road, while Munro cooked up the acid on the floor above in a series of attic rooms. In the evenings, Cuthbertson would unwind by playing Chopin on the piano. By the summer of 1976, hundreds of thousands of tabs were ready to go. For the UK, Cuthbertson churned out microdots, selling them to his distributors for around £170 per 1,000. For the international market, he tableted domes and pyramids. Some of the acid that went abroad was exported to Amsterdam and Australia by members of the UK supply chain. Otherwise, Todd relied on a long-established relationship he had with two Germans based in West Berlin. Sometimes he would go there – where an exchange would occur in an antiques shop – or they would visit him in London. This arrangement had begun in 1971 when one of the dealers who was helping Todd offload Solomon's stash decided to drop out. Up to then, he'd been selling 2,000 tabs a week to the West Germans. Rather than lose that connection, Todd took over from the dealer, visited the West Germans on their home turf, came to terms with them and opened an account at a branch of the Berliner Bank.

Todd's contacts – who were known simply as Carl and Gunther – had emerged from West Berlin's anarchist scene, which was closely related to the city's drug culture. By 1968, a number of anarchist communes had popped up across West Berlin and LSD – which was probably coming from Czechoslovakia – began to circulate among them. Over the next couple of years, the volume of LSD and hashish entering the city increased dramatically. During 1968, the West Berlin police carried out 140 drug-related arrests; in 1970, there were 858. This steep rise was replicated across the country, where the number of arrests leapt from 1,891 in 1968 to 16,000 in 1970. This increase in acid's availability coincided with the publication of an LSD guidebook – *Consciousness Expanding Drugs: A Call for Discussion* (1969) – by a Berlin-based author who'd just returned from two years in London. It contained chapters on biochemical manipulation, the legalisation of marijuana, psychotherapy and psychedelics, and applied mysticism. More generally, the link between drugs and radical social change was explored in *Love* magazine. The first issue featured a lengthy interview with Timothy Leary and a bold statement of intent: 'it is our obligation to break the antiquarian social and economic system … we have to force ourselves collectively to build a new world'. The next one ran articles about hashish, while a 1970 edition was devoted to LSD and offered 'Tips for Trips' to the novice user, advising them to 'linger around the centre of a big city' and 'observe environmental oscillations, the traffic flow, the cars, traffic lights and the people standing in front of them'.

During the summer of 1969, some of West Berlin communards formed a loose-knit organisation called the Central Committee of the Roaming Hashish Rebels. Its main aim was to bring political activists and long-haired dope smokers together. Aside from consuming hash and encouraging others to follow their example, the Central Committee was in the business of selling it; one Hashish Rebel recalled how they knew 'countless people we could sell shit to … you literally lived with and from dope'. At the same time, they tried to control the market and keep organised crime away from it 'so that no dealer mafia could be created'. Given the significance of LSD to the Central Committee's overall mission – they described taking acid as an 'act of revolutionary disobedience' – it made sense to apply the same policy to its supply and distribution.

Though it's hard to pinpoint their sources of LSD, Orange Sunshine appeared in West Berlin during 1970, which must have come from either Nick Sand's labs or from Kemp's apprenticeship with Stark in Paris. At some point, a group of them went to London for a few months and, according to one Rebel, 'looked at the whole English scene'. Though their visit slightly predates the beginning of Todd's acid career, it may well have been when they forged the connections that made it possible for them to buy LSD from a London-based dealer. This laid the groundwork for the trade between Todd and Carl and Gunther, who were almost certainly linked to the Central Committee of Roaming Hashish Rebels, given how relatively small and incestuous the West Berlin anarcho-hippy drug scene was at the time.

Not long after their return, the Hashish Rebels began contemplating a change of tactics. From the moment protests against the Vietnam War got into their stride, the West German police had reacted with considerable ferocity. This intense level of state violence had convinced some on the hard Left that terrorism was the only viable response. From the Marxist camp came the Red Army Faction – whose most notorious cadre was the Baader-Meinhof Gang. In 1970, they took up arms, declared war on the system, and became public enemy number one. After a series of escapes, ambushes and shoot-outs most of them were rotting in jail, held in isolation and deprived of their rights. In this fevered atmosphere, the Hashish Rebels felt compelled to strike back with firebombs. With each arson attack, however, they became a bigger target for the police to aim at. On 4 December 1971, four of the Rebels were involved in a gun fight with the cops; one was killed, three escaped. Following this confrontation, the Central Committee of Roaming Hashish Rebels dissolved itself and reformed as the Second June Movement, named in honour of a student who was murdered by an undercover cop during a demonstration on that day in 1967.

On 2 February 1972, they exploded a bomb at the British Yacht Club in West Berlin, which killed an engineer. A few weeks after this, a Second June Movement member was shot dead by police. A wave of arrests followed. The Movement took time to regroup and rebuild. On 27 July 1973, they robbed a bank, making off with 200,000 DM. On 4 June 1974, they murdered an informer. Five months later, their attempted kidnapping of the President of the West Berlin Supreme Court went badly wrong and the judge wound up dead. Lessons learned, their next effort was more successful. On 27 February 1975, they took a conservative mayoral candidate hostage and demanded the release of six of their comrades. Within a week, the Second June Movement prisoners had been flown to safety in the Yemen and the kidnap victim had been set free.

To what extent Carl and Gunther were involved in the Second June Movement cannot be established with any accuracy. They did, however, continue their partnership with Todd throughout the Kemp years, receiving regular consignments of microdots. Then in June 1976, a tall West German – who was identified as having links to terrorist groups – came to see Todd in London, stayed a few hours and left. It's not known what they discussed – or if the German was Carl or Gunther or a third party – but in all probability the main topic was the acid that was coming out of Todd's Seymour Road lab. Once the deal was struck, all it would take was a few short cryptic phone calls and the LSD would be on its way from Hampton Wick to West Berlin.

● ● ●

On 8 March 1976, Detective Inspector Dick Lee held the first full meeting of the squad he'd assembled to smash the microdot network. Lee and his officers were based on the second floor of a former police driving school in Devizes, Wiltshire. Selected from eleven different forces, the majority were from the south, the south-west and Wales, representing Avon and Somerset, Hampshire, Thames Valley, Bournemouth, Wiltshire, and Dyfed Powys. All of them were drug squad detectives – either sergeants or constables. Out of fourteen, three were women. Lee was assigned a personal secretary and Sergeant Julie Taylor was initially in charge of administration. An executive officer looked after their specialist photographic equipment and radio transmitters. The unit was given six cars – two Ford Escorts, two Hillman Avengers, an Allegro and a Mini – each with two radios: one worked over long distances, the other car-to-car. The only thing their mission lacked was a name. After a brief discussion, they settled for Operation Julie.

About a week earlier, Lee had finally got his hands on the material the CDIU had been withholding from him. Reluctantly, and under pressure from above, the CDIU relented and Lee gained access to the Gerald Thomas interviews, his personal papers that were on him when arrested – including lists of names and addresses – and details of the CDIU's somewhat half-hearted efforts to follow up on all this information. After its detectives had returned from seeing Thomas in Canada, it took another nine months before anything meaningful happened. In January 1975, the CDIU bugged Solomon's UK phone and that April they raided his empty Maida Vale flat, measures that merely confirmed that he was out of the country. In the case of Kemp and Bott, the CDIU's investigations added little to what Lee already knew. With only the Ladbroke Grove address to go on, the CDIU had no luck tracing their whereabouts until they got wind of the Range Rover crash. Kemp and Bott's cottage phone was tapped, but neither of them indulged in shop talk. The electronic eavesdropping was abandoned and Kemp and Bott were left to their own devices. Nonetheless, the files did provide Lee with a vital clue.

Thomas had briefly mentioned Paul Arnaboldi. The name rang a bell. A few weeks earlier, Lee had been informed by the Dyfed Powys Drug Squad that Kemp was making frequent visits to a manor house in Carno, which was owned by an American called Arnaboldi.

Joining the dots, Lee decided to arrange surveillance of the house just as Arnaboldi was taking up residence again and Kemp was embarking on the production run that been delayed because of the fatal accident. Buried in his basement lab – which he'd christened 'The Yellow Submarine' – Kemp worked forty-eight-hour shifts before being picked up by Bott in their Renault, ferried back to their cottage for twenty-four hours' rest and then returned to the manor. At night, Arnaboldi sat at an upstairs window watching for any signs of trouble. During the day, he stood on the roof – from where he could see for miles around – and pretended to be fixing the tiles. Despite these precautions, neither he nor Kemp paid much attention to the shabby mobile works caravan – with a drop-down table, office chairs, a gas stove and a kettle – that parked up outside the main gates in early April and stayed there.

Crammed inside was a five-man team. Posing as surveyors hunting for a fresh seam of coal, they spent the next five weeks taking photos, acting busy, maintaining their cover with the locals and waiting for something to break the monotony. At the beginning of May, they observed Kemp and Bott transporting bits and pieces of what looked like lab equipment back to the cottage: they were cleaning up. On 7 May, Kemp was seen greeting Bott with a triumphal hug, overjoyed that he'd completed the biggest manufacturing operation of his career: Kemp had converted 7 kilos of ergotamine tartrate into 1,800 grams of LSD, enough for nine million microdots.

The next day, Arnaboldi concealed 450 grams of Kemp's acid in his suitcases, loaded them into his car, locked up the house and drove away. At 4 p.m. on 10 May, he boarded a ferry at Southampton that was heading for Spain. With the coast apparently clear, Lee ordered a break-in. Having purchased some tools – hammers, screwdrivers, a drill and a flashlight – and protective clothing – Marigold rubber gloves and four black balaclavas – the detectives waited until 3 a.m. before entering the grounds. After throwing stones at various upstairs windows to check that nobody was home, two of them stayed on guard outside while the other two forced open the lounge window and crawled in. It took several hours of roaming the ghostly corridors and exploring the dust-laden crumbling rooms before they found the basement cellars, which were barred by a solid oak door fitted with a new padlock. Using the screwdriver, they removed it, went in, located the two rooms Kemp had used – now stripped bare and spotlessly clean – and gathered some microscopic samples from the drains and surfaces that indicated the presence of methanol, which was sometimes added into the mix during acid production. The next day, they broke in again and conducted a more thorough search. While inspecting an outside drain, they found the corpse of a dead mole that had been poisoned by pure LSD.

● ● ●

By 1974, the ever-elusive Ronald Stark had resurfaced in Italy. For official purposes, he favoured his fake British passport, issued in the name of William Terence Abbott. For day-to-day interactions with the locals, he alternated between several different incarnations: he was Maurizio Borghetti, or Carlo Rossi, or Giovan Batista Mita. Though he rented a small apartment in Florence, Stark spent the majority of his time in Rome, Milan and Bologna, where he stayed in grand hotels. He also had access to a country house in Tuscany. As usual, he mixed not only with the business and social elites but also with radical and revolutionary groups, effortlessly moving between the two.

At some point, he'd also acquired a partner and child, an American woman – Henrietta Ann Kaimer – and her little girl Leyla. Quite when and how Stark met Henrietta is a mystery, as is the exact nature of their relationship. There is no mention of her name by anybody from the Brotherhood, the Microdot Gang or Stark's business enterprises. He did, however, furnish Henrietta with a fake British passport in the name of Pauline Margaret Booth, which he probably obtained in spring 1973, the same time he got his. And they did travel together using these identities, because their British passports carried stamps from the Netherlands and Sweden. Whatever Stark felt for Henrietta and Leyla, the arrangement between them served a practical purpose; it was a lot easier to pose as a normal, respectable citizen with them at his side. A couple and their offspring were much less likely to draw unwanted attention than a single man in his 30s.

Stark had been active in Italy since the autumn of 1969. Initially, he was distributing the acid brewed up for him by the Swedish alchemist Tord Svenson in their Paris lab. Then, in 1970, he opened a safety-deposit box in a bank in Rome. Inside it he put the handwritten formula for synthesising LSD that Nick Sand had sketched out for Kemp at the beginning of his apprenticeship. Though the Brotherhood commandeered half of what Kemp produced in Paris there was still plenty left for Stark, and it's safe to assume he sold some of it in Italy. The same can be said for the vast amount of acid that came out of Stark's Belgium lab between the summer of 1972 and autumn 1973: documents and letters concerning his on-campus facility landed in his safety-deposit box in Rome, along with other items relating to his activities during this period, suggesting that, at the very least, he was making regular trips to Italy's capital city.

Once based in the country, it is unclear whether or not Stark ran an LSD lab. There are rumours that he was hoarding ergotamine tartrate in Lebanon. What he didn't have was a chemist and, though no doubt he could have found somebody local to train up, there's no evidence that he did. Instead, he focused on smuggling hashish. Since 1970, Stark had been trying to find a feasible way to manufacture dimethylheptyl, a mind-bending by-product of THC that was difficult and expensive to extract. His interest in it led him to investigate hashish oil, which he introduced to the Brotherhood. According to one of Stark's circle – who was a former colleague of both Nick Sand and Owsley Stanley the Third – Stark was fascinated by 'the more powerful THC derivatives' and, by 1972, had decided 'that the best raw material for making these derivatives was hash-oil'. Trading in large quantities of hashish 'for fun and profit' would allow him to continue his experiments.

Stark's source of hashish was Lebanon and his supplier was Niaf Al-Masri, one of the country's biggest exporters. Between 1972 and 1975, Stark – who spoke fluent Arabic – frequently stayed with the Al-Masri clan at their estate in Baalbek, a city on the north-eastern edge of the Bekaa Valley, which was the centre of hashish production in Lebanon. Running for 75 miles, the Bekaa Valley had the right climate and type of soil for cultivating cannabis and was predominately populated by Shia Muslims, whose livelihoods largely depended on the crop, which they grew for magnates like Al-Masri. By 1972, there were 965 square miles of cannabis fields in the territory under his control.

Al-Masri was typical of the major players in the Lebanese hashish trade, which had been dominated by big landowners and city merchants for over forty years. Their economic power translated into political power and many of them were members of the Lebanese parliament, the Chamber of Deputies. Al-Masri was the elected representative for his region and virtually untouchable. As a Federal Bureau of Narcotics agent concluded back in 1954, 'certain of these large traffickers are so influential politically … that one might well state that the Lebanese government is in the narcotics business'. Sporadic attempts to crack down on the growers had a limited impact and were often met with armed resistance. A well-meaning attempt to encourage farmers to cultivate sunflowers instead of cannabis petered out after a few years due to lack of take-up: sunflowers simply weren't as profitable.

Stark's alliance with Al-Masri came about thanks to a Brotherhood connection. In the early 1970s, Lebanon accounted for 25% of the world's hashish. At the time, it could be bought wholesale for as little as $15 a kilo: on the American market, the same amount would fetch $1,500. These kinds of margins caught the attention of the Brotherhood of Eternal Love (as well as the Bureau of Narcotics and Dangerous Drugs, which had three agents in Beirut), and it's estimated that the Brotherhood smuggled around 4,000 kilos of Lebanese hash into the US, quite possibly with Stark's assistance.

In the summer of 1970, a Brotherhood associate arranged to pick up 1,500 pounds of hashish – worth about $3.5 million – from Al-Masri. The Brother's plane, which had flown a circuitous route from Canada to an airstrip near Baalbek, was intercepted before take-off by Lebanese customs, who were driven away under a hail of machine-gun fire unleashed by the twenty-four armed men provided by Al-Masri. After this narrow escape, the plane was forced to land on Crete for refuelling and repairs, where it was met by Greek police. The smugglers were arrested and the hashish seized. As an international incident it was hard to ignore and in the Chamber of Deputies Al-Masri was accused of being behind the operation, charges he flatly denied even though there was evidence that his son had met the Americans in a Beirut hotel. With their Brother in a Greek jail, his friends asked for Stark's help. His lawyer in Paris – the always reliable Sam Goekjian – duly obliged. Hefty bribes were paid to the appropriate individuals and in autumn 1971 the Brother was released. As a thank you, he introduced Stark to Al-Masri.

Aside from this extremely beneficial relationship, Stark claimed that he acted as a financial advisor to Musa Sadr, an Iranian-born Shia cleric who was the spiritual and political leader of his community, and had close ties to the Syrian regime. Based in the Bekaa Valley, Musa Sadr had a private army of around 1,000 men and, though not directly engaged in the hashish business, he did not interfere with it either, while his troops helped defend the valley from intruders. How much Stark contributed to his war-chest is impossible to say. But being on the right side of Sadr offered some further protection and allowed him to move in and out of the Bekaa Valley unmolested.

Otherwise, Stark's natural habitat was the Casino du Liban in Beirut. The casino and hotel complex – which perched on a hill overlooking the Mediterranean – was granted a gambling licence in 1957 and opened its doors two years later. From then on, it welcomed a steady stream of celebrities and regional leaders – like the Shah of Iran and the King of Jordan – who were treated to top-class food and A-list entertainment. The Casino du Liban was also a favourite meeting place for diplomats, spies, hustlers and crime bosses, making it the perfect environment for someone like Stark. He boasted of brokering deals for the oil-rich sheiks and Saudi royalty who often stayed there.

Thanks to his influential allies, Stark was able to move as much hashish as he could manage for nearly three years. With two accomplices – and the blessing of the local mafia – Stark loaded Al-Masri's hashish into stolen luxury cars and ferried them from Lebanon to Sicily. Alongside the cars, Stark used yachts and even planes to transport tons of hash into the country. Life was good and, in February 1975, he and Henrietta and Leyla were enjoying a comfortable stay in a palatial suite at the Hotel Baglioni, the oldest and most prestigious hotel in Bologna – with a main lobby and restaurants decorated with frescos and Renaissance paintings – unaware that the local police had recently discovered several stolen high-end cars in a garage and pulled in one of Stark's smuggling partners, a professional car thief, for questioning. Further enquiries led them to the Hotel Baglioni and Stark's room, where they found forged documents, Stark's fake US passport, large sums of cash in numerous currencies, cocaine, morphine base and several kilos of hash.

Throughout, Stark and Henrietta stuck rigidly to their English personas, insisting they were who their passports said they were. But the cops were not convinced that the man they had arrested was in fact William Terence Abbott, so they sent a telex with his photo and details via Interpol to drug squads in London and Washington, who informed them that the man they had in custody was Ronald Stark, wanted fugitive and acid tycoon. Caught red-handed, facing a long spell in jail and the threat of extradition, Stark's future looked grim. But he wasn't ready to admit defeat. If there was a way to get himself out of this predicament, he was going to find it.

12

The Best-Laid Plans

Once Kemp had completed his marathon production run in his basement lab in the manor house, he and Bott swiftly concealed the evidence. Under the floor tiles in their kitchen, about a foot down, they hid a plastic box containing 1.3 kilos of LSD crystals, the equivalent of thirteen million microdots. In the garden, they buried two brown bottles beneath the compost heap by their potato crop; inside them was another 120 grams of crystal, roughly 1.2 million microdots. To finish the job, they smashed up their lab equipment and assorted hardware, and dumped the remains down a disused well.

Also concealed in the cottage were the various component parts of a crude tableting machine. However, Kemp and Bott were in no rush to convert their LSD. That could wait. More pressing was their deteriorating relationship with Solomon, who had agreed to put their product on the international market. To do this, Solomon had secured the services of Isaac Sheni, an Amsterdam-based Israeli in his early 30s who also maintained an address in north London. At some point, he is alleged to have bought the Microdot Gang's acid for sale on the continent, which may be why Solomon knew him. They could have run into each other socially in London. But exactly how they got together is anyone's guess. Sheni was a mysterious character. Known to law-enforcement agencies on both sides of the Atlantic as a major dealer in LSD, hashish and heroin,

Sheni always managed to stay out of their reach. There were persistent rumours that he actually worked for Mossad – the infamous Israeli secret service – either moving drugs on their behalf or reporting on his business associates. During this period, one of Mossad's strategies for undermining its enemies was to encourage their military personnel to take drugs. Operation Blade, which began in 1968 and ran for ten years, involved Mossad agents buying hashish in Lebanon and then employing dealers near Egyptian army bases to sell it to the soldiers inside them.

With Sheni on board, Kemp and Solomon agreed on a price: Solomon would pay Kemp $500 per thousand microdots. Unfortunately, they agreed on little else. The lingering animosity over the Gerald Thomas affair – Kemp blamed Solomon for bringing him into the gang, an accusation Solomon thought was grossly unfair – bubbled to the surface and their new partnership was in danger of collapsing before it had even begun. Luckily, there was an old mutual friend who was prepared to act as bridge between them and be their acid middle-man.

Dr Mark Campbell Tcharney had met Solomon and Kemp in Cambridge in 1969 when he arrived there to study medicine. The son of a diplomat, he attended grammar school before going up to university. After graduating in 1972, he moved to the capital, lived in squats and communes and completed his medical training at the East London Hospital. In 1974, he bought an isolated farmhouse for £25,000 that was about half an hour away from Kemp and Bott's cottage. The property had four acres of land and was perched on an exposed hilltop, screened by trees, with just a narrow lane leading up to it. Tcharney moved in with his partner Dr Hilary Rees and operated out of Shrewsbury Hospital as a part-time locum. Naturally, Bott and the two of them had a lot in common, especially once Bott began working as a doctor in the Accident and Emergency Department, Bronglais Hospital, Aberystwyth; she could swap stories with them at the end of a long shift.

Other than seeing Tcharney and his partner, which they did frequently, Kemp and Bott's social contacts were limited to their nearest neighbour, a couple with a young daughter: according to her, they were 'very friendly with Kemp and Bott, especially with Christine' and she recalled that, though Kemp was 'a little more reserved' and 'tended to stay in the background', Bott 'would often be walking past on her way to the mountain, sometimes walking her goats, and would always stop to chat to us'.

• • •

As a result of Kemp and Bott's low-key lifestyle, the team of Lee's officers watching them had little to report to their boss. Lee had set up surveillance on the cottage while Kemp was still commuting back and forth to his manor house lab. Keen to get eyeballs on them as quickly as possible, Lee took on a cold damp cottage with no sanitation, water or heating that was available as a summer rental, 200 yards from Kemp and Bott. Four officers, posing as fishermen on holiday, moved in for a two-week stay. As an observation post it left a lot to be desired. There were no windows facing Kemp and Bott's place. To overcome this handicap, they drilled a small hole through the slate roof and poked a telescope out of it, which allowed an officer – who was perched on the top rung of a ladder positioned by the loft entrance – to peer through the other end. At night, they were restricted to taking note of any vehicles entering or leaving the property, a thankless and pointless task. When the fishermen's time was up, two sets of 'married couples' took up residence and continued the watching brief. Frustrated by the limited views on offer, Lee opted to try and get a microphone near to Kemp and Bott's cottage. Lacking the necessary gear, Lee got permission from the Home Office to visit a secret research centre and walked out with £6,000 worth of state-of-the-art surveillance kit: motorised cameras, lenses, telescopes, miniaturised microphones, transmitters and receivers.

Lee was hoping to take advantage of the fact that most evenings Kemp and Bott sat out on their makeshift porch and talked for hours. Wearing soft-soled shoes and black clothes, Lee and another officer crept onto Kemp and Bott's land at 3 a.m. one night with the aim of planting a bug by a dry stonewall about 10ft away from where they sat and chatted, but as Lee stealthily paced out the distance he noticed the bedroom window was wide open: the slightest noise might wake the sleeping couple. Lee retreated carefully to the wall where his colleague was waiting with the listening device. After a few moments' cautious digging and scraping the rocky earth to make a hole with their trowels, the fear of being overheard became too much to bear and they retreated. Undeterred, Lee decided to try again the next day. The best moment to strike would be while Bott was delivering Kemp to his basement lab, giving them roughly an hour and a half before she returned. An observer posted on a nearby hill watched for

Bott's Renault, while a female officer sat in a car ready to block her arrival if needed. As it was, Lee and his team-mate got in and out with plenty of time to spare, leaving the bug where they'd intended to the night before. That evening, as Kemp and Bott settled on their porch, Lee and his colleagues huddled round their receiver waiting to hear voices but all they picked up was bird song. By mistake, they'd hidden a microphone that lacked the range they needed to pick up anything useful.

Meanwhile, a few miles away at Llanddewi Brefi, two of Lee's undercover hippies were trying to form a relationship with Smiles. For accommodation, Lee furnished them with a used transit van, which they decorated with appropriately psychedelic colours, images and slogans. Inside, they made do with a couple of old mattresses, some blankets and a primus stove. They had fake driving licences and criminal records for drug offences registered at Bristol Crown Court. Getting a fix on Smiles was not a problem. Something of a local celebrity, he was loved for his flamboyance and care-free attitude to money, lighting cigarettes with £5 notes, dishing out whiskey to pensioners, giving random gifts – like the watch off his own wrist – and stuffing charity boxes with cash. The undercover officers hung out in Smiles' favourite haunts – his local, the New Inn; the Railway and the Red Lion in Tregaron; and the Black Lion in Lampeter, where he bought champagne by the bucket-load – but struggled to get close to him. Smiles was wary of fresh faces and kept well clear of them. Realising it was going to take time to land him, the hippy cops began to make themselves known on the local scene, hoping that word of their authenticity would get back to Smiles. On 21 June 1976, Midsummer's Eve, they attended a 10 p.m. screening of the cult movie *Performance* (1970) at the village hall in Pontrhydfendigaid which, according to one of them, was 'like a scene out of Woodstock'. Around 100–150 hippies showed up for the film. The room was thick with hashish smoke. Joints were in constant circulation and a young woman with flowers in her hair offered them some magic mushrooms.

Earlier that month, Lee had shifted his surveillance of Kemp and Bott's cottage to a new site. Aside from the inconvenience of the vacation rental, the fortnightly turn-around of pairs of couples had hit the buffers: there were no more female officers available. Lee chose Bronwydd, a 400-year-old stone-built farmhouse half way up a mountain with two bedrooms, which was available to rent for £10 per week. It was 2 miles from Kemp and Bott, and had outbuildings where the team could conceal multiple vehicles. The interior, however, was even less welcoming than the previous location. When it rained, the kitchen flooded. The only fireplace had a chimney breast made of woven willow brands that produced so much smoke and soot that the front door had to be kept open when it was lit.

In order for his officers to stay there for the long haul, Lee invented a cover story and gave himself the lead role. He was a Mr Calvert, the owner of an import–export business and keen ornithologist who was hoping to recover from a traumatic divorce in peaceful and tranquil surroundings. Though primarily there for relaxation, Mr Calvert intended to continue running his firm and would be receiving visits from colleagues as well as having his male assistant staying with him at the farmhouse. They moved in at the end of June and immediately set about spreading word of their arrival, putting down roots in the bar of the Talbot Hotel in Tregaron, where they spent every lunchtime and evening, and built a rapport with the landlord and his wife. Though none of the other regular punters questioned their identities, a few found them almost too convincing; two single men shacked up like that could mean only one thing – they were homosexual. Knowing that such an assumption might damage their prospects of being accepted by the community, Lee replaced his assistant with a female officer who acted as his secretary. She proved popular with the locals at the Talbot and it wasn't long before she and Lee were taking part in raucous after-hours drinking sessions.

As they bedded in, Lee pondered another attempt at putting a microphone close to Kemp and Bott's porch. The main obstacle was the formidable mountain that separated their cottage from his base at Bronwydd farmhouse and blocked any signals from travelling directly between them. To overcome this problem, Lee and his team would have to plant a receiver on top of the mountain, which could pick up Kemp and Bott's conversations and relay them back to Bronwydd, which was 600 yards away from the peak. Working from the top down, they successfully buried the cable, but woke the next day to find 100 yards of it had been uprooted and destroyed by hungry sheep. When the same thing happened again, they laid the cable above ground by lacing it through wire fencing. This painstaking task was performed in scorching heat and took six days of sweat and toil; by the end, they were wearing nothing but swimming costumes, layers of mosquito repellent, and gauntlets and wellington boots to guard against the adders that nestled in the thick fern that covered the lower levels of the mountain.

Compared to that, hiding the bug close to Kemp and Bott's cottage was child's play. With everything ready, Lee and his exhausted colleagues sat round their receiver, switched it on and were struck by the stirring sounds of a Welsh male voice choir. Switching it on and off again made no difference. All they heard were the choir's harmonious voices. As before, sheep were the culprits. They'd chewed through the cable's insulation and turned the mountain-top transmitter into a giant aerial that was faithfully broadcasting Radio Wales.

● ● ●

From the beginning of Operation Julie, Lee was convinced that Kemp was in charge of producing the LSD for a network that had a central hub in London, where the as-yet-unidentified 'Henry' had overall control of supply and distribution. Supporting his theory was material given to him by the CDIU. In April 1974, a young Englishman was arrested on arrival in Australia with 1,500 microdots. In exchange for a lighter sentence, he told his captors that he'd got the acid from the Last Resort restaurant in Fulham, though it had originally come from Wales. In response, the CDIU tapped the premises' phone and raided it, but found nothing.

To help follow these leads, Lee would have normally turned to the Metropolitan Police and its drug squad. However, Lee had kept them away from Operation Julie for a reason; they were riddled with corruption and malpractice. Standard procedure involved finding a dealer, protecting their supply in return for a slice of their profits and information about their rivals, who would then get busted, giving officers the chance to sell on some of the drugs seized. Higher up the food chain, the dynamic former head of the drug squad and several of his key personnel had been hauled through the courts for overzealous and criminal behaviour. One of the CDIU officers who'd gone to Canada to speak with Gerald Thomas was later convicted of accepting bribes from pornographers while working for the Obscene Publications Squad. As far as the Microdot Gang were concerned, Lee had word from a trusted informant that they had friends inside Scotland Yard.

However, he had another option: HM Customs & Excise, the organisation that policed the country's borders and was on the frontline of the war on drugs. To tackle the smuggling of contraband into Britain, HM Customs & Excise had established the Investigations Branch in 1946. By the time Lee got in touch, it had been renamed the Investigations Division and had a dedicated drugs taskforce with six separate teams comprising sixty men and two women. The first thing it did was confirm Lee's doubts about the Metropolitan Police's reliability, telling him that 'substantial corrupt payments had been made to London police officers for protection by the LSD distributors'. Next, the Investigations Division gave him a file they'd compiled on Russell Stephen Spenceley, based on a report they'd been given by a recently retired Thames Valley Drug Squad detective. In it, Spenceley was named as one of the key players in an LSD ring operating between London and Reading circa 1971–72.

Intrigued, Lee invited the former Thames Valley cop in for a chat. Apart from what Lee had already gathered from his report, the source said that a man named 'Henry' was manufacturing the acid that Spenceley was selling. The son of a farmer, Spenceley had dropped out of Chelsea College of Science and Technology in 1969 and immersed himself in London's drug scene, where he met and befriended Smiles. Todd recruited Spenceley as a dealer when he was in the process of moving the yellow capsules full of Solomon's share of Kemp's Paris acid. In 1972, Spenceley moved to Reading and on 14 March was convicted at Sandwich Magistrates' Court for cannabis possession and fined £20. The following year he relocated to Woodstock in Oxfordshire and then, in 1974, to Glynrichet Fach, a small hill farm about 8 miles from Smiles in Llanddewi Brefi. While he ran a small car-delivery service, his wife worked as a nurse at a local care home. Once Todd got the Hampton Wick lab up and running, Spenceley was ready to take on his former role. He enjoyed the money the LSD business made him, travelled extensively – Europe, Scandinavia, Africa, America – and shared Todd's love of high-class dining; Spenceley's favourite restaurant was La Sorbonne in Oxford. Run by a French chef, La Sorbonne regularly made the *Michelin Guide* and was popular with local celebrities.

During the course of Lee's conversation with the retired Thames Valley officer, he mentioned that a certain Andy Munro was linked to the all-important 'Henry'. Lee recognised the name from the lists found on Gerald Thomas. He had his officers drop in on Munro's Clapham flat, only to find his brother and girlfriend and no sign of the chemist. Clearly, all roads led to 'Henry' and Lee made it his priority to track him down. Several of Thomas' anecdotal remarks to his CDIU interrogators hinted that the connection between 'Henry' and Solomon and Kemp was Cambridge. Two of Lee's detectives combed through the court records for the city and the whole county going back ten years but came up with nothing. They talked to members of the Cambridge Drug Squad, who had only vague memories of Solomon and a bloke called 'Henry' – though one did recall the arrest in Cheltenham of eight people from Cambridge for possession of cannabis. Lee's officers went straight to Cheltenham, rifled through the records, and found what they were looking for. In July 1970, Henry Barclay Todd was part of the group that was caught and then acquitted. Not quite daring to believe that this was their man, they asked round the station for any further details and were rewarded with the revelation that Todd was accompanied by a young American woman – Solomon's daughter.

Included in the local county court records of the case was a postal address for Todd in the East End of London. After sitting on it for a week and talking to the other residents in the building, it was obvious that Todd had not lived there for years. A thorough trawl through the relevant public records revealed that Todd always used that address on official documents, with one exception. On an application to have his young daughter added to his passport – dated 20 March 1975 – Todd had supplied a contact number that did not match the East End address. It was the phone number of his flat at 29 Fitzgeorge Avenue in Earl's Court. Within a few hours, a surveillance van was parked outside. That evening, they watched as Todd drove up, got out of his car and entered the building.

● ● ●

By the spring of 1975, Ronald Stark was adjusting to life at Don Bosco prison in Pisa. Deploying his near-perfect Italian, Stark got a job with the prison barber – which put him in a position to hear all the latest gossip – and used his language skills to help other inmates with their legal documents. Having found his feet, Stark proceeded to forge an alliance with high-ranking members of the Red Brigades, a Marxist-Leninist guerrilla group that was engaged in a bitter struggle with the Italian state and had gone from humble beginnings to achieve national and international notoriety. The Red Brigades were formed in the autumn of 1970 by three sociology students who had experienced the pitched battles between radicals, striking workers and the police that had erupted across Italy in the late 1960s. The Red Brigades' founders felt that the traditional parties of the Left were too wedded to the system to contemplate revolution. It was down to them to defend the proletariat, while hitting the capitalists where it hurt.

At first, the Red Brigades focused on sowing discord at the various Fiat car plants, factories and subsidiaries in Turin that together accounted for half the city's workforce. Industrial relations were fraught and Fiat hired known fascists to try and control their employees. The Red Brigades organised rallies, handed out leaflets, set fire to some cars belonging to much hated managers and planted firebombs under Pirelli trucks. These early actions were followed by their first exercise in kidnapping. On 3 March 1972, they seized their target – an executive at the Italian subsidiary of Siemens – and released him twenty minutes later. Between February and December 1973, they carried out three more kidnappings: a manager at Alfa Romeo; someone from Fiat's personnel department; and the provincial secretary of a fascist trade union. Having gagged him, shaved his head and removed his trousers, they tied him to a pole next to the gates of the Fiat factory and left him to rot.

Up to this point, none of their captives were held for more than eight hours and none of them were particularly newsworthy individuals. This changed when the Red Brigades grabbed Genoa's right-wing attorney general on 18 April 1974 and kept him for thirty-five days. They interrogated him, put him in front of a revolutionary tribunal and demanded the release of eight of their comrades. The whole incident was extensively covered by the press and prompted a massive crackdown. Though most of the Red Brigades were already underground after a series of raids and arrests the previous year, many of them were flushed out of hiding and joined the growing number of them languishing behind bars.

Stark went about winning the confidence of the Red Brigades prisoners by talking up his connections to the Popular Front for the Liberation of Palestine (PFLP). This line of approach was guaranteed to impress the Red Brigades as they regarded the PFLP as both an inspiration and brothers-in-arms. The PFLP had emerged in the wake of the Six Day War, June 1967, a stunning victory for the Israeli army over the combined forces of Egypt, Syria and Jordan. This had caused thousands of Palestinians to join the exodus that had begun during the 1948 Arab–Israeli War, when around three-quarters of a million were driven from their homes and into exile. While most went to Jordan, around 100,000 entered Lebanon.

The PFLP was a largely independent group within the PLO – which had been founded three years earlier – and combined Marxist-Leninism with Arab nationalism. In their opening statement, the PFLP declared that they were at 'the beginning of a new stage of revolutionary work in which the masses would assume responsibility for leading the fight against imperialism and Zionism through revolutionary violence'.

To carry out actions on an international stage, the PFLP created a Foreign Operations cadre with bases in Jordan – where members of West Germany's Red Army Faction and the Roaming Hashish Rebels went to train. Aside from hit-and-run attacks on targets within Israel, the Foreign Operations unit specialised in hijacking passenger planes. Their campaign began in Rome on 23 July 1968 when they boarded El Al flight 426, diverted it to Algiers and kept it there for thirty-nine days. The next two attacks were at Athens and Zurich airports, where planes were assaulted on the runway, causing two deaths. On 29 August 1969, they took control of TWA flight 840 at Los Angeles International airport and held it hostage for forty-four days. Six months later, they opened fire on a passenger bus at Munich airport, killing one and wounding eleven. Then, on 6 September 1970, they pulled off their most audacious heist yet, the simultaneous seizure of three flights to New York. A Pan Am jet from Brussels airport was diverted to Cairo; in Frankfurt, a TWA plane was seized and rerouted to Jordan; and a Swiss Air flight from Zurich suffered the same fate. All three were blown up a few days later. Not content with this haul, the PFLP attempted to hijack a British Airways plane at Heathrow on 9 September, but never got off the ground.

On 17 September, the King of Jordan ordered his troops to uproot and expel the Palestinian guerrilla forces in his country, which by now amounted to thousands of fighters, mostly congregated in refugee camps. The activities of the Palestinian resistance had provoked Israel to repeatedly invade the monarch's territory, and its calls for proletarian revolution threatened to undermine his hold on power, while the recent hijacking extravaganza only added to the pressure on him to act, as did the fact that the PFLP had already tried to kill him twice. Over the course of an eleven-day battle – that became known as Black September – Jordanian soldiers killed anywhere between 2,000 and 20,000 Palestinians. Many more fled into Lebanon, swelling their numbers there to about 400,000, roughly one-sixth of the population. The surviving guerrillas went with them. The PFLP established its HQ in Beirut and located its military bases and ammunition dumps in the Bekaa Valley, home of the Lebanese hashish trade and close to the cannabis fields owned by Al-Masri, Stark's former business partner.

Because of his frequent trips to see Al-Masri, Stark would have learnt about the PFLP's presence in the area. There is also the possibility that Stark got to know them because groups like the PFLP regarded drug smuggling as a useful source of income. In the spring of 1971, eight men from Lebanon – who claimed to be working for the PLO – were arrested at Heathrow airport with eight suitcases containing 145 kilos of hash. Some years later, a US Senate Committee report stated that 'the PLO has been involved in worldwide drug trafficking' selling its merchandise in 'Britain, Sweden, West Germany, Canada and the United States'.

There was also a considerable overlap between drug running and gun running. The same suppliers often made use of the same routes and personnel, and the two commodities were interchangeable; drugs were exchanged for weapons and vice versa. As the Red Brigades were increasingly in need of guns, Stark's offer to connect them to the PFLP would have been extremely enticing, and there is evidence that Stark was not simply telling them what they wanted to hear. During 1970, while Stark was spending chunks of time in the UK, Special Branch – who were responsible for countering domestic terrorism and political subversion – ran a check on him. It concluded that he was buying and selling guns for the PLO, a subject that Stark had raised with Steve Abrams, his host at Hilton Hall. Abrams remembered a 'conversation' between them about the 'PLO and arms deals' that seemed to him to be more than just idle banter.

Overall, Stark gave the Red Brigades inmates enough reasons to invite him into their inner circle. The importance of this union for Stark's future increased when his new friends were joined by Renato Curcio, their leader and founder member. Curcio was initially taken prisoner in the autumn of 1974, but on 18 February 1975 he was busted out of jail by his wife and comrade, Mara Cagol. After two of her team, dressed in workmen's overalls, cut the prison phone-lines, they broke in brandishing machine-guns and liberated Curcio. Having freed her husband, Cagol was trapped by police in a remote farmhouse on 5 June, wounded and executed on the spot. Curcio, meanwhile, evaded the authorities until 18 January 1976. Holed up in a flat in Milan, he fought a twenty-two-minute gun battle before surrendering.

Stark was introduced to Curcio and soon won him round by showing him a secure cryptographic system for encoding radio messages. In return, Curcio told him about a plan to assassinate Judge Francesco Coco, who was due to preside over the trial of the Red Brigades prisoners. Stark spied an opportunity. He was scheduled to go to court himself in July and information like this might work in his favour. Through a prison guard Stark arranged a meeting with officers from the Interior Ministry's anti-terrorism squad, who passed what Stark told them to Pisa's state prosecutor. However, Stark's powers of persuasion were not enough to convince the prosecutor; he mistrusted Stark's motives, questioned his credibility and disregarded his warnings. But on 8 June 1976, Judge Coco met his end. Returning home from work, he entered the side-street that led to his front door with his bodyguard beside him. As they walked along, three men armed with automatic weapons appeared from beneath some arches ahead of them, walked on a few paces, turned and discharged their magazines, instantly killing the judge and his guard. Though Stark had been proved right – and the authorities were sufficiently worried about his safety to transfer him to Bologna jail – it made no difference when he stood trial a few weeks later. Realising his gambit had failed, Stark declared that he was a political prisoner and refused to recognise the court's right to try him. Stark was sentenced to fourteen years in jail and fined $60,000.

Over a year had passed since Stark's arrest, yet at no point had the US government expressed any interest in extraditing him. Aside from the indictments for conspiracy to produce and distribute LSD that concerned Stark's Belgian lab and his collaboration with Billy Hitchcock, Nick Sands and the Brotherhood, the Feds were keen to question him about his part in the hashish oil trade. On 6 August 1975, the DEA in Los Angeles issued a warrant against him for organising an amphetamine ring. Five weeks later a New York City court found him guilty of making false statements on a passport application. Despite all these outstanding charges, nobody was in any hurry to make Stark pay for his crimes. Apparently, the US authorities were quite content to leave Stark exactly where he was.

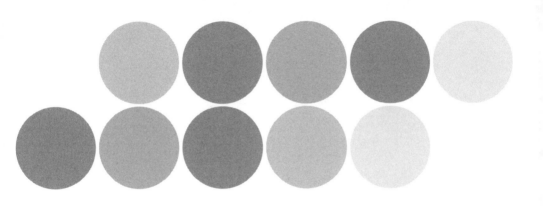

Part Four

COME-DOWN

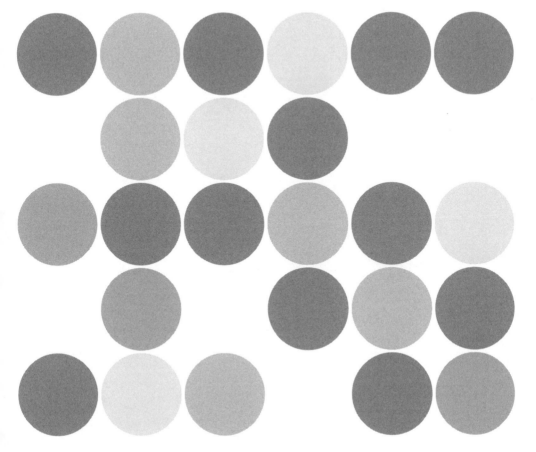

13

Race to the Line

As Lee pieced together a rough biography of the Microdot Gang and the true extent of its activities, its access to foreign markets and intricate financial arrangements, he kept encountering Stark and the Brotherhood. The more he learned, the more convinced he was that they were behind the success of the UK network. Yet the picture Lee had was partial and incomplete. He'd approached the Italian authorities about Stark, but they were reluctant to share any of the evidence they'd gathered. The other potential source of information was the DEA, who proved more accommodating. Lee was given the chance to benefit from its accumulated wisdom and in mid-September 1976 he landed at San Francisco airport, where he was greeted by his hosts, DEA agents who had previously worked on the Brotherhood of Eternal Love investigation. Aside from sharing numerous bottles of whiskey with him, the DEA agents gave Lee access to all the Brotherhood case files and told him about their current operation – code-named Centac X – aimed at a new LSD network that had risen from the ashes of the Brotherhood, drawing on the expertise of several of those who'd avoided capture. They'd busted two of its labs, seized 40 tons of chemicals and equipment, and believed that the gang were getting their LSD crystals from Europe and also dealing in guns.

After stop-overs in San Diego and Houston, Lee headed to Louisiana to track down the man whose information had set him on the trail of the Microdot Gang. Gerald Thomas was not expecting visitors. He'd gone out of his way to make his small apartment a refuge, tucked away in Baton Rouge – where he'd got a regular day job as a chemical engineer – trying to stay as invisible as possible, certain that his former comrades had put a price on his head because of his decision to co-operate with the Canadian authorities. Having served seven months of a fifteen-month sentence, Thomas was released on parole and deported to the US. So far, his past had not caught up with him, yet here was somebody knocking on his door. Breaking into a cold sweat, Thomas answered it and was relieved to find a middle-aged English detective on his doorstep and not a hitman.

Over the next forty-eight hours, Lee patiently probed and prodded Thomas as he told his story: his scientific background; falling under the influence of Huxley and Leary; visits to Millbrook and meeting Solomon and Arnaboldi; and being reunited with them in Majorca. At this point, Thomas lied about his whereabouts between leaving Majorca in 1969 and moving to London in 1972. Thomas claimed he spent the whole period in Baton Rouge, deliberately editing out the fact that he'd made regular trips to the UK; hung out at Solomon's Grantchester cottage; been introduced to Stark; and was aware of the deal struck between Stark, Solomon and Kemp to produce acid in Paris. Otherwise, he mostly stuck to the truth, adding little to what he'd told the Canadians and the detectives from Scotland Yard.

Nevertheless, Thomas had given Lee some insight into the inner-workings of the gang and its origins, and he left Baton Rouge reasonably satisfied with what he'd learnt. Lee ended his trip at the DEA's forensic laboratory in Washington, where he was shown examples of LSD that had been sent there for analysis, including some of Kemp's handiwork, which had been found all across America – in New York, California, Kansas and Illinois – bearing images of pyramids, dragons and Santa Claus.

● ● ●

In deepest Wales, two of Lee's surveillance team were positioned on top of the mountain overlooking Kemp and Bott's home waiting for them to leave in their Renault and take one of the roads out of the valley. On their signal, several of their colleagues were poised to enter the cottage grounds and plant a tiny microphone – enclosed in a waterproof tube – in the guttering above the frame of a small window that Kemp and Bott would leave half-open and was ideally placed for picking up their conversations either upstairs or downstairs.

Lee had authorised this mission after a long and fruitless summer during which his team had endured a record-breaking heatwave. Conditions at the Bronwydd farmhouse had not been pleasant. The water in their well dried up and their crude outside toilet was besieged by swarms of flies and bluebottles. With drought setting in, water was also an issue for Kemp and Bott. To maintain their vegetable garden, Kemp had to get it from a river about a mile away, using a truck to cart it back to their thirsty crops. To avoid having to do this in the future, Kemp set about digging his own well, employing a divining rod to locate a decent source of water. Otherwise, they tended their goats and chickens and, aside from Tcharney and his partner, their only visitors were the odd stray hippy stopping to buy their goat's milk.

This lack of any incriminating activity was praying on Lee's nerves; hopefully a successfully placed bug would end the monotony and release his officers from purgatory. So when his watchers saw Kemp and Bott drive off in the direction of Aberystwyth, his men got the all-clear and – armed with a ladder – raced to the cottage to execute their plan, which involved running the cable through joints in the stonework leading up to the window. But on closer inspection, they saw that there was no way the cable would fit in the guttering. Determined not to leave empty-handed, one of them took advantage of an open bedroom window, climbed inside and did a sweep of the downstairs, copying down telephone numbers, names and addresses that he found in a diary by the phone.

All things considered, this was a decent result and compensated somewhat for the continued failure of the two hippy cops based near Llanddewi Brefi to attach themselves to Smiles. However, they were getting closer by gaining the confidence of two locals – called Happy and Blue – who did a bit of business with Smiles. Blue was the more significant of the two, and the undercover detectives managed to arrange a hashish deal with him having produced a large lump of it – borrowed from an evidence room – to prove that they were serious.

Blue often discussed his relationship with Smiles, but the man himself continued to keep his distance, until one afternoon they spotted him walking beside the road outside Lampeter and offered him a lift. Smiles accepted, but as soon as he sat in the passenger seat he demanded to know if they were undercover cops. Too stunned to speak, one of them burst into nervous laughter and Smiles' question remained unanswered for the rest of the journey.

As it was, progress was made in Smiles' case thanks to Martyn Pritchard, who had returned to the West Country after a brief spell in west London researching the drug and party scene and gaining valuable intelligence. Based in Bath, Pritchard discovered that the Chippenham–Frome axis which he'd previously encountered was no longer operating, but in Hankerton, a small village in Wiltshire, a couple of dealers were flogging 1,000 microdots a week plus amphetamines and cannabis. After a few weeks carefully establishing his credentials, Pritchard engineered an invitation to their house at 29 Chapel Lane, an attractive cottage with a substantial garden, which contained a swimming pool, cannabis plants and a chapel. They chatted and smoked for a few hours and Pritchard convinced them to sell him 500 microdots for £160. Then, in an effort to make himself a fixture in their lives, he flirted shamelessly with the sister of one of the dealers – who lived there too – and offered to help renovate the chapel, in exchange for LSD.

On the basis of Pritchard's regular reports, Lee felt it was worth asking the Home Office if he could tap the dealers' phone. In the same way the British government officially denied the existence of its intelligence services, it also refused to admit it employed electronic surveillance, a fiction sustained by the fact that any material gathered by it was inadmissible in court. As a result, all requests for it had to be sanctioned by the Home Office first. Permission granted, Lee's decision paid off handsomely: the two dealers from Hankerton spoke openly about their business and made the error of phoning Smiles to order 3,000 tabs of LSD. Smiles was furious they'd contacted him at all and even more annoyed that it was about such a trivial amount of acid. Rather than let them come and collect it, Smiles told them he'd mail it to a friend who'd deliver it by hand, and warned them to never call him again, under any circumstances.

Though this was an important development, it meant little if Lee couldn't tie the West Country-to-Wales supply line to Todd in London, something that was proving difficult to do, despite the fact that Todd was under surveillance twenty-four hours a day with officers on foot, on bikes, and in cars and vans following his every move. It didn't help that Todd spent the summer doing nothing except enjoy himself, eating at his favourite restaurants and shopping at his favourite stores while Lee's watchers boiled in the heat: inside their van the temperature regularly hit 100 degrees centigrade. They installed electric fans, swallowed salt tablets and pints of water, and stripped down to the bare essentials. Unable to leave the confines of the van, in case they were spotted, they kept an eye on Todd through a small peephole. Finding a decent parking space was a constant headache. Yet so far, they had nothing to show for their efforts.

The obvious way to penetrate behind Todd's respectable front would be to bug his phone. Though getting Home Office approval wouldn't be a problem, all monitored calls were fed through a central switchboard at Scotland Yard, increasing the chances that Todd might get to hear about it through the grapevine. Faced with this dilemma, Lee compromised. He asked the Post Office to put a meter on Todd's phone that recorded the exact time that calls were made or received, clocked their duration and registered the numbers involved. While this was a helpful innovation, Lee was not satisfied with the information it was providing him. He wanted more. Rather than risk exposure by following standard procedure, Lee turned once again to HM Customs & Excise.

Since 1946, HM Customs & Excise had the right to run phone taps and four of its officers occupied a cramped room in a nondescript office block in Chelsea – nicknamed 'Tinkerbell' – a former Department of the Environment building that had been redesigned and re-equipped by boffins from the Government Communications Headquarters (GCHQ) and housed operatives from MI5, MI6, Special Branch and Scotland Yard. By 1976, the HM Customs & Excise listeners had been absorbed into its Investigations Division and concentrated exclusively on drug trafficking. Less ponderous and slow-footed than the other agencies camped in the building, the dedicated staff of the Drugs A for Alpha team – as they were known – reacted in real time to intercepted conversations, giving Lee up-to-the-minute feedback on Todd's telephone activities.

By October, the bug was in place and at 11 a.m. on 2 November it paid dividends. Todd called a hi-fi supplier about a piece of stereo equipment he'd sent for repair. While going over details of his order, Todd couldn't remember which address he'd given them, Earl's Court or Seymour Road. Once Lee heard that Todd had access to another dwelling, he dispatched a surveillance squad to Seymour Road and had the Post Office put a meter on the phone-line. With no reason, as yet, to believe otherwise, Lee assumed that the house in Hampton Wick was where Todd intended to tablet the acid that Kemp had made in Wales. The thought that they were working separately never occurred to him.

● ● ●

Despite the Operation Julie team's failure to observe Kemp and Bott doing anything even vaguely criminal, they had succeeded in remaining undetected. As far as Kemp and Bott were concerned, it was safe to go ahead and begin tableting their LSD. During November 1976, they removed thirty moulds and some small perforated boards they'd kept hidden under their compost heap, and assembled a crude tableting machine in their kitchen. Working steadily they could produce 50,000 microdots every three hours. Within a few months, they'd accumulated nearly 400,000 microdots, which Kemp gave to Dr Mark Tcharney, his close neighbour and old Cambridge friend. Tcharney passed 200,000 of them to Solomon, who sold them to Sheni, the Israeli dealer from Amsterdam. In the process, Tcharney also made contact with Sheni and sent another 183,000 his way. At the same time, Tcharney and Kemp began considering the possibility of using Tcharney's farmhouse as the site for a new lab.

Soon there was enough money in Kemp and Bott's pockets to justify a trip to their Swiss bank. With £16,000 worth of Dutch currency in her suitcase and the key to their safety-deposit box, Bott arrived in Zurich on 8 February 1977. She checked into the Hotel Plaza and was soon interrupted by Swiss customs police who wanted to inspect her belongings – a random check, nothing personal. Bott held her nerve and told them that the cash belonged to her sister, a medical practitioner. The cops were satisfied with her explanation and left. Rattled by this unexpected intrusion, Bott phoned Kemp that evening. He reassured her that it was probably just a routine search; the main thing was they hadn't found the key to their safety-deposit box. Around lunchtime the following day, Bott left the hotel, walked to the Kantonel Bank and put the Dutch guilders into the safety-deposit box. Mission complete, she returned to the UK via a deliberately circuitous route, boarding a Calais to Dover ferry two days later.

Another financial matter Kemp and Bott were anxious to resolve was the sale of the Carno manor house, which had been on the market since the summer. While it stood empty there was always the danger that the cops might come snooping round. Arnaboldi had flown over from Spain in October and he and Kemp had met with their estate agent. By mid-January, they had a buyer, who had taken possession of the manor house but not parted with any money for it. Arnaboldi returned to Wales to force the issue. The buyer refused to back down and they had a furious argument that ended when he threatened to call the police. On 12 March, Arnaboldi was back for another try. This time the buyer was more amenable and agreed to settle up within a few days, much to Kemp's relief. He was looking to terminate his relationship with Arnaboldi because the American kept pestering him to tablet his share of the Carno acid as he lacked the means and the knowledge to do so. Kemp firmly refused and, after they'd finally shaken hands with the buyer, he hoped he'd never have to see Arnaboldi again.

● ● ●

During the last months of 1976, Todd was putting together the lab at Seymour Road so Munro and Cuthbertson could hit the ground running. Posing as Mr Blunt of the fake firm Inter-Organics Ltd, Todd ordered supplies of chemicals and lab equipment from the same firms and companies that he'd bought from before, and made a trip to Switzerland to stock up on ergotamine tartrate. He flew to Bordeaux, picked up a brand-new Volvo from Cuthbertson's place in the Dordogne, and drove it to Basel and straight to his supplier of choice – Dolder AG. Todd got out of his Volvo and went in the main entrance. Moments later, he re-emerged with two employees and entered a nearby bar. After half an hour, they came out and returned to the office. Todd reappeared almost immediately carrying a bulky brown paper bag, which was packed with ergotamine tartrate. The following day, he boarded a ferry to Dover, having mailed the ergotamine tartrate to his preferred courier company in Paris, which would forward it to the UK for Todd to pick up at a later date.

As soon as Todd had fitted Seymour Road out with what Munro required, the chemist got cracking. With his part of the process complete – and supremely confident that once set in motion the network would run itself – Todd found time to play rugby for the London Scottish third team, until a leg injury sidelined him, and plan a mountaineering expedition to the National Park of Northern California, paying for a climbing friend to go there and survey the terrain for him. In the meantime, Cuthbertson returned from France and started tableting Munro's acid the minute it was ready, mixing the liquid LSD with calcium lactate to help prepare it for his hungry tableting machine. In total, Munro and Cuthbertson got through 15 kilos of ergotamine tartrate, enough for twenty million tabs, and, once Cuthbertson had accumulated hundreds of thousands of them, he would bury them in a prearranged spot in the countryside near Reading.

A long-term colleague, who lived in the area, dug them up and then reburied them in hidey-holes in Berkshire and Hampshire, where they were collected by the owner of the Last Resort in Fulham, who forwarded them to a contact in Amsterdam for distribution across mainland Europe and Scandinavia. Cuthbertson's contact gave the remaining microdots directly to Spenceley – who drove down to Reading to collect them in person. Between the end of November and 19 December, Spenceley met Smiles on three separate occasions in three different pubs: the Ram Inn, Lampeter; the Drover's Arms, which was in a tiny hamlet of eight houses, 6 miles from Llanddewi Brefi; and the Black Lion, Lampeter. During their first rendezvous, Spenceley handed Smiles a plastic shopping bag that had 50,000 microdots concealed inside resealed tins of baby food. The next two times, Spenceley gave him 100,000. In return, Smiles paid Spenceley £170 per 1,000 microdots, then sold them on to dealers in London, Birmingham and Swindon for £200 per 1,000.

Thanks to the fact that Lee had already applied for and obtained taps on both Spenceley and Smiles' phones, his officers were present to witness each of these handovers. Meanwhile, the undercover hippies – who'd since moved from their camper van to a terraced two-bed stone cottage close to the heart of Llanddewi Brefi – had finally bonded with Smiles after a confrontation in the New Inn. Smiles had once again pointed the finger and accused them of being cops, which prompted one of them to fly into a rage, pin Smiles up against a wall and threaten to cave his teeth in if he ever accused them of that again. Shocked and apologetic, Smiles dropped his defences and invited them to join his life of endless partying. Long nights together would begin with a tour of the area's pubs and end with smoking sessions at Smiles' house, which had a whole room dedicated to Hindu gods and a papier-mâché sculpture of Jimi Hendrix upstairs.

By now, the undercover detectives had ceased trying not to inhale. During a booze- and dope-fuelled card game, one of them was passed a chillum loaded with premium-grade hashish. A few puffs sent his head into a whirl and he began to hallucinate; according to him, sounds became distorted, his playing cards 'appeared huge and out of proportion' and 'the Queen of Diamonds was smiling' at him. Seeking sanctuary in the bathroom, he retched violently into the toilet bowl and watched in amazement as 'a large dragon's head' rose out of it with 'red eyes and fire spitting forth from its mouth'. The whole experience seemed to last for hours; but when he rejoined his companions they'd barely noticed he'd gone.

Throughout all this socialising, Smiles declined to discuss business with them, until one evening in January. After a few hours drinking in various pubs, they went back to Smiles', where he offered them high-quality cocaine. Having snorted some lines, Smiles and company headed to a restaurant in Lampeter for a slap-up meal – his treat – while one of the hippy cops stayed behind to babysit Smiles' daughter. During their high-spirited dinner, Smiles spoke openly about his plan to exchange LSD for cocaine. Meanwhile, back at Smiles', the child-minding under-cover cop was taking advantage of their absence; he searched the premises and found a bag full of cash and a cereal box stuffed with around 1,000 microdots. This was the moment they'd been waiting for and they quickly relayed the news to their boss. But Lee was disturbed by this turn of events. Worried they were getting in too deep, he was also concerned that Smiles' potential cocaine supplier was an American with heavyweight mafia connections. His men were entering dangerous waters. The evidence against Smiles was already damning enough, so rather than continue to jeopardise his detectives' safety – and sanity – Lee pulled them out of Llanddewi Brefi.

In London, the HM Customs & Excise Alpha squad kept Lee up to date with Todd's calls to chemical firms and lab equipment companies. When he headed to Switzerland to obtain ergotamine tartrate, Lee's men were right behind him. In Hampton Wick, the surveillance team at Seymour Road noticed the arrival of a tall man in a leather jacket whose car was registered to a certain Brian Cuthbertson. Lee ran background checks, assembled a picture of Cuthbertson's long history with the Microdot Gang and even had French police search his house in the Dordogne, though nothing of consequence was found. Put together, these new developments suggested that Todd might be doing more at Seymour Road than simply tableting Kemp's acid. This possibility became harder to ignore when Lee and his watchers in Hampton Wick managed to identify the scruffy young man who was frequently spending the night at Seymour Road.

One morning in December, four cars and ten officers were in position ready to tail their target as he left the house and made the five-minute walk to Hampton Wick station. Once inside, he purchased a one-way ticket to Clapham Common. A detective standing behind him in the queue noted the destination and radioed it through to the waiting cars that sped off at full pelt to try and reach Clapham Common before the train did. Lee and one other cop followed the man onto the platform, keeping a discreet distance. The train arrived after ten minutes and pulled into Clapham Common twenty minutes later. The target was the last passenger to get off and exit the station. The police cars, which had negotiated dense south London traffic to arrive with just seconds to spare, disgorged two officers – one who fell in behind their man, the other in front of him – who followed their quarry for half a mile until he reached his flat. As soon as Lee heard what the address was, he realised the person they'd been shadowing was none other than Andy Munro.

The addition of Munro to the equation appeared to confirm that Seymour Road was acting as an acid lab. Yet Lee stuck stubbornly to his theory that Kemp produced and Todd and his crew tableted and supplied: one network, not two. This misconception clouded his judgement and made him view each fresh discovery from that perspective, obscuring the truth and delaying the resolution of the investigation, putting almost intolerable demands on his task-force. At Bronwydd in Wales, morale was low. Winter was doing its worst. The snow was so thick they had to abandon their cars and get a Land Rover. The farmhouse was perpetually cold and damp. Water ran down the walls. Mould was forming.

Freezing nights were spent crawling around the perimeter of Tcharney's land, searching for signs that a new lab was being prepared. In London, the surveillance teams had taken up residence in a three-bedroom house in Hendon – borrowed from the RAF – where eighteen of them shared one small bathroom and kitchen. There weren't enough beds to go around so one of them slept in a cupboard, another in an alcove under the stairs, and another in the linen cupboard on the landing. Though everybody was given a few days off at Christmas, most of the Operation Julie team were too exhausted to enjoy it.

By then, Lee's superiors were running out of patience. They wanted action. At a meeting held on 2 February 1977, he was given thirty days to wrap up the operation and make the arrests. But even with the clock ticking, Lee was hesitant, unwilling to strike until the last possible moment. He let his officers follow Bott on her trip to Switzerland, and arranged for the local police to pay her a visit in her hotel room. In Carno, he persuaded the troublesome buyer to let things proceed smoothly and watched Arnaboldi and Kemp complete the sale of the manor house. In London, his detectives observed how Munro and Cuthbertson rarely left the house on Seymour Road anymore, and listened to recorded conversations about thousands of tabs of acid changing hands. But still Lee insisted on waiting, his indecision agonising for his officers, especially those stationed in Hampton Wick, who kept telling their boss that LSD was being manufactured right under their noses.

It was only when Lee was presented with incontrovertible proof that there were two LSD factories that he reluctantly admitted that he was wrong. On 17 March, scientists at a government lab informed him that there were two sorts of microdots in circulation: Kemp's – which were extremely pure – and Munro's – which were diluted. But having held off for so long, Lee was in danger of missing the boat altogether. Both Todd and Cuthbertson had booked holidays to the Bahamas and Todd had cancelled the milk deliveries at Seymour Road. On the afternoon of 23 March, the watchers in Hampton Wick tailed Todd – in his Volvo – and Cuthbertson – in a transit van – as they left Seymour Road and parted company, only to come together again on the M4 motorway outside London, and then take the A33 to Reading. On the outskirts of the town, they turned into an industrial estate and approached Smallmead, a municipal rubbish dump. Todd parked his Volvo and joined

Cuthbertson in the van as he drove into the tip. Together they unloaded some black plastic bags, piled them in a heap and set fire to them. This drew the attention of the onsite bulldozer operator who sidled over and told them they couldn't burn garbage there. Todd suggested he might like to use the bulldozer to bury it instead and slipped him £5. The council worker did as he was asked, and Todd and Cuthbertson left in their respective vehicles.

One of the cops – who'd followed them to the dump and witnessed what happened – approached the bulldozer driver and gave him £10 to dig the bags up again. Inside were traces of calcium lactate, tablet moulds, plastic floor covering, protective gloves and an assortment of microdots and domes. The next day, Munro loaded his car with more plastic bags, went to a refuse tip in nearby Kingston and left them there. The cops retrieved the bags, which were full of smashed-up lab equipment. Todd and his colleagues were cleaning house. Within twenty-four hours, there might be nothing left to find. It was time to bring the hammer down.

14

Busted

At 8 p.m. on 25 March 1977, three sets of officers assembled at Seymour Road. One group entered through the French windows, another through a side entrance, while Lee and the others came in through the front door. The reaction to this sudden invasion was mixed. Munro was dazed and confused. Cuthbertson became agitated when his wife – who happened to be there – was also put in handcuffs, announcing her innocence to anyone who'd listen. Todd was calm and apparently unruffled.

Around ten hours later, just before dawn, officers in Wales crashed in on Kemp and Bott. According to one of the arresting officers, Kemp was 'so sure that he would never be traced he thought we were busting him for having cannabis or something minor like that' and asked whether he'd be back the next day to feed his animals. It was only when they crossed the Severn Bridge into England that Kemp grasped the gravity of the situation. A few miles up the road from Kemp and Bott, Tcharney was taken into custody. As were Smiles and Spenceley. In Reading, Todd's key distributor was dragged out of bed. In Hankerton, the duo of dealers were led away, as was the owner of the Last Resort in London. In total, 180 officers raided 87 different addresses and made 120 arrests.

David Solomon, who'd been something of an afterthought during the final stages of Operation Julie, enjoyed another twenty-four hours of freedom before the net closed on him too. Early on Sunday morning,

27 March, Solomon received a call from Wales alerting him to the danger he was in, but he failed to react quickly enough and, two hours later, the police came knocking on his door. Arnaboldi was picked up in Majorca, held for a few days and released; Spain had no extradition treaty with the UK for drug offences. Nevertheless, Arnaboldi immediately quit Deya, flew to Zurich and then onto New York, where DEA agents intercepted him, searched him and found nothing incriminating. Arnaboldi travelled to Miami and disappeared out of sight. As for Sheni, the Israeli dealer, he was nowhere to be found.

The core group of prisoners were taken to Swindon police station where they underwent five days of interrogation. Within twenty-four hours, the Hankerton boys, Spenceley, Smiles and Munro had all admitted to being part of the LSD network going back a number of years. Solomon initially denied any involvement with Kemp but then quickly conceded defeat. Tcharney admitted to his role selling Kemp's acid to both Solomon and the Israeli Sheni, and offered to take police to the spot on his land where there were 50,000 microdots. Cuthbertson had the same idea as Tcharney, except when he took officers to a clearing in a wood outside Reading to show them the location of a massive stash, he couldn't remember where he'd buried it. A return visit was arranged, but Cuthbertson was still unable to find the right spot.

At which point Todd entered the picture. So far, he'd refused to discuss anything until he'd spoken with his lawyer, deflecting his interrogator's questions and not giving an inch. But neither the cops nor Cuthbertson had given up hope of unearthing the LSD; so Lee asked Todd if he wouldn't mind lending a hand. For all his defiance, Todd realised the hole he was in and was looking for ways to improve the odds in his favour. The next day, 31 March, Todd accompanied Cuthbertson and his escorts back to the woods. After conferring, Todd and Cuthbertson found what they were looking for; 12 inches below ground was a black plastic bag. Inside it were three plastic, cylindrical containers: inside them were 250,000 domes and microdots.

Following close on their heels was Todd's distributor, the Reading-based Leaf Fielding. When he arrived at the University of Reading in 1966, Fielding had already rebelled against his boarding school education and become an anarchist. In the summer of 1967, he took acid and saw that 'all creation is a shimmering dance of energy'. Like Solomon, Kemp and Bott, Fielding thought LSD could heal the world's wounds; it was a 'tool that could help us see a way back from the brink'. He dropped out, did random jobs and bummed round Europe, getting into a number of drug-related scrapes along the way. Back in Reading, and at a loose end, Fielding was approached by his friend Brian Cuthbertson, who got him to sell Solomon and Todd's yellow LSD capsules. In 1971, Cuthbertson gave Fielding some of Kemp's brand-new product, which he thought was 'excellent' and 'the best' he'd ever had. For the next two years, Fielding tableted the Microdot Gang's acid. In 1975, Cuthbertson offered him the role of key distributor in Todd's new network. By then, Fielding had opened Reading Wholefoods – initially as a stall before becoming a shop – and needed the money to keep it afloat. After his arrest, on the fourth day of interrogations, Fielding informed Pritchard about another stash in Caesar's Wood, stuffed inside two packets of Winalot dog food. Inside each of them were fifty small plastic bags containing a total of over 100,000 microdots and domes.

Bott was also persuaded to give away the whereabouts of some of her hidden treasures – the brown bottles of LSD crystal and the tableting moulds concealed under the compost next to Kemp's potato patch. During her interrogations, Bott was reserved, polite but unapologetic, as she tried to explain that making LSD 'was my contribution to society' because using acid 'lifts the veil and one sees the truth'. Her faith in the rightness of her cause remained strong even when confronted by the cold reality of prison. From her cell in Bristol, she wrote to Kemp about how 'all those we reached with our acid, lovingly produced, will feel united in support of truth and that vision we share of mankind living in harmony'. Kemp's reply to her was similarly defiant: despite the fact that 'the forces of repression are firmly in control' he remained convinced that they had 'started something no one can stop'.

Throughout his interrogations, Kemp had played it tough. Brooding and resentful, he conceded as little ground as possible. According to one of the cops shut in a room with him, Kemp was 'the hardest man' he'd 'ever interviewed'. Kemp's 'mind was razor sharp and, although extremely egotistical about his acid manufacture, he constantly analysed the questions put to him and from this built a picture of what the police knew'. Kemp vehemently denied that he was mainly in it for the money and gave the same reasons for his actions as Bott, wishing he could 'turn on' the cops so they could see the light. The one time he lost control was when he expressed his feelings about Gerald Thomas, 'the guy who's put us all here': Lee remembered Kemp calling Thomas a 'bastard' and a 'slimy creep', and muttering darkly that he was 'a dead man'. When pressed by Lee, Kemp said arrangements had already been made to have Thomas killed – 'it's been seen to' – though claimed he had no direct involvement with organising the planned hit.

Thomas' betrayal wasn't the only one to trouble Kemp. After several months in jail, and with plenty of time to ponder their plight, one of the Microdot Gang – whose identity has never been revealed – told their lawyer about the thirteen million microdots worth of LSD crystals under Kemp and Bott's kitchen floor. To add insult to injury, word reached the police that Kemp had secreted £16,000 in the boot of his car, which friends had subsequently concealed under a stone by a river. However, when the cops located the money, there was only £11,000 left: somebody had stolen £5,000 from Kemp's nest-egg.

● ● ●

During the weeks that followed the arrests, teams of forensic experts picked over Kemp and Bott's cottage and 23 Seymour Road. By 3 April, the house in Hampton Wick had been stripped clean of dismantled lab equipment, empty chemical bottles and general rubbish. All that was left to remove was the carpet, whose fibres were still impregnated by the pure liquid LSD that Munro had tipped onto it. Three uniformed officers, who weren't wearing protective masks or gloves, pulled up the carpet and sealed it in a large polythene sheet. As they did, they each absorbed a mighty dose. The results were instantaneous. Convulsed by hysterical laughter, they decided they'd better get some air and clear their heads, ending up at the Angler's pub by Teddington Lock, where their pints of beer changed shape – one said his resembled the FA Cup – and every noise was unbearably magnified. Escaping out into the night, they sought the sanctuary of Seymour Road. The 'pavements felt soft' like 'an expensive carpet', 'flowers and trees came to life', and a pile of logs resembled a herd of deer. Back at the house, their buoyant mood turned ugly and, in a blind panic, they called a police surgeon who told them to go straight to Kingston Hospital. Once they'd recovered, their nightmare quickly became a funny story to be endlessly retold, and they were happy to share it with the press: *The Liverpool Echo* recounted their surreal escapades under the headline 'Operation Julie and its lighter moments'. However, one of them felt compelled to visit Leaf Fielding in jail and tell him that the whole trip had been 'a profound experience' that had made him discover that 'life was a deeper and more subtle business than he'd imagined'.

Despite the stunning amounts of acid already recovered, Lee was not satisfied and carried on with the investigation. Having put pressure on the prisoners and the Swiss authorities, Lee managed to gain access to their bank accounts and safety-deposit boxes. Aside from 1.2 kilos of ergotamine tartrate, Kemp and Bott had deutschmarks, share certificates and stocks and bonds with a total value of around £55,000. Solomon had accumulated least of all – he had £7,000 in his account. Todd had assets worth £307,000 in the Vontobel bank, at the same branch where Cuthbertson kept roughly £150,000 and a kilo of pure gold. Of special interest to Lee was the fact that Kemp, Bott, Solomon and Todd had signed up with these Swiss banks as early as 1971 when he suspected that they were still connected with Stark and the Brotherhood.

This aspect of the case continued to bother him. Kemp had written two versions of his acid career for Lee, and both skirted round the truth about his partnership with them. Kemp said he was contracted by Stark to work on THC, not LSD, and had no idea that the Brotherhood were involved until he arrived in Paris in 1970, where he watched its chemists in action and learnt enough to branch out on his own after returning to London. But thanks to the appearance of a new witness – a woman Lee referred to as 'Nancy' – he knew Kemp was lying to him. Nancy had been part of Solomon's Grantchester scene in the late 1960s and had met Kemp, Gerald Thomas, Stark and Todd. She knew all about how the Microdot Gang had come together as a result of Solomon's quest to tablet and sell his portion of the LSD Kemp had made in Paris for Stark and the Brotherhood. Unfortunately for Lee, the Director of Public Prosecutions decided not to use her testimony because it was tainted by her close association with the accused.

By autumn 1977, Lee had run out of rope. As far as his superiors were concerned there was nothing worthwhile to be gained by pursuing these new leads. Operation Julie was brought to a close and the team disbanded. Of the twenty-six members of the squad, almost a quarter resigned. One of those to quit the force was Martyn Pritchard, the hippy cop. Back in uniform and on traffic patrol, he was unable to adjust to such mundane duties after his adventures working undercover: 'I could never go back to being a copper after those kinds of experiences.' Taking advantage of the intense media interest in the case, Pritchard did a deal with *The Daily Mirror* newspaper and co-authored a no-holds barred account of his double-life with one of its journalists. *Busted: The Sensational Life-Story of an Undercover Hippie Cop* was published in 1978 by Mirror Books and the paper ran a series of feature-length pieces about it; one full-page spread featured a picture of Pritchard in hippy mode, leaning back in a chair, naked from the waist up, with long bedraggled hair and a neatly cropped moustache, staring into the camera as if he was posing for an album cover.

In his conclusion to the book, Pritchard expressed his belief that marijuana was a benign drug – 'in my opinion, the guy with a little cannabis who goes home, listens to his stereo music and turns on with a joint, isn't doing any harm' – but stopped short of recommending decriminalisation. Though proud of what Julie had achieved, he acknowledged that 'there must be quite a few people on the fringe of the distribution network that got away' and the operation had been a 'failure' where 'the money' was concerned. His boss felt the same way. Like Pritchard, Lee could see no future for himself in the force. After being denied a promotion, he resigned in January 1978 – barely a week before the Microdot Gang trial began – and teamed up with a journalist from *The Daily Express*. The book they produced together – *Operation Julie: How the Undercover Police Team Smashed the World's Greatest Drug Ring* – was an incredibly detailed and thorough account of the investigation, which covered every twist and turn, every advance and every false step, leaving the reader in no doubt that Lee thought it had ended prematurely, with much still unknown.

Lee's misgivings, however, were not merely confined to procedural issues. He was suffering from a deeper malaise. True, he'd taken a vast quantity of drugs out of circulation, but he'd also locked up a group of phenomenally bright people who no doubt would have contributed to society if they hadn't been seduced by LSD. And what about acid? Should it really be treated in the same way as heroin and cocaine? Or did it have a useful function to perform? Seeking answers, Lee spent an evening with the renowned psychiatrist R.D. Laing, long-term friend of Solomon and, for one day only, Stark's analyst. Lee and a colleague were due to arrive at Laing's London home at 7 p.m. They showed up three hours late, leaving ample time for Laing, his son and Steve Abrams – formerly of SOMA and Hilton Hall – to work themselves into a lather; Laing's son remembered that 'paranoia was the order of the day'.

This state of high anxiety was largely due to Laing's recent encounter with the police. In the spring of 1976, they arrested him for possession of around one hundred single-dose bottles of Czech LSD. Much to Laing's relief, the case was thrown out of court because the acid had been legitimately acquired back when he had a licence to use it for clinical purposes. Even so, the prospect of entertaining the lead detective from Operation Julie – who had considered interviewing Laing about his relationship with Solomon – gave them all the jitters.

Over the course of a night's hard drinking, Lee and Laing debated the pros and cons of LSD. According to Laing's son, 'the intricacies of Operation Julie were laid out from Inspector Lee's side' while Laing described 'the psychoanalytical theories behind the use of LSD'. When Lee asked Laing to explain the meaning of the word 'ego', Laing came up with twenty-nine different definitions. Unable to match the cop's stamina and capacity to soak up alcohol, Laing puked at 4 a.m. By 6 a.m., he was lying flat on the floor. Despite this rather undignified end to their discussion, Laing's son was left with the impression that 'Operation Julie had somehow changed Lee's perspective on the world'.

● ● ●

As far as David Solomon was concerned, the trial of the Microdot Gang was not only about their future, but also about the survival of the LSD counter-culture he'd been part of for over twenty years. Realising that public opinion would play a crucial part in the outcome, Solomon did his best to mobilise support. There was talk of a book about the case and efforts to organise a defence fund. On 29 April 1977, Solomon wrote to the editor of the Ladbroke Grove-based *Homegrown*, which billed itself as 'Europe's first dope magazine'. Solomon had met the editor to talk about making a contribution to its maiden issue just two weeks before he was arrested. In his letter, Solomon issued a plea for help. Given the immeasurable debt 'famous pop artists and groups' like Bob Dylan, the Rolling Stones and the Beatles owed to LSD, it was 'morally unthinkable' for them not to rally round and make 'sizeable contributions to help pay our immense legal bills and keep our families fed and housed'.

Though Solomon could count on *Homegrown* to do what it could, the groundswell of protest he'd hoped for did not materialise, and the former champions of LSD were nowhere to be seen. Instead, the tone of much of the public debate was dictated by a nakedly hostile press, both national and local. During the week that followed the arrests, *The Daily Mirror* came out all guns blazing. On 30 March, it claimed that £10 million worth of LSD had been recovered so far, while two days earlier it had reminded its readers about the terrible things acid was capable of: 'LSD users have turned killer under the spell of a bad trip. Some thought they could fly and jumped from windows and roofs. Others have seen their friends as horrific monsters and killed them.'

The Microdot Gang trial began on 12 January 1978 at Bristol Crown Court and, as Solomon predicted, LSD joined the defendants in the dock. Kemp and Bott spoke passionately about its virtues and emphasised the importance to them of producing the finest acid possible: Bott said that Kemp 'wanted his stuff to be not only good but the best'. This line of argument was bolstered by a witness from the drug charity Release, who agreed that the purity of Kemp's microdots reduced the risk of bad trips. The head of the Drug Dependency Unit at University College London stated that it was absurd that LSD had the same Class A status as heroin and coke, given it was probably less harmful than alcohol or cigarettes.

But the aging judge – for whom the drug culture was an utter mystery that frightened and baffled him – would not even consider the possibility that LSD might have any positive effects, and his grave disposition and rigid attitudes dominated proceedings. The oppressive atmosphere in court was captured by a writer from the underground paper *The International Times*. Noting how the crown prosecutor 'sometimes glances nervously at the dock as if expecting the prisoners to levitate', his article compared proceedings to an 'old witchcraft trial' where defendants were accused of flying, 'intercourse with the Devil' and putting 'spells on people'. Like them, the Microdot Gang were being persecuted for having 'a different belief system' and committing the crime of 'heresy'.

Destroying Bott's credibility was an important part of the prosecution's strategy as she had chosen to plead not guilty – along with Cuthbertson and Spenceley. This was cause for concern. The case against her was weak. She was guilty of knowing what her life-partner was doing and supporting him throughout, yet her hands-on involvement was limited to driving him back and forth to his manor house lab. Had she shown regret or remorse, or put the blame squarely on Kemp's shoulders, she might have received a more sympathetic hearing. As it was, Bott stood her ground and refused to play the victim. Even so, there was the fear that her unblemished record as a doctor, serving her community, would play in her favour. The prosecutor warned the jury that they had 'to remember she is no ordinary doctor' like the one 'you go to consult when you're ill', but a 'person with no moral scruples'.

The jury agreed and found her guilty, much to the press's delight. *The Belfast Telegraph* ran with 'Drugs Plot Doctor Found Guilty'. *The Liverpool Echo* – which referred to her as a 'varsity girl' – carried the headline 'The Final Trip: Doctor Bott Guilty'. *The Daily Mirror* called her 'Doctor Chick', drew attention to the '£45,000 in cash and bonds' in her Swiss safety-deposit box and featured a picture of her face next to photos of the Carno manor house and Seymour Road, alongside yet another article about 'The Horrors of LSD', which claimed that 'takers have been known to ... chew a hand to the bone believing it was an orange' or 'truss and prepare a baby for roasting, believing it was an oven ready chicken'.

Stewing in his cell in Horfield Prison, Kemp decided to fight back. He wrote a fifty-three-page statement that he intended to read out in court, until his lawyer persuaded him not to. Instead, he sent his manuscript to *The Cambrian News* and, as the trial reached its climax, the paper published an in-depth article – 'Microdoctrine – The Beliefs Behind Kemp's LSD' – summarising his arguments and quoting them at length. The accusation that acid had made him a rich man had got under his skin and he addressed it head on: 'I have no hidden stash of LSD money, I have no secret bank accounts, in any foreign country, no valuable assets, such as jewellery, coins or stamps. I own no property nor even a car' – declining to mention that the majority of his assets were in Bott's name. He conceded that some people did suffer an adverse reaction to LSD but claimed he'd never seen it happen to anyone he knew. He described the personal benefits of taking LSD – it 'helps one realise that happiness is a state of mind' and acts as 'a signpost pointing a way to self-discovery' – and emphasised the role it could play in raising awareness about the ecological crisis facing humanity and the 'urgently necessary' changes that had to be made 'if we are to have any chance of solving the pressing problems of the modern world'.

The article came out on the same day as the defendants were sentenced. In his summing up on 8 March 1978, the judge reserved his harshest comments for Kemp, scolding him for wasting his 'considerable talent' on 'a false ideal'. Todd had an easier ride as the judge could at least understand his motivation, which rested on the fact that dealing acid was 'an easy way to make large sums of money'. As for Munro, the judge thought it was 'a disaster' that he had 'allowed himself to become enmeshed in crime'. More generally, he regretted having to punish 'people with excellent characters' and 'excellent qualifications' with 'severe sentences' that would place them in the same penal category as murderers, armed robbers and rapists. But he did anyway. Kemp and Todd were given thirteen years; Cuthbertson got eleven; Solomon, Munro and Spenceley each received ten; Fielding and Smiles, eight apiece.

The press reacted with unrestrained glee. *The Daily Mirror* thought 'the country should be celebrating', not least because the Microdot Gang had been stopped from realising its 'crazy ambition' to 'blow a million minds' by dumping LSD into Birmingham's water supply. Other papers concentrated on Kemp and Bott. *The Daily Express* published excerpts from their letters. *The Coventry Evening Telegraph's* coverage focused on 'The Lovers who Plied Drugs', while *The Liverpool Echo* had several pages devoted to the 'Two Lovers and their £1m Drugs Racket' that described their student days together at Liverpool University, how they got sucked into taking drugs, and Kemp's early failed attempt to make acid 'in the basement of a Liverpool house'.

The next day, Bott stole the headlines. She was the last defendant to hear their fate. Any hopes of leniency were dashed when the judge declared that she only had herself to blame for the position she was in; Bott was 'a clear-headed and very sensible woman' who could have 'kept out' of 'the conspiracy' if she'd 'wished to do so'. For her minimal participation in the Microdot Gang, the judge sentenced Bott to nine years in prison.

• • •

A few months after the trial ended, *Homegrown* magazine brought out its third edition. Alongside pieces about the Smokeybears – a legalise cannabis direct action group – UFOs and the US Army's secret LSD experiments, the issue's lead article – 'The Acid Alchemist Affair' – was all about the Microdot Gang. Accurate and well-balanced, it pointed out that the Julie investigation relied on the deployment of barely legal electronic surveillance, observed how the issue of police corruption had been conveniently ignored and asked whether a criminal court was the appropriate venue for passing judgement on LSD, a substance that 'has its roots in the metaphysical, in the spiritual' and 'moves mysteriously in the caverns of the mind'. After all, if acid really was 'the key to the Doors of Perception' then it was a matter for philosophers and theologians, not lawyers and politicians.

Homegrown's point of view was largely ignored as the popular press continued to get mileage out of the case. A battle had been won but the war on drugs was not over. There were alarmist articles about a new LSD threat coming from America, and in the autumn of 1978 there was a resurgence of interest in the case to coincide with the publication of Lee and Pritchard's books. Lee's *Operation Julie* was promoted by his sponsor – *The Daily Express* – and was widely reviewed. The *Daily Mirror* and *Sunday Mirror* gave Pritchard's *Busted* acres of space: one feature focused on the 'elusive', 'greedy' and 'cunning' Todd, who acted as the network's 'hidden brain'. Almost a year later – in September 1979 – the Microdot Gang were in the news again. Two of them – probably Todd and Cuthbertson – had asked to see officers from Operation Countryman, a major enquiry into corruption within the Metropolitan Police. Though the pair had nothing to say that directly related to the Countrymen investigation (and a police spokesman told the press that 'there was no suggestion' that any of the Julie team were corrupt), the prisoners did direct them to another hoard of buried LSD, the biggest so far: one million tabs in a large glass jar buried in a wood near Bedford.

For decades after this, the belief persisted that there were still hundreds of thousands of the gang's microdots waiting patiently to be discovered. In the meantime, anybody who wanted to copy Kemp's world-beating recipe for LSD could refer to the widely reported testimony given by a government forensic scientist during the trial. On the stand, the expert listed the ingredients Kemp used, explained how he went about synthesising them together to manufacture his unique acid and confirmed that 'it was of a very high quality'.

15

Agency Man

In July 1977, Stark was in Bologna jail complaining to officers from the Interior Ministry's anti-terrorism unit. He was annoyed because they hadn't taken the information he'd given them about the Red Brigades seriously enough. They'd failed to act on his warning about the assassination of a senior judge and his prediction that the Red Brigades would kidnap a high-profile politician. If the Interior Ministry wasn't prepared to appreciate what an asset he was, Stark was ready to bypass them and channel his intelligence to the CIA via the American diplomatic personnel who regularly dropped by to see him in jail, continuing a relationship that had begun even before his arrest in February 1975. Lodged in Stark's safety-deposit box was correspondence between him and US counsels based in Rome and Florence. Replying to a request from one of them for his thoughts on whether the army was capable of taking control of Italy, Stark answered that 'the only important transition that is needed is still distant'.

Stark's enigmatic response to the embassy official almost certainly refers to a right-wing coup that was set to take place in 1974, before being exposed and swiftly shut down. The plotters behind it were a diverse mixture of members of the military, the secret services, the police, the judiciary, the civil service and a variety of fascist groups, such as the Italian Social Movement-National Right (Movimento Sociale Italiano,

MSI). Formed in 1946 by Mussolini's former henchmen, the MSI was a legal fascist party that consistently polled around 5 per cent of the national vote and was strong in Naples, the south and Sicily. Running in parallel to the MSI were extra-parliamentary organisations committed to the destruction of democracy like the Black Order, the Mussolini Action Squads, the Armed Nazi Group and the Rosa dei Venti.

This unholy alliance had already attempted to overthrow the government in 1970. Though they failed, they continued to pursue their so-called 'strategy of tension': according to a US Senate report on terrorism in Italy, this meant 'the indiscriminate use of explosive devices' to 'create panic' and force the 'adoption of strong measures by the government, including the intervention of the … conservative military establishment'. Beginning on 12 December 1969 with a bomb in a bank in Milan that killed sixteen and injured seventy, the 'strategy of tension' set off a vicious cycle of repression and reprisal: each horrific incident – like the spate of attacks on trains full of trade union representatives in October 1972 – raised the temperature of political conflict, creating the impression that the country was spiralling out of control, and by 1974 the conspirators believed conditions were ripe to try and seize power again.

As a prelude to the coup attempt, there were two bomb outrages: on 28 May, there were eight dead and a hundred wounded in a piazza in Brescia; and on 4 August, there was an explosion on the Italicus Express train that killed twelve and injured another forty-four passengers. Because of these atrocities, the authorities were on the alert for any repeat of the 1970 plot, and on 31 October 1974 they arrested General Vito Miceli, the head of Italian Military Intelligence and one of those planning to overthrow the state. Miceli was believed to be behind the Italicus train attack and the escape of two of the seven PLO operatives who perpetrated the 1973 Fiumicino airport massacre, chucking incendiary devices into a Pan Am Boeing 707 and incinerating thirty-two people.

Miceli's name made several appearances in Stark's personal papers, and there is evidence that Miceli sought help from Stark's partner in the Lebanese hashish smuggling racket, the architect Count Roberto Fiorenzi. Their colleague, the car thief who stole the vehicles they hid their hash in, claimed that Stark had told him that one of the organisers of the carnage at Fiumicino airport had stayed briefly at Count Fiorenzi's home on the island of Syracuse before slipping out of the country.

Prosecutors who examined this accusation were fairly sure that it was Miceli who'd asked the Count to shelter the fugitive. The Count was also known to have been at the same hotel at the same time as the right-wing terrorists responsible for the Italicus bombing were preparing the attack.

The common denominators that brought together men as different as Miceli, the Count and Stark were the drugs, guns and money that moved between the mafia and far-right groups through covert channels. At the centre of this maze was the secretive P2 masonic lodge: it had between 1,000–2,000 members, an elite of senior figures from the armed forces, the civil service, the Chamber of Deputies, business, industry and the mob. Miceli joined the P2 lodge in October 1971, when he was appointed head of Military Intelligence. The Count was almost certainly involved with P2, as were three others whose names appeared in the documents seized from Stark: an aristocrat with links to the aborted 1970 coup; the President of the Sicilian State Mining Company who had mafia ties and fled to Lebanon after becoming embroiled in a financial scandal; and Salvo Lima, Sicily's most powerful politician, a former mayor of Palermo and close friend of the mafia.

Any intelligence Stark had about these sorts of individuals would have been of interest to his friends in the American consulates. The US regarded Italy as a crucial battle ground in the Cold War, and its priority was preventing the country from turning Left and from 1947 the CIA was largely responsible for implementing this policy. Its station head in Italy during the 1950s wrote that the country had played host to 'the CIA's largest covert political action program undertaken until then, or, indeed since'. By the early 1970s, the CIA had decided that the far-right's 'strategy of tension' was the most effective way of keeping the Left out of government. In February 1972, Miceli was given $800,000 to coordinate anti-communist propaganda. During a TV interview, an ex-CIA contractor – who worked as a freelancer for the agency – said that he handed over millions of dollars a month to the P2 masonic lodge to finance drug trafficking and 'create a situation that would favour the outbreak of terrorism in Italy and in other European countries'.

But Stark's relationship with the murky netherworld of the P2 masonic lodge was of no benefit to him in jail and there is no evidence that he discussed it with the Interior Ministry's anti-terrorist squad. Nevertheless, his decision to collaborate with them seemed to pay off because in

September 1977 his sentence was reduced from fourteen years to five. After that, Stark saw no further need to meet with them, and they didn't seem that concerned about his sudden silence. The Interior Ministry was not especially impressed by what he'd had to say and doubted its reliability. An outline of the Red Brigades' organisational hierarchy that Stark had provided them with – featuring two distinct operational tiers commanded by a Military and Industrial Information Centre based in Rome – did not correspond to their understanding of it or how the Red Brigades actually functioned, with interlocking cells arranged horizontally within a vertical pyramid structure. According to a local prosecutor who looked into Stark's affairs, much of what he revealed about the Red Brigades was 'imaginative or already known and of public domain, or has never been verified'.

● ● ●

Freed from the obligation to play nice with the authorities, Stark befriended Enrique Paghera, an anarchist who belonged to a group called Revolutionary Action, which aimed 'to wage the armed struggle for a free and equal society'. Revolutionary Action were international in outlook, recruited foreigners and fostered ties with anarchists in other countries. When Stark began cultivating Paghera, Revolutionary Action had not been in existence long and, despite its lofty ambitions, had so far concentrated on settling petty vendettas. Paghera remembered how Stark would spend hours discussing his vision for a global non-Marxist rebel alliance, a band of terrorists capable of waging war on the system. To show Paghera he was serious, Stark concocted a way for Paghera to form an alliance with the PFLP.

Stark gave Paghera a hand-drawn map of one of the PFLP's bases in the Bekaa Valley – within the territory controlled by his former source of hashish – a letter of introduction and the phone number of a Libyan embassy official in Rome who could help Paghera get where he needed to go. Though several officials from the Libyan embassy visited Stark in Bologna jail, it's not clear how or when he established this connection. The Libyan regime at the time supported the Palestinian cause and the destabilisation of Western societies, providing aid and sanctuary to a variety of terrorists. According to a report produced by the International

Association of Chiefs of Police, Libya had been an 'intermediary in the purchase of weapons' by 'the Red Brigades ... and Revolutionary Action' from 'the Popular Front for the Liberation of Palestine'. The weapons, 'which range from automatic rifles to portable missile launchers', were shipped by boat and 'deposited along the southern Italian coast at selected locations'.

On his release, Paghera intended to follow Stark's instructions but was arrested in April 1978 with the map in his pocket. Paghera pointed the finger at Stark, who now faced charges of 'armed banditry'. However, the investigation that was launched to establish the extent of Stark's crimes was abandoned after only a few weeks when the judge in charge of the case was killed in a car accident. Instead, Stark appeared before the Court of Appeal in October, a right due to anyone who had completed three years in custody. Rather than grab the chance to talk his way out of prison, Stark put on a bizarre and apparently self-defeating performance. Speaking Arabic throughout the proceedings, Stark informed the court that he was in fact Ali Khoury, a Palestinian refugee and member of an international terrorist group based in Lebanon.

Though his adoption of a fake Palestinian identity seemed to make no sense, Stark was preparing the ground for his parole hearing the following spring, where he was hoping to convince the presiding judge that he had been working undercover in Lebanon on behalf of the American government since the early 1970s. Judge Floridia, who was in charge of Stark's parole hearing, was inclined to believe him, having been won over by what he called 'an impressive set of scrupulously enumerated proofs' that showed that 'Stark had entered the Middle East drug world in order to infiltrate armed organisations in that area and gain contacts and information about European terrorist groups'. Judge Floridia also noted that Stark had personal contacts with a number of American officials and received 'periodic payments' from 'Fort Lee', which was 'known to be the site of a CIA office'.

Taking all this into account, Judge Floridia concluded that 'from 1960 onwards Stark belonged to the American secret services' and granted him parole on the condition that he showed his face at a police station every week or so. Stark left jail on 11 April 1979 and immediately checked into a hotel before being taken ill with heart problems, aggravated by the Reiters Syndrome – a severe form of arthritis – that had troubled him for years. On 24 April, Stark discharged himself from hospital and promptly vanished. On 17 May, the Chief of Bologna police telexed the Interior Ministry to tell them that 'a reliable confidential source has reported that Ronald Stark … was in a position to leave the country with the assistance of American personnel'. The telex went on to identify 'Pisa and Vicenza' as possible points of departure as they both were close to US airbases.

● ● ●

If Judge Floridia's assertion that Stark had been employed by the US intelligence services since 1960 was true, it would mean that, from the beginning, Stark's whole extraordinary career was masterminded by the CIA. Yet Stark's life in the early years of that decade gave little indication that this was the case. Stark was in Washington, and he did have a government job, but he was arrested and convicted for making a false application for a position at another state department. Though this might have been an elaborate CIA ruse to furnish its new agent with a criminal record, it seems excessively convoluted. There remains the possibility, however, that after he was convicted for fraud and the judge decided that he needed therapy rather than jail, Stark was given LSD while receiving treatment at the New York State Psychiatric Institute, which ran LSD trials on its patients that were funded by the CIA as part of its decade-long experiment with acid.

By the beginning of the 1950s, the CIA was trying to perfect 'enhanced interrogation' by combining drugs – including cocaine, marijuana, heroin and mescaline – with sleep deprivation, hypnosis and sensory overload at Camp King, an off-the-grid facility in West Germany. During 1953, the CIA decided to expand its mission to find what a senior agency official called 'material' that 'could potentially aid in the discrediting of individuals, eliciting information, implanting suggestion and other forms of mental control', and a programme with the code name MKUltra was launched with a starting budget of $300,000 under the auspices of the Technical Services Division. Though the majority of documentation concerning MKUltra was destroyed, as many as 149 subprojects have been identified, around fifty of them relating to LSD and four of them to magic and magicians.

The man chosen to run the programme was Sidney Gottlieb, a bio-chemist who had studied plant diseases and the metabolism of fungi. Gottlieb had been in charge of MKUltra's predecessors – Project Bluebird and Project Artichoke – and had a special interest in LSD, which he'd taken for the first time in 1951; according to Gottlieb, he experienced 'out-of-bodyness', 'a sense of well-being and euphoria' and felt 'as though' he was 'in a kind of transparent sausage skin' that covered his 'whole body'. Gottlieb was certain that LSD was the key to mind control; a truth drug; a brainwashing tool; a means to erase identity and rebuild a person from the bottom up.

To convince others of LSD's unique properties, Gottlieb acid-tested his colleagues, influential agency personnel (including the head of counter-intelligence who was treated to spiked Cointreau at the secluded Deep Creek Lodge), and other members of staff, often without their knowledge, with results that were sometimes tragic – the suspicious suicide of one unwitting subject – and sometimes farcical; a search party was required to comb Washington's streets after a hapless CIA desk jockey's coffee break turned into a nightmare. Having drunk the dosed liquid, he realised he was tripping but couldn't handle it and fled the building. Once outside, 'every automobile that came by was a terrible monster with fantastic eyes' and he was forced to hide each time one passed by, trapped in 'a dream that never stops'.

Beyond the confines of the CIA, Gottlieb proceeded more cautiously. He introduced LSD to selected doctors, one of whom was based at the New York State Psychiatric Institute, where Stark would later undergo his judge-appointed therapy. With money from MKUltra, the Institute initiated acid testing, which was still happening when Stark was there. Otherwise, Gottlieb sought controlled settings where the patients were unable or unlikely to complain. In that respect, prisons were ideal. In 1953, a doctor at the Addiction Research Center in Lexington, Kentucky, wrote to the CIA and gained Gottlieb's support for Subproject 73, a pro-gramme of experiments on prisoners with pre-existing drug problems. Seven African-American inmates were given very concentrated doses of LSD for seventy-seven consecutive days, during which they were kept awake with electric shocks.

At Atlanta Federal Penitentiary, the Chairman of the Department of Pharmacology at Emery University – who specialised in schizophrenia

– ran an even more grotesque series of trials. A Boston hoodlum, who was doing time for armed robbery and hijacking trucks, was one of twenty volunteers who took acid every day for fifteen months straight. The young gangster kept a diary and wrote about 'hours of paranoia and feeling violent' and 'horrible periods of living nightmares and even blood coming out of the walls' as 'guys turned to skeletons in front of me'. By the end of it all, he was depressed and suicidal, while two of his fellow inmates were reduced to 'growling, barking and frothing at the mouth'. Word of these kinds of experiments filtered through the federal prison system and the use of LSD became fairly standard procedure, though little evidence of the full extent of it has survived. Nevertheless, there is a chance that Stark encountered these practices after he took up residence in Lewisburg State Penitentiary; he was sent there after breaching the conditions imposed on him by the New York judge and spent time in the prison's psychiatric wing.

While these subprojects served their purpose, Gottlieb was anxious to monitor the effects of LSD in real-world settings and chart how it altered the behaviour of unsuspecting civilians. In the summer of 1953, he hired George White, a Federal Bureau of Narcotics agent who had made a name for himself busting jazz musicians, including Billie Holiday. White, who took a liking to acid and nicknamed it 'Stormy', rented an apartment in Greenwich Village. Posing as either a bohemian artist or a merchant seaman, White trawled the bars, picking up a motley crew of drunks, gamblers, prostitutes and pimps, and lured them back to his place to party 'til dawn. Once inside, his guests consumed booze laced with LSD and White would perch on a portable commode in front of a two-way mirror and watch events unfold.

In 1955, White moved to San Francisco to become the Federal Bureau of Narcotics District Supervisor. Always looking for new opportunities, Gottlieb acquired another LSD 'safe house' on Telegraph Hill to explore what a CIA psychologist referred to as 'the combination of certain drugs with sex acts' and the 'various pleasure positions used by prostitutes'. Decked out with red curtains and large mirrors, White's brothel had a fully stocked bar and an array of sex toys, leather gear and pornographic movies. The prostitutes, hand-picked by White, were paid £50–100 per client and were encouraged to get them to open up and chat after sex, pillow talk that was picked up by the four microphones disguised as wall outlets that were connected to two tape recorders situated in a listening post next door. Subproject 42 – which became known as Operation Midnight Climax – ran until 1965 when the San Francisco acid trap closed for good. Its equivalent in New York was shut down a year later. Given Stark's predilection for sex, drugs and the seamier side of life, it's not beyond the realms of possibility that at some point he found himself drinking spiked cocktails in the Greenwich Village pad.

While these various subprojects were set in motion, Gottlieb was looking for ways to extend the reach of MKUltra and encompass a broader cross-section of society. To encourage LSD testing on campuses and in clinics, Gottlieb set up the Human Ecology Fund. Through it, money for research was funnelled either directly to applicants or through established funding bodies – such as the Geeschichter Fund for Medical Research, the National Institute for Mental Health, and the Office of Naval Research – and then dispensed to suitable candidates. For its first year, the Human Ecology Fund was administered by a doctor at Cornell University Medical Center, and this prestigious institution continued to employ LSD after its initial involvement with MKUltra. While Stark was under orders from the New York judge and receiving treatment at the New York Psychiatric Institute, he was allowed to work as a janitor at Cornell University Medical Center and often posed as a medical student so he could observe the doctors at work with their patients.

There was, however, one serious flaw in Gottlieb's approach: what if there wasn't enough acid to go round? The CIA had been getting its LSD from the Swiss firm Sandoz, but its stockpiles were not sufficient to satisfy Gottlieb's requirements. During 1953, Gottlieb contacted a leading American chemical firm – the Eli Lilly Company – and asked it to try and create a synthetic version of Sandoz's acid and its crucial organic element, ergotamine tartrate. By the end of 1954, the Eli Lilly Company had completed its task and, with an investment of $400,000 from Gottlieb, began mass production. With its source of supply secured, the Human Ecology Fund was able to be as generous as its budget allowed. There was no shortage of takers. Acid subprojects of one sort or another popped up across the country at forty-four colleges and universities, fifteen research organisations and twelve hospitals.

As many of the participants in these programmes were civilian volunteers – mostly students – they stopped short of the kind of sadistic abuse that was inflicted on prisoners. However, there were exceptions, especially when it came to vulnerable people who could be convinced to sign away their rights. Across the border, at the Allen Memorial Institute of Psychiatry, McGill University, Montreal, Dr Ewan Cameron persuaded as many as 300 schizophrenics to place their sanity in his hands. Cameron had written to the Human Ecology Fund and in early 1957 Gottlieb awarded him a $69,000 grant to pursue Subproject 68. Cameron had developed a technique he called 'psychic driving', designed to totally dismantle a patient's sense of self, strip them to the core and render them as malleable as putty. With their ears, eyes and skin covered, his victims were locked in a 'sleep room' for anywhere between a few days and a few months. Injected with LSD, they were blasted with heat and intense red light, and were forced to listen to tapes of Cameron's voice intoning the same phrases and monologues over and over again for hours on end. The results weren't pretty: Cameron observed that one of his patients – a 19-year-old honours student – had been turned into 'a woman who sucked her thumb, talked like a baby, demanded to be fed from a bottle, and urinated on the floor'.

By 1960, Gottlieb and those around him were having second thoughts about LSD. The intention had been to use it to control minds, but it was more and more obvious that they couldn't control what it did to people. The results were entirely unpredictable; there was no way of knowing how any one individual might react to it; and the insights they might have while hallucinating rarely had any obvious application as far as the CIA were concerned. In 1963, MKUltra was officially brought to an end and its subprojects slowly wound down over the next couple of years. Given that Stark served the various stages of his sentence – both in clinics and prison – during this period, it's entirely possible that he caught the tail-end of the programme.

Yet Stark may well have been exposed to LSD some years earlier. According to him, he was given psychoactive drugs by a New York psychiatrist in the mid-1950s, when Stark was in his late teens, recovering from the recent death of his father and coming to terms with the realisation that he was bisexual. At that moment, acid and the other psychedelics were not as commonly used by psychiatrists as they were later in the decade. In New York, those that did employ them were encouraged to do so by an influential doctor who had guided Gottlieb through his first acid trip, and gave MKUltra LSD to his colleagues and to members of his Long Island social circle. Stark never named the psychiatrist who offered him the drugs, or described the effect the treatment had on him or whether it was repeated more than once. Even so, considering what he went on to achieve, it would be strangely appropriate if it was the CIA that had inadvertently started Stark's long love affair with LSD.

16

Wild Card

Amsterdam, 1982. Dutch police arrest a man for possession of considerable amounts of hashish, cocaine and heroin. Though the trafficker claims to be a Palestinian refugee, closer inspection reveals that he is the fugitive Ronald Stark. The US government is alerted. DEA agents arrive in Holland and escort their prisoner back to America, landing at JFK airport on 13 July 1983. Stark was placed in a San Francisco jail to await trial on the LSD conspiracy charges involving Nick Sand, Billy Hitchcock, the Brotherhood and his Belgian lab. Stark opted to defend himself and filed a discovery motion for access to the state's evidence against him, which was denied. On 8 December 1983, he appeared in court. The judge began by rejecting Stark's motion to dismiss the charges 'on various grounds related to the delay in prosecution', but then went on to make an extraordinary statement. Because of 'the nature of the government evidence' and 'problems that have arisen locating key witnesses abroad as well as important documentary evidence', the case could not 'proceed to trial'. The charges were dropped. Stark was a free man.

The US authorities may have decided to let Stark off the hook, but their Italian equivalents had not forgotten him. On 18 September 1979, the US legation in Bonn informed the FBI that Stark was 'being sought on an arrest warrant issued by the magistrates' court in Italy' and 'therefore requested personal background re subject, to include description, photograph, and fingerprints, if available'. This request was passed onto the Department of Justice who asked the Immigration and Naturalisation Services about the various passports Stark used 'and was advised that no record could be located concerning Ali Khoury', the Palestinian that Stark had impersonated during his appeal hearing a year earlier. On 14 December, the FBI informed Bonn that Stark was a potential terrorist who was wanted by the DEA, and sent over copies of his fingerprints, photograph and records of identification.

A few weeks later, the Italians launched a major judicial enquiry into the circumstances surrounding the violent death of Aldo Moro, one of the country's most prominent politicians and the leader of the Christian Democratic Party. On 16 March 1978, Moro was snatched by members of the Red Brigades. On 9 May, his body was discovered in the boot of a Renault, riddled with bullets. The Aldo Moro Commission's main concern was to establish whether or not the Red Brigades really were responsible for what happened to Moro. On the morning he was taken hostage, Moro was on his way to the Chamber of Deputies to vote on a deal that would bring the Italian Communist Party (Partito Comunista Italiano, PCI) and the smaller Socialist Party into a coalition government. Moro's unwavering support for what was known as the 'historic compromise' made him a lot of enemies, the usual suspects who had orchestrated and carried out 'the strategy of tension' since the late 1960s. Among many aspects of the affair that looked suspicious – important clues were mislaid or ignored and there were unnecessary delays in acting on vital intelligence – the kidnapping itself came under scrutiny. What concerned the commissioners was the sheer speed and deadly efficiency with which it was executed, as if it was the work of trained professionals and not an assortment of left-wing guerrillas. Even at the time, many questioned whether the Red Brigades were capable of pulling off such an audacious and lethal operation.

Three cars and a Honda motorbike descended on the Via Fani – about a quarter of a mile from Moro's home – on that dreadful morning. Four men carrying bulging briefcases and dressed in blue uniforms that resembled those worn by the staff of a local airline assembled outside the closed Olivetti café next to where a Fiat 132 – plus driver – was parked. A further two assailants were with their driver in a Fiat 128, waiting by a news-stand. Stationed nearby was a white car with false diplomatic plates; a woman behind the wheel, her male accomplice in the passenger seat next to her.

Moro set off at 9 a.m. Aside from his driver, there were two body-guards with him – one in the back and one in the front – and two more in an Alfa Romeo following behind. Once the kidnap squad's motorcycle rider had signalled Moro's imminent arrival, the white car pulled out in the middle of the road and began a manoeuvre designed to halt Moro's convoy in its tracks. Seeing the obstacle ahead, Moro's driver braked. The doors of the white car flung open and the woman and her comrade leapt out, levelled their sub-machine guns at Moro's vehicle and started shooting. At that moment, the four uniformed men came charging over, all guns blazing. In under half a minute, nearly a hundred bullets were fired, roughly a third of which hit their targets. Four of Moro's companions were killed instantly. The fifth died later in hospital. A barely scratched Moro was bundled into one of the cars and the kidnappers drove at top speed to a sparsely populated suburb where they transferred Moro to a VW minibus and spirited him away and into captivity.

Almost exactly a year later – and shortly after Stark left Italy for good – copies of an anonymous leaflet were left in two phone booths in Florence. On the following day, 16 May 1979, the police were called and they went and collected the leaflet. The leaflet may have contained just one para-graph of prose, but it was enough to set alarm bells ringing. It announced that 'the real man who organised the Via Fani massacre and the kidnap-ping of Aldo Moro is an Italian American who is very close to Ronald Stark'. The leaflet said the perpetrator's name was 'David', an 'ex-marine in Vietnam with the rank of captain' who was 'lately a military advisor to the Central Intelligence Defence of West Germany'.

The ruthlessly accurate shooting that dispatched Moro's bodyguards pointed to the presence of at least one highly skilled marksman. Over half the bullets fired came from a single weapon. Stark did know some-body called David who was part of his entourage and had been spotted with him in Lebanon and Belgium. But as Stark was in jail at the time of the kidnapping, the Moro commissioners were inclined to dismiss the leaflet as a hoax, especially when they realised who was responsible for writing it. Born in Glasgow, Martin Woodrow Brown was 60 years old when he accused Stark of being linked to the Moro affair. With a background in cryptography, acquired during a stint in the army, Brown had worked as a civil engineer in the US and Canada during the 1950s and 1960s before returning to the UK in 1968. Despite owning a home in Scotland and having money in the bank, Brown chose to live like a hobo, wandering round Europe and building a large library of material: according to British intelligence it contained 'numerous newspaper cuttings concerning terrorism and organised crime'.

What puzzled the Italians about Brown's allegations was that he seemed to possess the kind of knowledge that would only have been available to an insider, hints of which were revealed in letters he wrote to a Christian Democrat senator prior to penning the offending leaflet. Yet Brown had nothing further to say about Moro, so the Commission let the matter drop, reassured by the fact that British intelligence thought he was 'mentally unbalanced' and 'unreliable'. After Brown's death in 1986, the British secret service took the trouble to comb through his possessions and the vast amount of papers and documents he left behind. According to its report about what the British found, the Italian Interior Ministry noted that Brown had linked Moro's death with the assassination of John F. Kennedy, predicted a terrorist attack on a Concorde jet, and made numerous false statements 'about murders, drug trafficking' and 'the poisoning of elephants'.

As it was, the Aldo Moro commissioners were much more interested in Stark's involvement with the far-right and far-left and whether he fraternised with them because he was a CIA agent. In their two-and-a-half-page analysis of this issue – *Il Casa di Ronald Stark* – the commissioners examined his drug smuggling partnership with the aristocratic architect who had alleged links to several fascist bomb attacks; his alliance with Enrique Paghera and the planned collaboration with the PFLP in Lebanon; and the fact that Stark had met with Libyan diplomats, causing the commissioners to wonder if 'Stark was one of those from the CIA who was later accused by President Carter of having carried out, unknown to the American government, subversive activities in Europe in collaboration with the Libyan services' or 'was an agent in charge of sowing false "Libyan" traces in order to discredit' the Italians.

In making their conclusions, the commissioners were caught in two minds. On the one hand, the US authorities had 'never admitted that Stark was an American agent, and moreover affirmed that they were seeking his arrest'. On the other hand, 'no request for extradition was ever made, while the cordial relations with senior American officials are documented, both during his incarceration and before his arrest'. Added to this were Judge Floridia's comments at Stark's parole hearing about him being in the CIA since 1960. Stark denied this in court, but then so would any CIA operative who was put in the same position. Given the agency's history of meddling in their country, the commissioners were prepared to take seriously the Soviet claim that 'Stark's activities in Italy' was further proof that the CIA were 'supporters of terrorism'.

The Aldo Moro Commission completed its work in 1983 and its findings were made public the following year. At the same time, a prosecutor from Bologna had reopened the 'armed banditry' case against Stark and was seeking his arrest for breaking the conditions of his parole and escaping justice. But when the prosecutor applied to the US authorities for the right to extradite Stark, he was told that Stark had passed away on 8 May 1984. On his death certificate, it said that Stark had died of a drug-induced heart attack – either cocaine or heroin or a combination of both – aggravated by his long-standing health issues.

The timing of Stark's sudden departure from this earth at the age of 46 was extremely convenient for anyone worried about what he knew about the poisonous underbelly of Italian politics. That November, a US Senate Judicial Committee submitted a rigorous and detailed report on 'Terrorism and Security: The Italian Experience'. It included a section that recounted how Enrique Paghera was arrested with 'a Palestinian training camp map', and described his 'contacts with Libyan elements'. What the report failed to mention was that Ronald Stark, an American citizen, was the brains behind the operation. This was either a genuine oversight or a deliberate omission: an attempt to write Stark out of history, made easier by the fact that he was not around to set the record straight.

Though it's tempting to think that Stark was silenced to remove the risk of him revealing the ugly truth about the CIA's activities in Italy, and his death was caused by the unseen hand of the American state, it's just as likely that Stark never worked for the CIA; instead, the CIA worked for him. Aligning himself with what many thought was an almost omnipotent organisation that was able to bend the world to its will added to Stark's aura of invincibility. However the chips fell, he would always come out on top thanks to his friends at the agency. An old colleague of

Stark's – an acid alchemist who'd assisted Owsley Stanley the Third and worked with Nick Sand – thought that he was a 'very charming' and 'very intelligent pathological liar', who was a 'world class con artist and not a CIA agent' and claimed 'involvement in the intelligence community to impress people'. A former Brotherhood member echoed this when he remarked that Stark could have been 'employed by an American intelligence agency that wanted to see psychedelic drugs on the street. Then again, he might have tricked the CIA, just like he fooled everyone-else'. Sand believed that Stark liked 'cloaking all of that in this air of mystery which it wasn't at all. He told me that he worked for the CIA but he was so entranced by his own mental manipulations he obviously didn't know who he was himself so how could anyone-else know?'

Stark's abrupt end robbed him of the chance to tell his story. To this day the CIA denies having any record of him. The DEA never responds to requests for information. A tranche of heavily redacted FBI documents that were released in 2010 shed some light on corners of Stark's life but add up to nothing that substantial and mostly relate to the Italian author-ities' requests for information about him. If anything, these declassified files demonstrate how little the Feds had on him. In 1976, the FBI was following up on warrants issued against Stark for passport fraud. In the vain hope of finding something solid to fasten onto, the FBI expended time and resources on a thorough investigation of the life of Leonard Ennis Stark, a Texan who happened to be born in the same year as his namesake; lived in Seattle; had never left the US except for an eight-day vacation to South America in 1969; and had never been arrested by the police. It seems Stark's movements were as much of a mystery to the FBI as they were to everyone else.

● ● ●

Whatever Stark was, he wasn't a hippy. Love and peace were not on his agenda. No doubt his main allegiance was to himself and serving his own interests (Sand called him 'a glutton for power, for money, for sex, for sensation' who 'got greedy and ripped me off'), but Stark's actions were also dictated by his peculiar brand of anarchism, which was drawn from the revolutionary blueprint outlined in Heinlein's sci-fi novel *The Moon is a Harsh Mistress*. As far as Stark was concerned, LSD was not a mystical panacea for the West's spiritual ailments; it was a means to accelerate the collapse of society, clearing the way for a new beginning.

Stark was not alone in believing that acid was a weapon of destruction, and he probably supplied LSD to the Up Against the Wall Motherfuckers, a loose-knit collection of activists who gained a great deal of attention in the late 1960s, largely because of their name, and inhabited an area of New York – the Lower East Side – that was familiar to Stark. The Motherfuckers advocated 'Acid Armed Consciousness' and declared that they were 'the eye of the revolution'. Embedded in their racially mixed poverty-stricken community, the Motherfuckers wore black and learnt karate. Their Action Committee for Immediate Defence (ACID) organised neighbourhood patrols. They used donations to set up free stores, free food programmes, free clinics and pay for legal advice. To gain publicity for their cause, the Motherfuckers performed symbolic acts of vandalism. During the 1968 New York garbage strike, they collected piles of rubbish, carried them on the subway to the Lincoln Center – which was hosting a gala event – dumped them all into the fountain outside and set fire to them.

Inevitably, the Motherfuckers were constantly being arrested and harassed by the police. By 1969, they'd quit New York, hit the West Coast and reformed as the International Werewolf Conspiracy. Inviting 'werewolves of the world' to 'join our feast', the group described its followers as the 'ultimate horror show' with 'Hideous Hair & Dangerous Drugs', and declared that they were ready to 'drink the magic potion and become the spectre that haunts Amerika', while 'baying at the moon' with 'fangs sharpened' and 'claws dripping'.

The International Werewolf Conspiracy's blood-curdling pronouncements were primarily an act of cultural terrorism. In the years that followed, a small proportion of activists practised actual terrorism, and Stark consistently chose to associate with radical groups that were committed to the armed struggle. There is evidence that indicates that Stark intended to get involved with the Angry Brigade. During his spell in London in 1970–71, Stark gravitated towards *Frendz* magazine and hung round its Ladbroke Grove office. According to Steve Abrams, Stark helped bankroll its early issues, paid the staff's wages and hired them a fleet of cars. The *Frendz* team were not only fans of the Angry Brigade, they were part of the same social scene. Over the course of its campaign of direct action, the Angry Brigade targeted the bosses of car manufacturers who were locked in pay disputes with their workers. Among Stark's personal effects were the contact details of Lord Donald Stokes, the Chairman of British Leyland.

In Lebanon, Stark was not content with hashish smuggling. It appears that he moved guns as well and sought to forge a relationship with the PFLP, one of the most effective terrorist groups in the region. Incarcerated in an Italian jail, he gave his support to Revolutionary Action and chose to betray the Red Brigades, who were Marxist-Leninists and therefore the natural enemy of any self-respecting anarchist. Aside from having fundamentally different philosophies, anarchists nursed bitter memories of the savage repression dealt out to them by the forces of Marxist-Leninism during the Russian Revolution and the Spanish Civil War.

How much Stark actually achieved as a result of these liaisons is open to question. Ultimately, his most significant contribution to the upheavals that shook Western societies during that era was as a producer and distributor of black-market LSD. His labs in Paris and Belgium were responsible for staggering amounts of acid and comfortably out-classed the competition. In the UK, the Microdot Gang would never have prospered as it did without Stark's input. Not only did Stark give Kemp the chance to learn his trade, he showed him and the others how to operate on a global scale. When pressed by the Julie team about the Microdot Gang's fondness for the Swiss banking system, Kemp – in an unguarded moment – admitted it was 'a throwback from the Stark days'. In the end, it's no exaggeration to say that, between 1968 and 1975, Ronald Stark turned on the world.

Epilogue

If You Go Down
to the Woods Today ...

On 17 July 1979, Christine Bott was escorted from her prison cell to London and appeared before the General Medical Council Disciplinary Committee. It proceeded to strike her off the medical register and remove her right to practise as a doctor for what the Committee called 'reprehensible and irresponsible' behaviour. The hearing was considered newsworthy by the press and *The Belfast Telegraph* observed that Bott's hair was long and she was 'wearing an orange floral dress and a black jacket'. *The Daily Mirror* went with the headline 'Operation Julie Doc Struck Off' and featured a picture of her in profile with the tagline 'Christine Bott: On Her Way Back to Jail'. According to *The Birmingham Post*, her solicitor told the General Medical Council not to 'write her off' as she 'hoped to apply to get back in the future and would be keeping up with medical developments while in prison'. Four years later, Bott was out on parole, living in York and working as a volunteer with people with learning disabilities. Desperate to get her medical licence back, she'd submitted her case for reconsideration. On 23 July 1983, *The Liverpool Echo* reported that Bott 'sat impassively' throughout the proceedings and 'failed to have her name restored to the medical register'.

When Kemp was released from jail having served the bulk of his sentence, he and Bott were briefly reunited before going their separate ways. Too much time had elapsed. Too much distance had grown between them, cutting them adrift from their shared past as the ideals that had bound them together withered in the intervening years. Both were ready to move on and forget. Kemp idled for a while, travelled and spent some years in Goa, before a period in Spain, returning eventually to the world of regular office work. Bott ended up in Ireland, where she was able to put her medical training to use and to live a quiet and solitary existence. It's believed she passed away in 2018.

David Solomon was released in 1983 and returned to New York and his beloved Greenwich Village. He frequented the city's jazz clubs, wrote the occasional piece on the music he adored, and died aged 81 on 26 April 2007. *The Villager* printed a short obituary honouring Solomon's achievements as an 'editor, jazz critic' and 'psychedelic sage' without mentioning the Microdot Gang, Operation Julie or his subsequent imprisonment. Solomon is best remembered for his anthologies on LSD and marijuana, which remain invaluable introductions to the drug culture of the 1960s.

Todd did seven and a half years inside. When he got out he embraced his one great passion – mountaineering. In 1988, he scaled Annapurna, and a year later he went up Everest for the first time with a team of Polish climbers. The experience left Todd dissatisfied. He thought the trip was badly run and expeditions like that 'needed to be properly managed'. Never one to shy away from a challenge, Todd set up his own climbing firm – Himalayan Guides – and in 1995 he took his first party up Everest. Todd charged $29,000 per person, considerably less than his competitors. For that, his clients got their all-important climbing permit – which Todd sourced from the Nepalese authorities – their base-camp tents, a cook to make their meals and oxygen tanks, masks and regulators. From the start, Himalayan Guides gained a reputation for skimping on the essentials and using substandard oxygen equipment. Known to the Everest community as the 'Toddfather', the 'mayor of base-camp' or simply 'the Governor', Todd got into trouble when a 22-year-old British climber – who was kitted out with one of Todd's oxygen rigs – went too far up the mountain too late in the day. He never returned. His death was reported in *The Sunday Times* along with questions about Todd's safety procedures. Todd dismissed the accusation of negligence as 'absolute nonsense'.

An American journalist wasn't so sure. Installed in base-camp, he began investigating Todd's business. The big Scotsman was not amused, punched him in the face and threatened to kill him if he didn't 'get the fuck out of camp'. The injured journalist went to the police, and on 18 July 2000 the Joint Secretary for Tourism informed Todd that he faced 'serious penalties'. On 6 November, the Nepalese Ministry of Tourism banned him from the country for two years and issued a press statement which noted that they'd previously 'warned Henry B. Todd several times to follow … norms and conditions'. Undeterred, Todd planned an expedition to Karakorum – a mountain in Pakistan – which went ahead in 2002. Ever the hustler, Todd continued to try and organise climbing excursions until age caught up with him and he retired to live in relative obscurity.

● ● ●

Over the years, many people have tried to get the key members of the Microdot Gang to talk about their LSD adventures, but they've never uttered a word. Every question rebuffed, every query rejected. The subject was completely off-limits. This decision reflected an understandable desire for anonymity, privacy and the chance to start again unencumbered by who they were and what they did in what must have seemed like a different universe. Yet Kemp, Bott, Solomon and Todd's decision to maintain a stubborn silence might not have been entirely their own. At the National Archives in Kew, there currently sit twenty-two files relating to Operation Julie that concern the gang and eight others who stood in the dock with them. But none of the files are open to view. Some have been sealed until 2054. The majority are under lock and key until 2060.

In the autumn of 2019, a journalist made a Freedom of Information Act request to the National Archives to try and obtain access to the files. The National Archives rejected his request, citing section 40(2) of the Act, which covers the 'personal data of third persons which it would be unlawful to disclose during the lifetime of the people involved'. In calculating what a 'lifetime' amounted to, the Act applied 'the 100 year principle'; if somebody 'named within the records were born under 100 years ago' they were considered to be 'still living'. The journalist was not convinced by the National Archives' response and challenged it. On 6 February 2020, he wrote to the Information Commissioner's

Office (ICO), which had the power to reverse the National Archives' judgement. The 'complainant' raised several legal technicalities and argued that disclosing the contents of the files was in the 'public interest' because Operation Julie had 'involved expenditure of considerable sums of public money' and unanswered questions remained about whether the Microdot Gang was 'associated with a US based criminal organisation'.

However, the Commissioner decided that these concerns were not serious enough 'to outweigh the subject's fundamental rights and freedoms' and dismissed the journalist's complaint. As the files contained 'personal data' – financial records, family and medical history, and 'political opinions' – as well as 'criminal defence data', the Commissioner concluded that the 'information remains sensitive' and releasing it would be 'unfair' and 'likely to cause damage and distress'.

Given this degree of secrecy, one can't help but speculate about whether the confidential contents of these files explains the gang's reluctance to speak. But, if so, why? And how could anybody involved in the investigation be under threat because of it? It's possible that one of the dozen defendants was a police informer. But if that was the case, why did it prove so difficult and time consuming to bring the gang to justice? Equally well, one or more of them could have had dealings with corrupt officers that might rebound on those involved. But the fact that drug squad personnel were on the take during the 1970s is hardly a secret: it was common knowledge at the time and nobody today would be shocked to learn that even Operation Julie had its share of bent coppers.

This leaves the intelligence services – MI6, MI5 and Special Branch – who nurse an unhealthy fear of their past coming back to haunt them. During that era, while working in the context of the Cold War, they were coping with political terrorism – whether Republican Irish, left-wing European or allied to the Palestinian cause – an upsurge in youth radicalism and a drug culture that was synonymous with rebellion and frequently overlapped with organised crime. As a result, they made clandestine alliances with the strangest of bedfellows, recruited the most unlikely candidates and risked embarrassment if these dubious sources were ever revealed. Detective Inspector Dick Lee certainly thought that the security services had allowed the Microdot Gang to go about its business unmolested because they were interested in the types of people the gang associated with.

While there is no evidence that Kemp and Bott had anything to do with the intelligence services, Henry Barclay Todd is a different matter altogether. A cursory glance at his CV is enough to raise an eyebrow or two. There was his itinerant background, marked by his early childhood in Malaya and then an adolescence spent at a grammar school in Scotland. His lost years in Paris. His fraud conviction for passing bad cheques. His trip behind the Iron Curtain to Prague in late 1968. His mountaineering, which provided perfect cover for visits to geopolitically sensitive areas. His long-standing association with West German dealers who had links to the Second June Movement. His relaxed response to the news of Gerald Thomas' arrest. The difficulties Dick Lee had locating him, despite his criminal record. The list goes on. Yet there is nothing resembling proof. Nothing but guesswork. The truth will have to wait until the government decides to open those files.

● ● ●

On 20 December 1995, *The Reading Evening Post* featured the headline 'Fears Over LSD Buried in the 70s' alongside an article about how the police had 'recently found 90 of the black microdots similar to those seized during Operation Julie', which they believed might be 'part of a missing cache of acid hidden in the forest of Pangbourne'. The prospect of these microdots being 'sold in Reading pubs and nightclubs' was a worrying one and 'medical experts' warned that the 20-year-old LSD 'could cause severe psychological problems, including paranoia or schizophrenia'. In the summer of 2017, one of the undercover hippy cops assigned to Smiles produced a memoir about his time as a member of the Operation Julie team. In it, he alleged that while in prison Kemp had told a fellow inmate that he'd hidden a million-pounds worth of his LSD in a wood close to the Carno manor house. *The Sunday Express* picked up the story and informed the local police. They acknowledged that there was now a risk that people would come looking for Kemp's acid and told the *Shropshire Star* that they'd alerted the current owners of the manor and reassured them that they'd be increasing the number of patrols in the area.

Though the legends about the Microdot Gang's missing LSD live on, their acid did not transform society in the way some of them hoped it would. An article in *The New Musical Express* – published almost imme-diately after their trial ended – bemoaned the fact that only 'a few short years ago Kemp and co. would have been hailed as "psychedelic outlaws". Now it seems most people are content to accept the official word on the subject and go back to their Bovril and bedroom slippers'.

By the late 1970s, the ideas that had inspired and animated acid culture were no longer considered relevant, dismissed as nothing more than fanciful pipe-dreams. Yet despite this, they have endured and still influence how we look at the world. As to whether or not the Microdot Gang were right to put so much faith in LSD, it's probably too early to tell. Though their mission ended in failure, they achieved their main aim: to bring LSD to the masses. For hundreds of thousands of people who experienced the Summer of Love and the Swinging Sixties second-hand – removed by age or distance from the heart of things – and yearned to be part of it all and enter an alternative world, the Microdot Gang's prolific output meant they had the chance to sample acid's mind-bending potential for themselves.

Sources

The main sources of information about the police investigation into the Microdot Gang are Lee, D. and Pratt C., *Operation Julie: How the Undercover Police Team Smashed the World's Greatest Drug Ring* (W.H. Allen 1978), and Laxton, E. and Pritchard, M., *Busted! The Sensational Life Story of an Undercover Hippie Cop* (Mirror Books Ltd 1978). For the experiences of one of the undercover cops assigned to Smiles see Bentley, S., *Undercover: Operation Julie – The Inside Story* (Hendry Publishing 2019).

Insights into the workings of Todd's network can be found in Fielding, L., *To Live Outside the Law* (Serpent's Tail 2012), while Ebenezer, L., *Operation Julie: The World's Greatest Drug Bust* (Y Lolfa Cyf 2011) focuses on the Welsh dimension of the story. Short biographies, photographs and other material about the Microdot Gang are at operationjulie.wordpress.com. Media coverage about Operation Julie and the Microdot Gang can be accessed at www.britishnewspaperarchive.co.uk.

To view descriptions of the sealed Operation Julie files at the National Archives visit www.nationalarchives.gov.uk, and to see the recent judgement to keep them closed – Decision Notice 11th December 2020 Ref: IC-44093-C2S4 – go to ico.org.uk. For legislation relating to LSD in the UK, go to www.legislation.gov.uk.

The history of LSD in the UK is well covered by Roberts, A., *Albion Dreaming: A Popular History of LSD in Britain* (Marshall Cavendish Editions 2012). For the UK festival scene in that era go to www.ukrockfestivals.com and www.meiganfayre.co.uk.

An essay on David Solomon's career, Black, D., 'From Acid Jazz to Acid Revolution: The Psychedelic Odyssey of David Solomon', *Rab-Rab: Journal for Political and Formal Inquiries in Art* no.5 (2019), is worth a read. The same author has spent several decades delving into the mysterious case of Ronald Stark, and his two books on the subject – Black, D., *Acid: The Secret History of LSD* (Vision Paperbacks 1998) and *Psychedelic Tricksters: A True Secret History of LSD* (BPC Publications 2020) – are essential resources. His conclusions about Stark appear in the short piece 'On Getting it Wrong and Getting it Right: Ronald Stark, LSD and the CIA', www.lobster-magazine.co.uk (2019).

For another angle on Stark, there is Lee, M., 'The Rasputin of LSD: The Story of Ronald Stark, the CIA Informant who Turned on the World', *The National Reporter* (Fall 1988). For an analysis of the more outlandish aspects of his career go to the anonymously curated site 'Ronald Stark – Brotherhood of Eternal Love, History', *The Brotherhood of Eternal Love Archives*, belhistory.weebly.com (2021).

The declassified FBI files relating to Stark are available at www.archive.org. The Aldo Moro Commission report, '*Relazione della Commissione Parlamentare D'inchiesta Sulla Strage di Via Fani sui Sequestro e L'Assassinio di Aldo Moro e Sul Terrorismo in Italia*', is at www.senato.it (1983). Further details about Stark's role in Italian extremist politics are in Willan, P., *Puppet Masters: The Political Use of Terrorism in Italy* (Authors Choice Press 2002). All the declassified CIA documents concerning MKUltra and Operation Chaos are at www.archive.org

On the same site you can find the US Senate Committee report on The Brotherhood, 'Hashish Smuggling and Passport Fraud: The Brotherhood of Eternal Love', www.archive.org (1973). For The Brotherhood story and its connection to Stark and The Microdot Gang see May, D. and Tendler, S., *The Brotherhood of Eternal Love: From Flower Power to Hippie Mafia – The Story of the LSD Counterculture* (Cyan Books 2007). For a slightly different perspective on the same events read Lee, M.A. and Shlain, B., *Acid Dreams: The Complete Social History of LSD, the CIA, the Sixties and Beyond* (Grove Press 1992).

The most comprehensive account of the life of Timothy Leary is Greenfield, R., *Timothy Leary: A Biography* (Harcourt Books 2006). Leary's thoughts about LSD, the individual and society were best expressed in his *The Politics of Ecstasy* (G.P. Putnam's Sons Ltd 1968) and *High Priest* (New American Library 1968). For a close-up, immersive view of the birth of West Coast acid culture see Wolfe, T., *The Electric Kool-Aid Acid Test* (Black Swan 1989). For US laws relating to LSD go to https://mn.gov

Bibliography

Books

Abella, A., *Soldiers of Reason: The Rand Corporation and the Rise of the American Empire* (Mariner 2009)

Abidor, M., *May Made Me: An Oral History of the 1968 Uprising in France* (AK Press 2018)

Andrews, G. and Solomon, D., (eds) *Drugs and Sexuality* (Panther Books 1973)

——— *The Coca Leaf and the Cocaine Papers* (Harcourt Brace Jovanovich 1975).

Ashley, M., *Transformations: The Story of the Science Fiction Magazines from 1950–1970* (Liverpool University Press 2005)

Aubrey, C., and Shearlaw, J., *Glastonbury: Festival Tales* (Ebury Press 2004)

Aust, S., *The Baader Meinhof Complex* (Bodley Head 2008)

Babbs, K., and Perry, P., *On the Bus: The Complete Guide to the Legendary Trip of Ken Kesey and The Merry Pranksters and the Birth of the Counter Culture* (Thunder's Mouth Press 1993)

Ballard, J.G., *Miracles of Life: Shanghai to Shepperton – An Autobiography* (Fourth Estate 2010)

Barber, P.W., *Psychedelic Revolutionaries: Three Medical Pioneers, the Fall of Hallucinogenic Research and the Rise of Big Pharma* (Zed Books Ltd 2018)

Barnes, M., *A New Day Yesterday: UK Progressive Rock and the 1970s* (Omnibus Press 2020)

Baumann, B., *How it all Began: A Personal Account of a West German Urban Guerrilla* (Arsenal Pulp Press 1981)

Beck, C.A., Emilia, R., Morris, L., and Patterson, O., *Strike One to Educate One Hundred: The Rise of the Red Brigades 1960s and 1970s* (Kersplebedeb 2019)

Becker, J., *The PLO: The Rise and Fall of the Palestinian Liberation Organization* (Author's House 2014)

Beckett, A., *When the Lights Went Out: What Really Happened to Britain in the Seventies* (Faber & Faber 2010)

Bedford, S., *Aldous Huxley: A Biography* (Chatto and Windus 1974)

Bender, C., and Harris, L. (eds), *Best of Homegrown 1977–1981* (Red Shift Books 1994)

Bentley, S., *Undercover: Operation Julie – The Inside Story* (Hendry Publishing 2019)

Beyers, R., and Orrill, R. (eds), *R.D. Laing and Anti-Psychiatry* (Perennial Library 1971)

Black, D., *Acid: The Secret History of LSD* (Vision Paperbacks 1998)

——— *Psychedelic Tricksters: A True Secret History of LSD* (BPC Publications 2020)

Blackburn, R., and Cockburn, A. (eds), *Student Power: Problems, Diagnosis, Action* (Penguin Books 1969)

Blake, M., *Pigs Might Fly: The Inside Story of Pink Floyd* (Aurum Press 2007)

Booth, M., *Cannabis: A History* (Bantam Books 2004)

Braden, W., *The Private Sea: LSD and the Search for God* (Pall Mall Press 1967)

Bugliosi, V., and Gentry, C., *Helter Skelter: The True Story of the Manson Murders* (Arrow Books 2018)

Burrough, B., *Days of Rage: America's Radical Underground, the FBI, and the Forgotten Age of Revolutionary Violence* (Penguin Books 2015)

Burroughs, W.S., *Rub Out the Words: Letters, 1959–1974* (Penguin Books 2012)

Carr, G., *The Angry Brigade: A History of Britain's First Urban Guerrilla Group* (PM Press 2010)

Castaneda, C., *The Teachings of Don Juan: A Yaqui Way of Knowledge* (Penguin Books 1968/1973)

Caute, D., *The Year of the Barricades: A Journey through 1968* (Harper Collins 1990)

Christie, S., *Granny Made Me an Anarchist: General Franco, the Angry Brigade and Me* (Scribner 2005)

Cox, B., Shirley, J., and Short, M., *The Fall of Scotland Yard* (Penguin Books 1977)

Davis, S.L., and Minutaglio, B., *The Most Dangerous Man in America: Timothy Leary, Richard Nixon, and the Hunt for the Fugitive King of LSD* (John Murray 2020)

DeGroot, G., *The Seventies Unplugged: A Kaleidoscopic Look at a Violent Decade* (Pan Books 2011)

Dunne, B., and Shoots, R. (eds), *The Red Army Faction, A Documentary History – Volume 1: Projectiles for the People* (PM Press and Kersplebedeb 2009)

Dyck, E., *Psychedelic Psychiatry: LSD from Clinic to Campus* (Johns Hopkins University Press 2008)

Ebenezer, L., *Operation Julie: The World's Greatest Drug Bust* (Y Lolfa Cyf 2011)

Ecologist The., *A Blueprint for Survival* (Penguin Books 1972)

Ellwood Jnr, R.S., *Religious and Spiritual Groups in Modern America* (Prentice-Hall 1973)

Feenberg, A., and Freedman, J., *When Poetry Ruled the Streets: The French May Events of 1968* (State University of New York Press 2001)

Fielding, L., *To Live Outside the Law* (Serpent's Tail 2012)

Frazer, A., and Gillespie, D., *To Be or Not to Bop: The Autobiography of Dizzy Gillespie* (Quartet 1980)

Gardner, J., *The Multiverse of Michael Moorcock* (Head Press 2014)

Gitlin, T., *The Sixties: Years of Hope and Days of Rage* (Bantam Books 1993)

Grathwohl, L., and Reagan, F., *Bringing Down America: An FBI Informer with the Weathermen* (Tina Trent 2013)

Graves, R., *Difficult Questions, Easy Answers* (Cassell 1972)

——— *Majorca Observed* (Cassell 1965)

Graves, W., *Wild Olives: Life in Majorca with Robert Graves* (Hutchinson 1995)

Green, J., *All Dressed up: The Sixties and the Counter Culture* (Jonathan Cape 1998)

——— *Days in the Life: Voices from the English Underground 1961–1971* (William Heinemann 1988)

Greenfield, R., *Bear: The Life and Times of Augustus Owsley Stanley III* (St Martin's Press 2016)

——— *Timothy Leary: A Biography* (Harcourt Books 2006)

Heinlein, R.J., *Grumbles from the Grave* (Del Ray 1989)

——— *The Moon is a Harsh Mistress* (Gollancz 1966/2008)

Higgs, J., *I Have America Surrounded: The Life of Timothy Leary* (Friday Books 2006)

Hoffman A., *The Autobiography of Abbie Hoffman* (Four Walls Eight Windows 2002)

Hofmann, A., *My Problem Child* and *Insights/Outlooks* (Oxford University Press 1979/2019)

Hollingshead, M., *The Man Who Turned On the World* (Blonde & Briggs 1973)

Homebrew Press., *Up Against the Wall Motherfucker! An Anthology of Rants, Posters and More* (Homebrew Publications 2007)

Home Office Report by the Advisory Committee on Drug Dependence, *The Amphetamines and Lysergic Acid Diethylamide (LSD)* (Her Majesty's Stationery Office 1970)

Huxley, A., *Island* (Vintage Books 1962/1994)

——— *The Doors of Perception and Heaven and Hell* (Vintage Books 1954/2004)

Jacobs, R., *The Way the Wind Blew: A History of the Weather Underground* (Verso 1997)

Jay, M., *Mescaline: A Global History of the First Psychedelic* (Yale University Press 2019)

Katz, R., *Days of Wrath: The Public Agony of Aldo Moro: The Kidnapping, the Execution, and the Aftermath* (Granada Publishing 1980)

King, R., *The Lark Ascending: People and Music in the Landscape of the Twentieth Century* (Faber & Faber 2019)

Kinzer, S., *Poisoner in Chief: Sidney Gottlieb and the CIA Search for Mind Control* (Henry Holt and Co. 2019)

Kirby, D., *Operation Countryman: The Flawed Enquiry into London Police Corruption* (Pen & Sword True Crime 2018)

Kleps, A., *Millbrook: A Narrative of the Early Years of American Psychedelianism* (OKNeoAC 2005)

Kurlansky, M., *1968: The Year that Rocked the World* (Vintage Press 2005)

Lachman, G., *Turn off your Mind: The Dedalus Book of the 1960s* (Dedalus Concept Books 2010)

Laing, A., *R.D. Laing – A Biography* (Peter Owen Publishers 1994)

Laing, R.D., *The Divided Self* (Penguin Books 1960/2010)

——— *The Politics of Experience and The Bird of Paradise* (Penguin Books 1967/1973)

——— *Wisdom, Madness and Folly – The Making of a Psychiatrist* (MacMillan 1986)

Laxton, E., and Pritchard, M., *Busted! The Sensational Life Story of an Undercover Hippie Cop* (Mirror Books Ltd 1978)

Leary, T., *Confessions of a Hope Fiend* (Bantam Books 1973)

——— *Flashbacks – An Autobiography: A Personal Cultural History of an Era* (G.P. Putnam's Sons Ltd 1983)

——— *High Priest* (New American Library 1968)

——— *The Politics of Ecstasy* (G.P. Putnam's Sons Ltd 1968)

Lee, D., and Pratt C., *Operation Julie: How the Undercover Police Team Smashed the World's Greatest Drug Ring* (W.H. Allen 1978)

Lee, M.A., and Shlain, B., *Acid Dreams: The Complete Social History of LSD, the CIA, the Sixties and Beyond* (Grove Press 1992)

Leone, M.P., and Zareksky, I.I. (eds), *Religious Movements in Contemporary America* (Princeton University Press 1974)

MacAdams, L., *Birth of the Cool: Beat, Be-Bop and the American Avant-Garde* (Scribner 2002)

Madge, T., *White Mischief: A Cultural History of Cocaine* (Thunder's Mouth Press 2001)

Marchetti, V., and Marks, J.D., *The CIA and the Cult of Intelligence* (Knopf 1974)

Marks, H., *Mr Nice – An Autobiography* (Vintage Press 1998)

Marks, J., *The Search for the Manchurian Candidate: The CIA and Mind Control* (Penguin Books 1979)

Marshall, J.V., *The Lebanese Connection: Corruption, Civil War, and the International Drug Traffic* (Stanford University Press 2012)

Marwick, A., *The Sixties: Cultural Revolution in Britain, France, Italy and the United States 1958–1974* (Oxford University Press 1999)

May, D., and Tendler, S., *The Brotherhood of Eternal Love: From Flower Power to Hippie Mafia – The Story of the LSD Counterculture* (Cyan Books 2007)

McDougal, D., *Operation White Rabbit: LSD, the DEA and the Fate of the Acid King* (Skyhorse Publishing 2020)

McKay, G., *Glastonbury: A Very English Fair* (Victor Gollancz 2000)

McNally, D., *A Long Strange Trip: The Inside Story of the Grateful Dead and the Making of Modern America* (Corgi Books 2003)

Melechi, A. (eds), *Psychedelia Britannica: Hallucinogenic Drugs in Britain* (Turnaround 1997)

Michell, J., *The Flying Saucer Vision* (Abacus 1967/1974)

——— *The View Over Atlantis* (Abacus 1969/1975)

Miles, B., *London Calling: A Countercultural History of London Since 1945* (Atlantic Books 2011)

Moorcock, M. (under pseudonym Colvin, J.), *The Deep Fix* (Compact Books 1963/1966)

Morgan, T., *Literary Outlaw: The Life and Times of William S. Burroughs* (Pimlico 1991)

Morley, J., *The Ghost: The Secret Life of CIA Spymaster James Jesus Angleton* (St Martin's Press 2018)

Nevala-Lee, A., *Astounding: John W. Campbell, Isaac Asimov, Robert A. Heinlein, L. Ron Hubbard and the Golden Age of Science Fiction* (Harper Collins 2018)

O'Neill, T., *Chaos: The Truth Behind the Manson Murders* (Windmill Books 2020)

O'Prey, P. (ed.), *Between Moon and Men: Selected Letters of Robert Graves 1946–1972* (Hutchinson 1984)

O'Reilly, T., *Frank Herbert* (Frederick Ungar Publishing 1981)

Palacios, J., *Lost in the Woods: Syd Barrett and the Pink Floyd* (Boxtree Ltd 1998)

Piggott, S., *The Druids* (Thames and Hudson 1975)

Reiss, S., *We Sell Drugs: The Alchemy of US Empire* (University of California Press 2014)

Richardson, P., *No Simple Highway: A Cultural History of the Grateful Dead* (St Martin's Press 2015)

Ridley, M., *Francis Crick: Discoverer of the Genetic Code* (Harper Perennial 2008)

Roberts, A., *Albion Dreaming: A Popular History of LSD in Britain* (Marshall Cavendish Editions 2012)

——— *Divine Rascal: On the Trail of LSD's Cosmic Courier, Michael Hollingshead* (Strange Attraction Press 2019)

Robinson, P., *Perry Robinson: The Traveler* (Writers Club Press 2002)

Rosak, T., *The Making of a Counter Culture* (University of California Press 1995)

Rudd, M., *Underground: My Life with SDS and the Weathermen* (Harper Collins 2009)

Sandbrook, D., *Never Had it so Good: A History of Britain from Suez to The Beatles 1956–1963* (Little Brown 2005)

——— *Seasons in the Sun: The Battle for Britain 1974–1979* (Penguin Books 2013)

——— *State of Emergency: The Way We Were – Britain 1970–1974* (Penguin Books 2011)

——— *White Heat: A History of Britain in the Swinging Sixties 1964–1970* (Abacus 2007)

Schaffner, N., *Saucerful of Secrets: The Pink Floyd Odyssey* (Harmony Books 1991)

Schildt, A., and Siegfried, P. (eds), *Between Marx and Coca-Cola: Youth Culture in Changing European Societies 1960–1980* (Berghahn Books 2006)

Schou, N., *Orange Sunshine: The Brotherhood of Eternal Love and its Quest to Spread Peace, Love, and Acid to the World* (St Martin's Press 2010)

Schumacher, E.F., *Small is Beautiful: A Study of Economics as if People Mattered* (Vintage Books 1973/2011)

Sciascia, L., *The Moro Affair* (Granta Books 2013)

Seymour, J., *The Complete Book of Self-Sufficiency* (Corgi Books 1976/1978)

Siff, S., *Acid Hype: American News Media and the Psychedelic Experience* (University of Illinois Press 2015)

Smith, E., and Worley, M. (eds), *Waiting for the Revolution: The British Far Left from 1956* (Manchester University Press 2017)

Smith, G. (ed.), *The Letters of Aldous Huxley* (Chatto and Windus 1969)

Smith, M.S., *Robert Graves: His Life and Work* (Hutchinson 1982)

Solomon, D. (ed.), *The Consciousness-Expanding Drug* (G.P. Putnam's Sons Ltd 1964)

——— *The Marijuana Papers: An Examination of Marijuana in Society, History and Literature* (Panther Books 1969)

Stevens, J., *Storming Heaven: LSD and the American Dream* (Paladin 1989)

Streatfield, D., *Cocaine* (Virgin Books Ltd 2002)

Sweet, M., *Operation Chaos: The Vietnam Deserters who Fought the CIA, the Brainwashers, and Themselves* (Picador 2019)

Talbot, D., *The Devil's Chessboard: Allen Dulles, the CIA and the Rise of America's Secret Government* (William Collins 2016)

Taylor, G.R., *The Doomsday Book* (Panther Books 1970/1972)

Thompson, H.S., *Hell's Angels* (Penguin Books 2009)

Turner, A.W., *Crisis? What Crisis? Britain in the 1970s* (Aurum Press 2009)

Walsh, P., *Drug War: The Secret History* (Milo Books 2018)

Weir, J. (ed.), *The Angry Brigade: Documents and Chronology 1967–1984* (Anarchist Pocketbooks, Elephant Editions 1983)

Wheen, F., *Strange Days Indeed: The Golden Age of Paranoia* (Fourth Estate 2010)

Widgery, D., *The Left in Britain 1956–1968* (Penguin Books 1976)

Willan, P., *Puppet Masters: The Political Use of Terrorism in Italy* (Authors Choice Press 2002)

Wolfe, T., *The Electric Kool-Aid Acid Test* (Black Swan 1989)

Woods, R.B., *Shadow Warrior: William Egan Colby and the CIA* (Basic Books 2013)

Worthington, A., *Stonehenge – Celebration and Subversion* (Alternative Albion 2005)

Zelko, F., *Make it a Green Peace: The Rise of Countercultural Environmentalism* (Oxford University Press 2013)

Articles, Papers, Documents and Theses

(*Note*: All material cited below is available to view or download online.)

Andrews, G., 'Strange Illuminations', *Psychedelic Review* Vol.1 no.1 (1963)

Anonymous, 'The Red Brigades – A Primer', www.cia.gov (1982)

Barcott, B., 'The Toddfather', www.outsideonline.com (2001)

Bartali, R., 'The Red Brigades and the Aldo Moro Kidnapping: Secrets and Lies', University of Sienna (2017)

Bates, R.C., 'Psychedelics and the Law: A Prelude in Question Marks', *Psychedelic Review* Vol.1 no.4 (1964)

Birmingham, J., 'William Burroughs and David Solomon', realitystudio. org (2009)

Black, D., 'From Acid Jazz to Acid Revolution: The Psychedelic Odyssey of David Solomon', *Rab-Rab: Journal for Political and Formal Inquiries in Art* no.5 (2019)

——— 'On Getting it Wrong and Getting it Right: Ronald Stark, LSD and the CIA', www.lobster-magazine.co.uk (2019)

Blewett, D., and Chwelos, N., 'Handbook for the Therapeutic Use of Lysergic Acid Diethylamide-25', maps.org/research-archive (1959)

Block, A.A., and Klausner, P., 'Masters of Paradise Island: Organized Crime and Neo-Colonialism in the Bahamas', *Dialectical Anthropology* Vol.12 no.1 (1987)

Bradley, M., and Leighton, A., 'Operation Julie', *International Times* Vol.4 Issue 6 (1978)

Brecher, E.M., 'LSD Today – The Search for a Rational Perspective', *The Consumers Union Report on Licit and Illicit Drugs, Consumer Reports Magazine* (1972)

British Goat Society, 'History of the British Goat Society', www. britishgoatsociety.com (2020)

Brockway, A., 'Christine Bott – LSD Scapegoat', babylonwales.blogspot. com (2012)

Buckingham, Captain L.A., 'The Red Brigades: A Description of a Terrorist Organization', MA/PHD Thesis, California State University, Sacramento (1982)

Cohen, S., McGlothlin, M.S., and McGlothlin, W.H., 'Short Term Effects of LSD on Anxiety, Attitudes and Performance', RAND Corporation (1963)

Connors, J.B., 'Duncan Blewett – Psychedelic Research in Saskatchewan in the 1950s', Psychology Colloquium, University of Regina (2014)

Crockett, J.H., Franzosa, Dr E.S., and Harper, C.W., 'The LSD Blotter Index', www.erowid.org (July 1987)

Deakin, R., 'The British Underground Press 1965–1974: The London-Provincial Relationship and the Representation of the Urban and the Rural', MA Thesis, Cheltenham and Gloucester College of Higher Education (1999)

Drug Times., 'History of LSD', www.drugtimes.org (2019)

Drury, J., 'Operation Julie: Police Patrols Up after Claims Large Stash of LSD is Still Buried in Woodland', www.shropshirestar.com (10 July 2017)

Editorial, The., 'Two New Laws Relating to Psychedelics', *Psychedelic Review* no.7 (1965)

Elston, M.A.C., 'Women Doctors in the British Health Services: A Sociological Study of their Careers and Opportunities', PHD Thesis, Department of Sociology, University of Leeds (1986)

Eszterhas, J., 'The Strange Case of the Hippie Mafia', *Rolling Stone* (December 1972)

Eubank, W.L., and Weinberg, L., 'Neo-Fascist and Far Left Terror in Italy: Some Biographical Observations', *British Journal of Political Science* Vol.18 no.4 (1988)

Fielding, J., 'Police Could Have Missed Huge LSD Drug Stash Worth Millions', www.express.co.uk (25 June 2017)

Flores, D.A.J., 'Black Mask and Up Against the Wall Motherfucker: An Avant-Garde's Revolutionary Last Stand', *Journal of the Lucas Graduate Conference* (2017)

——— 'Remaking the Body Politic Anew: King Mob, Echo and Up Against the Wall Motherfucker', *Venezia Arti* no.28 (2019)

Freax, P., 'Days in the Life … Friends Magazine', www.ibiblio.org (2020)

Friedman, B.H., 'Starting Out with Dr. Leary', *New England Review* Vol.27 no.3 (2006)

Frost, D., 'An Unintended Community in the Welsh Hinterland: Networks, Lifestyles, Relationships', www.researchgate.net (2019)

——— 'Mud on the Tracks: Organic Growers in 1970s Wales', www.researchgate.net (2016)

——— 'New Farmers, New Growers – the 1970s Organic Movement in West Wales' www.researchgate.net (2019)

——— 'Nobody's People: Immigrant and Organic Farmers in the Welsh Hinterland', www.tyn-yr-helyg.com (2018)

Gray, D., 'The Future of British Climbing in the 1970s', *Alpine Journal* (1973)

Grindon, G., 'Poetry Written in Gasoline: Black Mask and Up Against the Wall Motherfucker', www.gavingrindon.net (2015)

Handley, M., 'The Acid Alchemist Affair', *Homegrown Magazine* Vol.1 no.3 (Summer 1978)

Hodson, P., 'The 'Isle of Vice'? Youth, Class and the Post-War Holidays on the Isle of Man', *Cultural and Social History: The Journal of the Social History Society* Vol.15 no.3 (2018)

Hof, T., 'The Moro Affair: Left-Wing Terrorism and Conspiracy in Italy in the Late 1970s', *Historical Research* Vol.38 (2013)

Holden, P., 'Back to Earth', *The Financial Times Magazine* (October 2009)

Home Office Advisory Committee on Drug Dependence, 'The Wootton Report', www.ukcia.org (January 1969)

Horowitz, M., and Rein, L., 'Acid Bodhisattva: The History of the Timothy Leary Archives During his Prison and Exile Years, 1970–1976 – Part One and Part Two' www.timothylearyarchives.org (2015, 2016)

Institute of Palestine Studies, 'The Popular Front for the Liberation of Palestine (PFLP) 1967–Present', www.palestine-studies.org (2020)

Laing, R., 'Transcendental Experience in Relation to Religion and Psychosis', *Psychedelic Review* no.6 (1965)

Lee, M., 'The Rasputin of LSD: The Story of Ronald Stark, the CIA Informant who Turned on the World', *The National Reporter* (Fall 1988)

Linville, T.M., 'Project MKULTRA and the Search for Mind Control: Clandestine Use of LSD within the CIA', *History Capstones Research Papers 6*, Cedarville University (2016)

Marks, S., 'From Experimental Psychosis to Resolving Traumatic Pasts: Psychedelic Research in Communist Czechoslovakia 1954–1974', *Cahiers du Monde Rusie* Vol. 56 no.1 (Jan–March 2015)

Marsland, J., 'Kick it 'til it Breaks: The Social-Cultural Revolution of Britain's Angry Brigade 1967–1972', www.academia.edu (2020)

May, J., (writing as Dick Tracy), 'Operation Julie', *New Musical Express* (18 March 1978)

McGlothlin, W.H., 'Hallucinogenic Drugs: A Perspective with Special Reference to Peyote and Cannabis', RAND Corporation (1964)

——— 'Long-lasting Effects of LSD on Certain Attitudes in Normals: An Experimental Proposal', RAND Corporation (1962)

——— 'Towards a Rational View of Hallucinogenic Drugs', RAND Corporation and University of Southern California (1966)

McWilliams, J.C., 'The FBN, the OSS, and the CIA', *The Historian* Vol.53 no.4 (1991)

Moorcock, M. (author), and Cawthorn, J. (illustrator), 'The Sonic Assassins', *Frendz* no.15 (1971)

Morgan, C.S., 'The Story of the West Wales Hippie Invasion – Fun, Laughter, Misunderstandings and Acceptance', www.walesonline.co.uk (2015)

Morris, W., 'Spiel Appeal: Play, Drug Use and the Culture of 1968 in West Germany', *Journal of Contemporary History* Vol.49 no.4 (2014)

New York Times, 'Conspiracy Case on Margin Filed', www.nytimes.com (8 June 1973)

——— 'King of LSD and 7 are Indicted by U.S. in Drug-Ring Case', www.nytimes.com (27 April 1973)

——— 'Oil Millionaire Key in Drug Case', www.nytimes.com (28 January 1974)

Novak, S.J., 'LSD before Leary: Sidney Cohen's Critique of 1950s Psychedelic Drug Research', *ISIS* Vol.88 no.1 (1997)

Pickard, W.I., 'International LSD Prevalence: Factors Affecting Proliferation and Control', www.erowid.org (2008)

Popular Front for the Liberation of Palestine., 'Platform of the Popular Front for the Liberation of Palestine', pflpeng.wordpress.com (1969)

Popular Front for the Liberation of Palestine, Information Department., 'The Military Strategy of the PFLP', www.pflp-documents.org (1970)

Rees, A., 'Nobel Prize Genius Crick was high on LSD when he discovered the Secret of Life', www.mayanmajix.com (2004)

Roberts, A., 'Francis Crick, DNA and LSD: Psychedelic History in the Age of Science', psychedelicpress.co.uk (2015)

Rockefeller Commission., 'Special Operations Group – Operation Chaos', www.aarclibrary.org (1975)

Schor, L., 'A Life's Work – Maybe More: Duncan Blewett and LSD', www. researchgate.net (2002)

Scott, P.D., 'Deep Events and the CIA's Global Drug Connection', *Global Research Archives* (2020)

Siklawi, R., 'The Dynamics of Palestinian Political Endurance in Lebanon', *Middle East Journal* Vol.64 no.4 (2010)

Simenson, P., 'The Acid House', *Druglink* (January/February 2011)

Solomon, D., 'The David Solomon Papers 1963–1965', Purdue University Libraries, Virginia Kelly Karnes Archives and Special Collections (2011)

US Senate Committee., 'Final Report of the Select Committee to Study Governmental Operations with Respect to Intelligence: CIA Intelligence Collection about Americans – Chaos and the Office of Security', www.icdc.com (1976)

——— 'Hashish Smuggling and Passport Fraud: The Brotherhood of Eternal Love', www.archive.org (1973)

———, 'International Terrorism, Insurgency, and Drug Trafficking: Present Trends in Terrorist Activity', www.ojp.gov (1985)

———, 'Report to the President by the Commission on CIA Activities within the United States', Richard B. Cheney Files at the Gerald R. Ford Presidential Library (1975)

———, 'Terrorism and Security: The Italian Experience', www.ojp.gov (1984)

Villager., 'Obituary: David Solomon, Jazz Critic, Drug Guru, 81', Vol.77 no.9 (August 2007)

Ward, D., 'The Golden Age of British Climbing', www.ukclimbing.com (2014)

Weinhauer, K., 'Drug Consumption in London and Western Berlin during the 1960s and 1970s: Local and Transnational Perspectives', *The Social History of Alcohol and Drugs* no.20 (Spring 2006)

Zadeh, J., 'A Fateful Hunt for a Buried Stash of the Greatest LSD Ever Made', www.vice.com (2017)

Index

Note: *italicised* page references indicate illustrations.